The Real
Bettie Page

The Real Bettie Page

The Truth About the Queen of the Pinups

Richard Foster

CITADEL PRESS
Kensington Publishing Corp.
www.kensingtonbooks.com

CITADEL PRESS BOOKS are published by

Kensington Publishing Corp.
119 West 40th Street
New York, NY 10018

All Kensington titles, imprints, and distributed lines are available at special quantity discounts for bulk purchases for sales promotions, premiums, fundraising, educational, or institutional use.

Special book excerpts or customized printings can also be created to fit specific needs. For details, write or phone the office of the Kensington sales manager: Kensington Publishing Corp., 119 West 40th Street, New York, NY 10018, attn: Sales Department; phone 1-800-221-2647.

CITADEL PRESS and the Citadel Press logo are Reg. U.S. Pat. & TM Off.

ISBN-13: 978-0-8065-4011-5
ISBN-10: 0-8065-4011-7

First Citadel printing: January 1999

16 15 14 13 12 11 10 9

Printed in the United States of America

Library of Congress Control Number: 97-34620

Electronic edition:

ISBN-13: 978-0-8065-4012-2 (e-book)
ISBN-10: 0-8065-4012-5 (e-book)

To Dad and Lisa

Contents

··

Appendixes

Preface

BETTIE hotfooted it in '57.

It was thirteen years before I was born.

I knew her first as a footnote, then as a photograph: a smile trapped in glossy black-and-white amber. Then I wanted to know Bettie Page, the woman.

What I found were her secrets. The dark things she wanted no one to discover. And I worry now that I have betrayed her, though we've never met.

There are two Bettie Pages.

There's Bettie, the Queen of Curves—alternately known as just Betty or the Tease From Tennessee—who lives forever in a million cheesecake photos as the greatest American pinup queen. She's a swinging fifties chick who looks like the girl next door, yet tells you she knows the score. She winks, tosses back her famous gleaming black bangs, and flashes you her killer come-hither smile. Her curves entice, entrance, and devastate. She's a leggy, torpedo-chested weapon aimed at your heart. That Bettie is fun. She's bikinis and lace. She's cotton candy and a ride on the Tilt-a-Whirl at Coney Island.

For almost fifty years she's been a fantasy woman that everyday guys fall for, over and over, each generation protectively tucking her pictures in sock drawers and under mattresses like a revered love letter from our best flame. She's the only Bettie most of her legions of fans know.

But there's another Bettie—the one who's an old woman now. The real Bettie Mae Page—the Bettie who lived a life outside those pictures, wearing the same face and curves, watching her trademark looks deteriorate with age. The Bettie who lived a life that matched both her dark and malevolent bondage photos and her sunny, fresh-faced beach bunny shots. She's the Bettie that most of her fans might not want to know. She might not fit a fantasy, but she's the genuine article.

I first met "Bettie" when I was about twenty years old on a magazine cover in a comics shop. I had just broken up with the girl I thought I would marry. I took back the three hundred dollars I had put down on an engagement ring, sank it all on a stack of Frank Miller's *Daredevil* comics, and reignited an old love affair. As a small child, I had learned to read when my dad, a patrol cop, brought me home dog-eared copies of the four-color adventures of Batman and Superman, his boyhood heroes. I began amassing and hoarding comics in the obsessive way that people who lived through the Depression stock their pantries to overflowing. I was a restless, bookish kid hurting for adventure, and the X-Men, Spider-Man, the Flash, and their ilk gave me a massive fix. Sometime in high school, our friendship ended. At seventeen I sold all my comic books to make the rent one month. I sold cheap.

But three years later, I rediscovered my love, and this time I wanted to know more about the people behind the comics—the writers, artists, and their inspirations. A budding journalist, I interviewed comics legends to try to get closer. An interview with Marvel Comics' Stan Lee was my first published piece. Soon, in reading interviews with other comics movers and shakers, I saw a single name repeated over and over: Bettie Page. She was a muse for some, a model for others, the personification of sexiness for all. Though I don't remember exactly where I first saw Bettie mentioned, I quickly wanted to know more. I bought a copy of a red comic-size fanzine called *Betty Being Bad*. It was an ode to the Bettie Page mystique. I studied it over and over, memorizing the direction her curves took when stuffed into a teeny-weeny bikini. I basked in her smile. I pictured myself with her. I was hooked.

Before too long, I found a friend who shared my jones for Bettie, and who introduced me to *The Betty Pages,* a slick fanzine produced by Greg Theakston, a talented New York graphic artist with a taste for fifties pinup girls, and Bettie in particular. Theakston had written a series of entertaining articles called "The Case of the Missing Pin-Up Queen."

In 1957, on the brink of achieving her lifelong dream of success in movies or television, Bettie Page disappeared. Some of her old friends suggested she may have been rubbed out in a mob hit for being in the wrong place at the wrong time. Others said she had married, moved overseas, and settled down. Some said she was frightened after having been subpoenaed to appear before a U.S. Senate subcommittee looking into her bondage photos. They said she became a born-again Christian and turned her back on a life she no longer wanted to acknowledge. Theakston came close to her—real close. He found old boyfriends, photographers, and buddies. He had so many clues, I couldn't understand why he wasn't able to find her. What I didn't understand then was that he had already found the Bettie he wanted to know: sexy, eternally young, and mysterious. He chose not to go further. But I was still curious.

I was a college student learning the reporting trade by writing for anyone who would publish me. I figured I'd write a piece on the cult of Bettie. By 1992 her merchandise was raking in millions a year, trading in her image on T-shirts, figurines, posters, magazines, comic books, and more. Author Gay Talese had brought Bettie back to prominence in the seventies with a mention in his book about American sex, *Thy Neighbor's Wife*. Odes to her innocence had been written in magazines like *Playboy* and *Rolling Stone*. Artist Dave Stevens even resurrected the vintage Bettie as a character in his beautifully conceived comic book, *The Rocketeer*, which later became a Disney film of the same name, sans Bettie.

Guys like Theakston and Stevens fantasized about Bettie stepping into a B-movie time machine or living in suspended animation in some mad scientist's test tube, and popping back out fresh to them forty years later. I wanted to know who Bettie had become. I started calling around. I hitchhiked on Theakston's research, tracking down Bettie's younger brother Jack. He was a sixty-five-year-old retired sheet-metal worker living in Nashville, her hometown. He talked with me for a couple of hours, not giving much up, not telling me anything really personal. But he did tell me Bettie was alive and living in California, and he agreed to send a letter of questions to her for me. I didn't count on anything coming out of it. I interviewed local Bettie fans and worked on my cult piece. A month later, a six-page letter came for me, written in the neat, lined, precise cursive of a woman who was once a high school English teacher. It was signed, "Sincerely, Bettie Page." Written in the letter were details only the real Bettie would know. It told me much about her missing years, yet startlingly omitted the last thirteen years of her life. From that letter, I fleshed out her life story —most of it, anyway: husbands, jobs, homes, old friends.

I have a strange role in Bettie's life. I don't know her. I've never met her. We've never even talked on the phone. I've only interviewed her through that one letter, five years ago. Yet, through my research and my discussions with the people whose paths have crossed hers, I feel I know her life story as well as I know my own and those of my family members. And, in quiet ways, I have added to her story.

I don't believe I am really part of the Bettie Page story, so you will be spared much mention of me in this book, but my friends and editor have asked me to address this premise for posterity. Make no mistake: I am not nearly as significant as Dave Stevens, J. B. Rund, Greg Theakston, Olivia, or any of the other incredibly talented people who have helped bring Bettie to prominence through their care and diligence. But I take a certain amount of pride in knowing that in 1993 in *The Betty Pages*, I put together the first comprehensive biography of Bettie, revealing for the first time the real history of the Tease From Tennessee—her marriages and travels and, most notably, the first factual (though partial) account of what happened to her after her disappearance.

Now I'm finishing the job. Shortly after the last *Betty Pages* annual came out, I found out about the Secret—the biggest scoop in my life as a journalist. I had unearthed the fact that Bettie Page stabbed three people, was tried for attempted murder, and put in an asylum. It took me years to figure out how to tell the story, let alone reveal it fully. I am truthfully amazed that no one has told it before me.

It's hard to believe this has been such an ironclad secret. At least one source close to Bettie who was interviewed for this book hinted at knowing about a "skeleton in Bettie's closet," presumably her history of mental troubles in later life. However, the same person said that the skeleton wasn't relevant to her life or career, and asserted that it didn't add anything to our knowledge of who Bettie Page was and is, so it shouldn't be revealed.

I disagree. While I can respect the fans who, because of their long love affair with Bettie, think they must protect her from the world at all costs, I am a journalist. My job is to tell the truth, good or bad, as completely as I can. I believe that to gloss over twenty years of Bettie's life—nearly a full quarter of it—is a mistake. Bettie is the person she is today because of *all* her past experiences, and to deny her present and recent past is to deny the sum of those experiences. I didn't create her life story—she did, by living it. I would have loved it if I could have told you that Bettie was all sweetness and goodness, and had lived a saint's life. But like all of us, she's human, and I feel it's up to me to chronicle her story honestly—that means telling both the good and the bad.

In the only authorized biography of Bettie Page so far, penned by reporter Karen Essex and Bettie's controversial one-time lawyer and agent James Swanson, it was written that Bettie spent the years from 1978 to 1987 living with her brother Jimmie. Actually, she was incarcerated in a state mental hospital for most of that time. I can only hope that Bettie lied to Essex.

Not everyone will agree with my choice to tell Bettie's complete story, skeletons and all, and certainly not everyone will believe what a personal struggle and dilemma my decision to write this book has been. I know Bettie doesn't want her secret past revealed, but I opted for the truth, as completely as I could reconstruct it from the sources and information available to me.

Bettie described herself as "penniless and infamous" in a November 1992 audiotaped interview for *Lifestyles of the Rich and Famous* —her first semipublic reappearance. No one knew more than I did what secret message lay hidden in those words. I'm sure most viewers thought Bettie was referring to her notorious bondage modeling, or that as a born-again Christian, she was simply ashamed of her nude poses. I knew differently. I can almost see the desperate dance in Bettie's words in that interview and others I've read. She is twirling and spinning inside, hiding a secret from the world that she thinks will place her beyond redemption. However, to quote the old adage, I believe the truth will set her free.

Bettie has lived in nearly total isolation for the last few years, communicating with her fans only through audiotape and telephone interviews with journalists, for the most part. Only a lucky few insiders such as cartoonist Dave Stevens have gotten within her guarded domain to meet with her in person. Bettie has told friends and interviewers that she doesn't want the world to see her as she is today, gray-haired and overweight, a faded beauty. And to a large extent, I think that is the primary reason for her J. D. Salinger turn. She is constantly reminded of her past glories and wistfully wants the world to remember *them,* not the human being who remained long after the celluloid beauty disappeared from view.

I also think that Bettie is afraid of being discovered, afraid of her battles with mental illness being uncovered. At the same time, however, I must also believe that on some level she wants that, that she has been waiting for it. She has given us many hints. Her letter to me explains her later years in two cryptic lines: "I wish I could erase the years from 1979 to 1992. I have had much difficulty which I don't wish to make known." And in some sense, Bettie did erase those years, leaving any mention of them out of previous interviews and biographies. But, ask yourself, why would she say that at all? Why would she drop a hint like that, portentous of much more than simply a decade of living quietly with her brother?

Bettie was testing the waters, I think. Her whole life has been a pursuit for acclaim and acceptance. And I think in keeping with the low self-esteem that implies, she's worried that her fans will desert her if they find out about her past of violence and insanity. I know that won't happen. A Bettie Page fan is the most loyal of fans. I personally think the revelation will be a relief to her. And, maybe, an impetus to accept her fans' invitations to come out and greet the world.

I make no apologies for telling Bettie's story. I have tried to do so fairly and sympathetically, but I also haven't pulled any punches. Yes, Bettie was a victim. The abusive childhood and sexual assaults she endured were certainly contributing factors to her troubled later years. But I must honestly tell you that Bettie was also a victimizer, hurting people older and weaker than she. The two are certainly linked.

After we all know the truth, can we still remember Bettie solely as the beautiful girl-next-door who captured our hearts with her smile and curves? How can we reconcile Bettie Page, the black-banged wonder, the Dark Angel, the Queen of Curves, with Bettie Page, the tragic human being, haunted by demons we couldn't see?

We do it the same way we do with anyone we care about. We understand and offer forgiveness for sin and compassion for pain. Bettie the glamour girl will live forever, but the fragile human being will not. Her life span is limited, but our love doesn't have to be.

Acknowledgments

···

THERE ARE many people without whom this book could not have been written. I want to give very special thanks to some of them: Bruce Elliott, for introducing me to the Bettie Page mystery; Wilma Wirt, for her wisdom; Bill Loving, for his guidance and advice; my father, Roger Foster, for keeping me on track; my wife, Lisa, for her incredible patience and great copyediting; and Barry and Sharon Fogel for helping me find a publisher.

My special thanks also go to Gary Fitzgerald and Mike Lewis at the Carol Publishing Group; Dwayne Yancey and Rich Martin at the *Roanoke Times,* and especially to Greg Weatherford, Janet Giampietro, and Beth Barmettler at *Style Weekly.*

Finally, I want to thank everyone I consulted, interviewed, or talked to in connection with this project, including: Leonie Haddad; Harry Lear; Steve Brewster; Harlan Ellison; Steve Allen; Carl Arrese; Art Amsie; Don Whitney; Ellsworth Boyd; Ira Kramer and Paula Klaw; Greg Theakston; Bunny Yeager; J. B. Rund; Robert Blue; Bonnie J. Burton; Peter Smerick; Dr. Mary Clement; Walter Durham; Mary Ann Jetton; the people at the Multnomah School of the Bible, the Bible Institute of Los Angeles, and the Moody Bible Institute of Chicago; the staff at the Vanderbilt University Library; Cora Mae Harper at the Sumner County, Tennessee, Archives; Carol Kaplan at the Nashville Public Library; Chuck Mead of BR5–49 and Arista Records; Addison Yeaman Jr.; Hillard Elkins; Jack Bradley; Richard Merkin; J. S. Meggs; the Reverend M. O. Wright; Arden D. Patefield; James Hirsen; Charles Wilson; and Lady Kayla.

The Real
Bettie Page

1

· ·

Distant and Strange

LEONIE HADDAD was sixty-six years old and, for the first time in her life, alone. It was March 1982, and her husband had just died, leaving her by herself in the small two-bedroom rambler they had shared since they moved from Lebanon to the southwest coast of California thirty years earlier.

She couldn't bear to leave the little house on Linda Lane in the aging middle-class suburban neighborhood of Sunset Park in Santa Monica, even though it seemed much too big without her husband. However, the threat of crime from nearby Los Angeles, with its drug and gang problems, made Haddad afraid to live alone. So when a nonprofit housing service for the elderly said they had found a possible housemate for her, Haddad thought her problems had been solved.

The service sent Bettie Page.

Nearly fifty-nine, Bettie was a heavyset woman, about five-foot-five and weighing around 180 pounds. Accenting her plump, stern face, her dyed jet-black hair was cut in the trademark bangs that had once made her a famous pinup queen. Her skin was darkly tanned, and she wore pastel pants with a long-sleeved blouse in the springtime heat to hide her bulk.

"She was very heavy. Always she wear long sleeves, because her arms was big. She always wore pants and long-sleeved shirts," Haddad

3

recalled in broken English tinged with a Middle Eastern accent. "She had black, straight hair. She dyed it real black."

Though she was very late and not at all apologetic, Bettie, on first appearance, was a quiet, well-mannered woman who spoke earnestly about her devout faith in Christianity. She seemed like a good choice for a housemate to Haddad, who was so anxious to find someone to share her home that she had completely remodeled her spare bedroom with bright, expensive new furniture and a queen-size bed. "She was looking good, very normal," Haddad recalled. But as the old saying goes, sometimes first impressions can be deceiving.

Bettie moved in almost immediately, bringing her belongings in over thirty sealed boxes of various sizes, which she stacked around the bed like a cardboard fortress. "She had the boxes around her and she slept in the middle," Haddad said.

The lonely widow Haddad found Bettie lacking as a companion. Bettie was cold, distant, strange, and spoke little, usually only about her past, telling Haddad she had once been a famous pinup girl. She provided few details, and Haddad figured it must have been an exaggeration. "She told me, 'You've never heard of Bettie Page? I used to be a beautiful model,'" Haddad said. As for family, Bettie didn't say much, even though her brother Jimmie lived not far away. "She hate her mother," Haddad said. "I remember she said she doesn't like her mother." Most of the time, Bettie stayed cloistered in her room or on the brick patio of the house, which was surrounded with Haddad's carefully planted flowers.

Haddad quickly became concerned with Bettie's behavior, which was often bizarre and paranoid. Sometimes Bettie would lean toward Haddad conspiratorially and tell her that people were stealing from her, taking her clothes and her vitamins.

Though devoutly religious, Bettie never went to church. She spent long hours in the bathroom, talking loudly, as if preaching a sermon. She believed there were seven gods, and she spent much of her time dictating their rambling, disjointed gospels into a tape recorder. She told Haddad she planned to write a book about the prophecies they gave her.

"She used to go the bathroom and put a tape recorder with her. She wanted to write a book about seven gods," Haddad recalled. "One time I asked why she believed there was seven gods. She said, 'You don't know?' "

In a holdover from her modeling days, Bettie would eat only vegetables and health foods, and she kept the cupboards stocked full of them. She always cooked dinner at midnight or later, sometimes adding beef bones for flavoring, which left the little house and its furniture with a pungent, unpleasant smell. Bettie seemed unconcerned about cleaning and never unpacked the boxes in her room.

Tomorrow, she told Haddad, she'd unpack them tomorrow.

Once one of Haddad's friends came to visit but Haddad wasn't there. The friend rang the doorbell, seeing Bettie through the living-room window sitting in a chair and watching TV. Bettie never turned around or got up to answer the door.

Though Bettie had enjoyed the outdoors as a young woman, the Bettie that Leonie Haddad knew remained indoors for the most part, though she must have liked strolling Sunset Park's winding streets that led down to Marine Street, where local teens played ball at Marine Park. Her only visitor at Haddad's home was a state mental health caseworker who came to the house occasionally. Once in a while, Bettie and the social worker would go out for a vegetarian pizza.

Haddad wanted to know why the caseworker was visiting. She says the caseworker told her that Bettie was upset over a recent divorce and needed help. She told Haddad not to worry about Bettie's behavior; Bettie was just a little upset.

Soon after Haddad's conversation with the caseworker, Bettie was late coming home from shopping. Always worried about crime, Haddad sat up and waited for her. When Bettie finally arrived, Haddad sighed with relief and told her she had almost called the police. Bettie glared angrily at her and yelled, "No! No! Never call the police!"

"She never was nice. I never talked to her too much," Haddad said. "I tried to be good to her. It never entered my mind she was crazy."

On June 11, 1982, Haddad woke up at around 3 A.M. to a foul burning smell coming from the kitchen where Bettie was cooking. It was the last straw. She went back to bed, and the next morning, she called her son, who lived nearby. "She's a strange one, this one," Haddad told him in her broken English. Her son told her not to worry, he would tell Bettie to leave the next day.

"Bitch! Bitch! Bitch!" Bettie screamed from the kitchen doorway, where she had been eavesdropping. "It was the first time she was talking this language," Haddad said.

Before Haddad could hang up the phone, Bettie was in front of her. Haddad tried to calm her, to explain, but Bettie would have none of it. She stalked past Haddad, slamming the door to her bedroom fortress with an ominous echo.

At four o'clock the next morning, June 12, Leonie Haddad woke from a sound sleep and screamed. Bettie was on top of her in the darkness, sitting on her stomach, pinning her to the bed and brandishing a foot-long serrated bread knife.

"Don't scream. Don't shout," Bettie hissed quietly in her deep, slow Tennessee drawl. "God has inspired me to kill you!"

2

....

Who Is Bettie Page?

BETTIE PAGE's whole life culminated in her picking up that knife in the darkness to wreak terrible vengeance not just against Leonie Haddad, but against the demons that had been haunting her since she was a girl.

For six all-too-brief wonderful years, from 1951 to 1957, Bettie Page was the living Queen of Curves. She is said to have been the most-photographed model who ever lived. Because of her mystery and legend, she may be the most desired woman in the world; more popular today than she ever was in the 1950s, rivaling Marilyn Monroe and even modern-day beauties like Cindy Crawford.

Bettie was a sexual trailblazer in an era when everything was taboo. She broke the rules, perhaps without even understanding what they really were. Her pinups and bondage photos unleashed a Pandora's box of sex upon the world, where fetishism and nudity are no longer relegated to sleazy corners and sold under counters as they were in Bettie's day.

"The whole rock music and fashion industry today is in retrograde, stealing from Bettie Page," says painter Robert Blue, who has portrayed Bettie on canvas over the last twenty years. "What Madonna's doing today that looks so razor's edge was done in the 1950s by Bettie Page. There's nothing in rock and roll, no costumes or outfits in fashion that are more potent than Bettie Page in her six-and-half-inch heels and a whip."

Despite her historic role in forging twentieth-century America's sexuality, however, Bettie Page spent her life fleeing from her past, searching for a home, for stability, and for an acceptance that she never found . . . until now, perhaps, in her end of century celebrity.

From out of a childhood of poverty, misery, and sexual abuse, Bettie escaped through a string of failed marriages and the world of pinup photography, searching for the answer. She never got what she wanted. Ironically, the modeling that made her famous wasn't her dream. She really wanted to be an actress.

In her later years, Bettie sought the answer in religion, and when it still eluded her, she descended into a violent madness that led to years behind asylum walls. When she reemerged it was into a world that had made her its goddess.

She is timeless.

She is the greatest star that never was.

She is Bettie Page, Queen of the Pinups.

But to understand her, you have to know her whole story.

It starts in Nashville.

Edna Page eased herself carefully into one of the movie palace's smooth, plush velvet seats. Nine months pregnant, she could barely squeeze herself between the armrests.

It was a hot, early spring in Nashville and the twenty-three-year-old housewife was tired of being cooped up at home, pregnant, while she cared for her two-year-old son, Billy. She was ready for the familiar pain in her back to be gone and ready for her new child to be born.

She needed a night on the town to shake her cabin fever. When Roy, her twenty-seven-year-old husband, came home from his job at the auto garage, he could see that it would be in his best interest to take her out for the evening.

That morning, Douglas Fairbanks's new silent film *Robin Hood* debuted in an early morning sneak preview at the Loew's Vendome, the landmark four-story red brick gothic theater downtown. The film was shown at a discount price to encourage attendance, and everybody in town was talking about it. Newspaper ads and signs posted in diners and shops added to the excitement. Hearing his customers talking about *Robin Hood*, Roy probably decided it was just the thing for him and his wife to do that night. If so, he was in for a rude surprise, because *Robin Hood* would not begin its scheduled run for another two days.

Though he was most likely disappointed when he realized the theater was playing a comedy that night instead of the new Fairbanks adventure, Roy soon forgot about it, and settled down with Edna and their son, who was sleeping on Roy's lap. Roy and Edna gazed across the ornate six-hundred-seat auditorium, listening to the orchestra warm up. The theater darkened, and the immense crystal chandelier hanging overhead sent fragments of fading light sparkling over the moviegoers like stars playing on the surface of a night ocean.

Newsreels played first, flickering across the screen the faces of President Warren G. Harding and German and Soviet officials who had just signed a peace treaty. Next came a Mutt and Jeff cartoon, which would probably have been more interesting to the audience of country folk. The feature film was titled, appropriately, *Kick In*. Almost as soon as the film began, Edna went into labor.

Roy rushed her from the theater to a nearby hospital. At three o'clock the following morning, on April 22, 1923, Edna gave birth to a baby girl. They named the child Betty Mae Page according to her birth certificate, but when she became old enough to write, the spelling changed to Bettie. In later years, Bettie would often wonder if her love of movies hadn't started in the theater where her mother went into labor.

The second of six children, Bettie quickly learned she would have to compete for her parents' attention. New babies were born almost every other year, and Bettie was soon burdened with responsibilities like changing diapers and caring for the younger children. However, at age five, when she played the angel Gabriel in a church Christmas pageant, she found a way to get people to notice her. She would spend the rest of her life trying to recapture the same satisfaction she got that night as a little girl when her ears rang with the audience's applause.

Foreshadowing her own relationships later in life, Bettie's parents argued constantly. Edna Mae Pirtle had married Walter Roy Page to escape the life of an orphan, cared for by brothers and sisters after her mother's death when Edna was just three. Most frequently, she and Roy would argue over sex. His desires could not be satisfied and she wasn't always willing to try. Edna was eight months pregnant with Bettie's younger brother Jimmie when Roy threw her out of the house in the rain after she refused to have sex with him.

Many of Bettie's earliest years were spent shuffling through small dustbowl towns in Texas and Oklahoma as Roy, a decorated World War I veteran, traveled from job to job. With the advent of the Depression, work for auto mechanics had dried up; no one could afford to have their cars fixed. In 1930, Bettie and her family were living in a rented house in Tulsa when she saw something that disturbed her greatly: a house being moved on a truck. It upset her to see such a lasting thing become so transitory. It was a sign of things to come for Bettie, who would fruitlessly crisscross the country again and again in her adult years, searching for stability and a home.

But it also symbolized the present. The still-unemployed Roy couldn't make the rent payments on their home in Tulsa, and the family was evicted and thrown onto the street with their belongings. They found themselves miles from home with no money and no friends or family to help them. Roy came up with a drastic solution: he stole a car and loaded his family up and headed for his mother's place in Tennessee. His fledgling criminal career ended just a day later when the owner of the car, a deputy sheriff, hunted Roy down and arrested him. An Atlanta prison became his home for the next two years.

As for Bettie and her brothers and sisters, they stayed with their mother in Nashville at Roy's mother's house. Corilla Page owned a large, aging tenement house across from the state capitol, but she had little else in the way of worldly goods. The family got by, but barely, and Bettie became accustomed to wearing her mother's hand-me-down clothing, cut down to her size. Without money for toys or entertainment, Bettie and her siblings learned to be very creative in their games, and Bettie grew up with a daydreamer's mind.

Early on she showed an interest in art. But with nothing to buy pencils or paper, Bettie was forced to create new mediums. She used the natural oil on the skin of her fingers to draw on the porcelain cabinets in her grandmother's kitchen.

When Roy was paroled from prison in 1931, the family scraped together what little money they had left and moved about thirty miles west of Nashville, buying a forty-eight-acre farm. Despite the poverty that forced Bettie and her siblings to walk to school without shoes on their feet, life on the farm was idyllic at first. On warm afternoons after lunch, she and her school-age brothers and sisters ditched school and splashed in the creeks, or made up games like "fighting feathers," in which they would blow on chicken feathers and see who could keep them aloft the longest. In foot races, tall, slender Bettie could already beat her brothers. Other times the children would play horses or cowboys and Indians, creating hobby horses with sticks for bodies and corn silk for manes.

At age nine Bettie fell in love with a fifteen-year-old neighbor boy, Clarence Daubenspeck, who lived on a farm next to the Pages. The infatuation burnt out quickly, though, when Clarence smacked her on her left hand with a stone during a rock battle between the Daubenspeck and Page kids.

Life was not all play, however. The farm demanded hard work like fetching buckets of water from a faraway well, watering crops, and picking rocks out of the soil so it could be seeded and plowed. Roy Page promised his kids allowance money for the chores, and they kept a ledger, each tallying up nearly $300 before Roy reneged and told them he wouldn't pay. "Chummy," Roy would say (calling Bettie by his pet name for her), "you didn't really think I'd pay you for that, did you?" It was not the first time—or the last—that Bettie would feel used and betrayed by Roy.

Bettie's disappointment probably didn't make much of an impact on Roy, who was more interested in carnal pursuits. He had an eye for women and a natural wanderlust, and farm life was just too quiet for him. In 1933 Roy got caught rolling in the hay—literally—with a fifteen-year-old neighbor girl named Rosie. When the girl got pregnant and her father found out, he chased Roy across the Page farm with a shotgun. Edna broke every dish in the house in a torrent of rage, trying to hit Roy as he ran. Roy and Edna's marriage was over. In interviews later, Bettie would always remember her father as a "womanizer of the worst sort." It was the beginning of the most traumatic years of Bettie's already turbulent life.

Bettie's mother hitchhiked to Nashville and later sent for her children. Edna was hired as a beautician at a local salon and she moved her family into a small house outside the city. The poverty in the household now headed by Edna Page was extreme. She had to wash people's laundry at night just to keep up, and even that was not enough. Like many Southern families of the time, the children had no idea what it was like to live in a house with indoor plumbing. Stressed and exasperated by her circumstances, the slim, beautiful, and still-young Edna would take out her frustrations on her children, telling them she hadn't wanted so many kids, that they were accidents, and that she certainly hadn't wanted any daughters. Those words must have rung in Bettie's young ears as, strapped for cash and pressed by bill collectors, Edna put Bettie and her two younger sisters, Goldie and Joyce (or Love, as she was also known), into a church orphanage. Bettie's older brother, Billy, and her younger brothers, Jimmie and Jack, stayed behind to help with the chores. Bettie never forgot that abandonment.

But, with the resilience of childhood, the precocious ten-year-old Bettie soon made many friends at the orphanage through her natural gifts as an entertainer. She and her sisters made up a new game called Program, in which they would gather in a circle with the other girls and each would take a turn inside the circle, pretending to be a radio performer. Bettie put on elaborate shows, imitating radio performers like Fibber McGee and Molly, smearing shoe polish on her face to do Amos and Andy, and performing elaborate hula dances behind the church mothers' backs—to the giggles and delighted screams of her sisters and the other little girls.

Edna visited every Sunday, sometimes bringing candy, sometimes fruit or cookies, depending on how the week had been. She always assured the girls she would bring them back home as soon as she could. Shortly after Bettie's twelfth birthday, Edna made good on her promise.

The next years would be rough ones for Bettie. Money was still almost nonexistent. Getting an orange for Christmas was a happy surprise for the Page kids, Bettie has said in interviews. Still, Bettie admired her mother's independence and self-sufficiency, as Edna stubbornly refused all handouts except for a gift of groceries from local charity groups at Christmas. Edna was determined that life be as normal for her children as possible, and as she flowered into adolescence, Bettie seemed like an average little girl.

Like many young American girls, Bettie dreamed of riding horses, and she played dress-up and held fashion contests with her sisters. She plucked her eyebrows like her mother and started to wear makeup, and later took occasional guitar and piano lessons at a local community center, where she also learned homemaking skills. Her main passion, however, was collecting cigarette trading cards of movie stars. She put their pictures on her wall and sipped Hires root beer at drugstore counters, daydreaming of being discovered by Hollywood talent scouts.

For Bettie, the dream was probably more than an idle one. She yearned for escape. Shortly after she had turned thirteen, Roy had moved back in after falling on hard times, renting a room in the basement of Edna's house. According to interviews with Bettie, over most of the next year her father sexually abused her, trading her dimes for the cowboy movies in exchange for her silence. Even though he did not have intercourse with her, this was Bettie's first sexual experience, and it made her ashamed. It was the 1930s. Sex was taboo. No one had ever talked to her about it. When she had her first period, she was convinced she was fatally ill. The abuse she suffered at Roy's hands would follow her the rest of her life, undoubtedly contributing to her mental deterioration as an adult.

The frightened young teenager wished she could be somewhere far away from Roy, somewhere better. She spent every weekend mesmerized in the dark, looking for that place in local movie theaters, spellbound by Roy Rogers, Bette Davis, Katharine Hepburn, Clark Gable, and Humphrey Bogart. Bettie dreamed about being in their world. On the silver screen, there were no Roy Pages waiting to take advantage of you. No one would hurt her if she was a movie star, Bettie probably reasoned. By her early teens, Bettie knew the layout of each theater in town from the Vendome to the Knickerbocker to the Princess to the Paramount.

In contrast to her earlier and later years, and perhaps in reaction to her sexual abuse, Bettie became very introverted. A naturally intelligent girl, her head was perpetually buried in school books. She occasionally took some ribbing from other kids, but she found a protector in her brother Jimmie, a strapping boy, big for his age and quick with his fists. She didn't think she was any smarter than the other students, she just studied more. It was probably best that Bettie was studious, though, because her mother was very strict and wouldn't have allowed much else. Edna Page took the girls to Nashville's First Baptist Church every Sunday and spent the weekdays lecturing them about the wages of sin, which must have rested heavily on Bettie, who says she kept Roy's abuse secret for six decades.

At fourteen Bettie was selected to attend Hume-Fogg High School, the oldest high school in Tennessee and a school that drew talented students. Its other alumni include the late entertainer Dinah Shore. Bettie joined the student council as its secretary-treasurer and was very active at Hume-Fogg, preferring it to home, where she was lost in a sea of siblings and had to put up with Edna . . . and Roy.

Showing a natural propensity toward English and writing, Bettie joined the reporting staff of the school paper, the *Fogg-Horn*, in her sophomore year. By the next year, she was one of its two editors. Often she stayed after school into the evening, working on the paper and its layout. The year she graduated, her efforts were rewarded by the National Scholastic Association, which gave the student paper a first-place award. Bettie was obsessed with the better life that could be offered to her after high school, and when many girls were thinking of marriage and families, she was dreaming of careers and adventures, of fame and fortune. Consequently, Bettie joined almost every organization the school had to offer, while keeping up her excellent grades in hopes of winning the school's valedictorian scholarship.

She edited the school's yearbook, *Echo*, was program chairman of the college club, and was a regimental sponsor for the three high school ROTC chapters in Nashville. By this time, Bettie had developed a curvy silhouette. With her hair parted in the middle and brushed back into dark, flowing wings, she resembled a young Judy Garland.

Marching in uniform alongside the boys at ROTC parades, her extraordinary beauty captured a lot of attention. But the boys who pursued her hit a brick wall. Edna forbade her to date. Ironically, Bettie, now the most popular girl in school, was probably the most lonely. Edna's cruel protectiveness knew no bounds: Bettie wasn't even allowed to go to her own senior prom.

3

....

Bettie and Billy

"HEY, BEAUTIFUL! Are there any more at home like you?"

Bettie looked up from her book, startled. It was a month before her high school graduation, and she had been walking down the road in Shelby Park, taking advantage of the spring weather to memorize a debate-club speech about federally owned railroads. A small convertible roadster had screeched to a halt beside her, shattering the solitude. The tall, thin, black-haired country boy riding in the passenger seat was the one calling her.

Bettie sighed, annoyed. "Yes, there's two, and they're both prettier than me. Why don't you go look for them?"

"Look, sister, I'm sorry. We was just having fun. Whatcha reading?" He tossed the basketball he was holding in his lap as he spoke, catching it in his hands. He was good-looking, Bettie noticed, but he also looked just a little mischievous.

"It's a debate-team speech. What did you think it was, football plays?" Bettie said playfully as she lowered her book. He was Billy Neal, he told her, and he played football and basketball at East High School. Bettie stood in her sweater and skirt, her feet shifting nervously in her bobby socks and black-and-white saddle shoes. She and Billy spoke for a few more minutes, and then Bettie excused herself to catch a bus. Billy watched her walk to the park entrance and take her place beside the bus stop sign, lifting her book up in front of her face again.

Billy asked his friend to drive over to her. "Hey, come on, Bett-ey," he said with a thick country accent. "Git in and we'll take yuh home."

Bettie looked at the boys cautiously and figured they were pretty harmless—besides, she never really got to meet boys outside of church and school. She hopped in the backseat and the trio chatted with brief interruptions as she gave them directions. As they came to the road leading to her house, Bettie yelled out, "Stop the car! Stop the car here!" The two boys looked puzzled.

"I thought you said you lived down the next road," Billy said.

"I do. But Mama doesn't allow me to date. I'll have to get out here."

About a week later, Billy was playing basketball with Frank Duncan, a friend who went to Bettie's high school. "Hey, Frank, you know a girl who goes to Hume-Fogg by the name of Bettie Page?" he asked.

"Heck, yeah, I know her," Frank said, looking at Billy like he had just asked if Frank knew that air was for breathing. "Everybody knows Bettie." While Frank was distracted, Billy took the opportunity to get past him to score.

"Well," Billy said, throwing the ball back to him, "What's the chance of me getting a date with her?"

"Everybody tries to date Bettie," Frank said, out of breath. "Only her mother won't let her date anybody."

"Well, I'm going to date her," Billy said, as he took the ball from Frank and sent another score swishing through the basket.

Billy started playing hooky from school, hanging around Hume-Fogg in hopes of seeing Bettie again. He was two years older than Bettie and a year behind her in school. If he had devoted the amount of attention to his studies that he did to pursuing Bettie, he could've been a rocket scientist. And his persistence paid off. Bettie agreed to go to the movies with him on a Saturday afternoon.

Bettie was seventeen years old and about a month away from graduating high school when she had her first date. Billy was fascinating to Bettie, who yearned to see the world instead of just watching it on a movie screen. He told her how he had spent the last two summers hitchhiking cross-country and taking odd jobs. While traveling through California and Arizona, he told her, he thumbed rides with Lew Ayres, Clark Gable, and William Holden. Bettie was in love.

The next weekend, Bettie sneaked away from her mother's watchful eye and met Billy at the movies for a double date with Frank and his girlfriend Toni. None of them had any money, so Betty turned on her charm and, batting her eyelashes, asked the usher if she and Toni could use the ladies' room. Then the two girls sneaked back to the exit and let Billy and Frank in the theater.

Before too long, Billy and Bettie found ways to go dancing on double dates at the Pines and the Palms, Nashville-area ballrooms where Snooky Lanson, a popular big-band singer, performed. Sometimes Bettie left her house secretly for nighttime picnics at Nashville's Percy Warner Park, where she and Billy would roast hot dogs and marshmallows and Billy taught her new dance steps to big-band music played on an old, hand-cranked Victrola. On one of these excursions, Billy borrowed a friend's car and Bettie lost her virginity in the backseat to the country-boy athlete.

Inevitably, Bettie's whirlwind affair with Billy caught up with her. Her mother heard about Billy and confronted Bettie as he dropped her off at home one night. In May 1940, about a week before graduation, Edna told Bettie she could never see Billy again. Bettie stormed out of the house, taking with her only the clothes on her back. It wasn't the first time Bettie and Edna had battled. As her own beauty faded, and Bettie's grew, Edna had begun treating Bettie less like a daughter and more like a rival. The two had come to blows the year before, when Edna's boyfriend, a young man in his twenties, had tried to force himself on Bettie in his car. Bettie not only had to fight him off, but later had to battle Edna as well. When Edna found out, she tore into her daughter like a tiger, ripping one of Bettie's most beloved sweaters from her chest and tearing at Bettie's breasts with her fingernails in a jealous rage. Bettie was thrown out of the house and had to live with her father until Edna relented months later.

After Edna forbade her to see Billy, Bettie again moved in with her father and former abuser, Roy, and his second wife, Lulu, a good woman who liked Bettie and looked after her. Billy took a part-time job and bought Bettie a few secondhand dresses so she would have clothes for school.

For some time before she met Billy, Bettie had been pursuing another love of her life: acting. She had performed in a two-act mystery called *The Tiger's Claw* at Hume-Fogg and had quickly moved on to roles such as Shakespeare's Lady Macbeth, and Kate Pettigrew, the lead in *Berkley Square*. She said in her yearbook that she dreamed of singing torch songs with a big-band orchestra, and hoped to study at a conservatory, even though she now admits she couldn't carry a tune.

Shortly before her graduation, Bettie skipped a two-hour art lab to practice in final rehearsals for the school's senior play, *Oh, Clarissa!* It cost her an A in the class and the school's valedictorian scholarship, which went to the school's Civitan medalist, Barton Murphy.

The night before graduation, a Saturday, Bettie was fighting a bad cold and riding home on a bus with Roy. She was steamed because he had waited until the last minute to buy her a graduation dress, but after a lot of frantic looking, she had finally found it—the perfect dress. She reached down at her feet to pick up the bag to have another peek at it when she realized it wasn't there. She thought Roy had picked it up, and he thought she had it. Roy Page told the bus driver to stop. He and Bettie ran down the street back to Morris's Dress Shop, where she had bought the dress, but the store was already closed for the weekend. Through the window, they could see the bag with Bettie's dress sitting on the counter.

They couldn't reach the store owner by phone, and Bettie, who now had no white dress to wear to graduation, was inconsolable. The next morning, in desperation, and still coughing and sick from the cold that had kept her awake all night, she went to the YWCA and knocked on doors at random, asking if any of the ladies there could loan her a dress. One woman took pity on the seventeen-year-old and lent her a formal white organdy gown.

On June 6, 1940, at Nashville's War Memorial Auditorium, Bettie delivered her salutatory speech, "Looking Forward," and received a scholarship from the Daughters of the American Revolution to attend the nearby George Peabody College for Teachers. It should have been one of the happiest moments in her life, but Bettie wept. Voted smartest and most likely to succeed by her classmates, Bettie graduated second in her class with a 97.19 grade-point average. The class valedictorian's grade-point average was less than a quarter of a point higher than hers. Also, Edna had not even bothered to attend her graduation.

In her senior will, Bettie left nothing to rising seniors because, she said, she had everything and was taking it with her. Everything that is, but the prestigious scholarship to Tennessee's Vanderbilt University that went to the valedictorian. Still, her classmates believed that Bettie had a grand future in store. They predicted that in 1970, thirty years in the future, Bettie would star with Mickey Rooney in a remake of *Ninotchka*.

During the summer, Billy and Bettie danced at local dance halls and made love in the park. They had fewer problems from Roy Page than they ever would have had from Edna, but Billy and Roy still clashed fiercely, and it would certainly have been worse had Billy known about the abuse. Once Bettie came to Billy in tears because Roy had called Billy a no-good, black-headed son of a bitch. That was all Billy needed. Despite the fact that Bettie's father was a sturdy bearlike man, weighing about 240 pounds to Billy's gangly 135, Billy burst into Roy's auto shop ready to fight, a tire iron in his hand. Roy was sitting near the pot-bellied stove in his office, playing cards on a nail barrel with some friends.

"I hear somebody called me a no-good son of a bitch," Billy said to him.

"You been talking to Bettie, I guess," Roy said.

"Yeah, well, I don't appreciate what you said to her or me," Billy shot back. Roy started to get up from behind the barrel, but Billy hefted up the tire iron. "Don't move or your head's busted," Billy said coolly.

"I never did have no more trouble out of him after that," Billy said years later in an interview with *The Betty Pages*. Roy told Bettie she could do what she wanted, he was tired of fooling with her.

In the fall, Bettie started classes at George Peabody. She had a promising career as an English teacher ahead of her, but she hadn't abandoned her dreams of stardom. Just as she had done in high school, she immersed herself in drama. She was secretary of the Peabody Players, the campus drama club, from 1943 to 1944, and she acted in seven plays while at Peabody including Noël Coward's *Cavalcade*, performed in the school's Demonstration Auditorium, and Thornton Wilder's *Ah! Wilderness!*, which was based on a Willa

Cather novel. A review in the campus newspaper, the *Peabody Reflector*, praised her role in another play, *Love From a Stranger*: "As a silly, none-too-bright maid, Bettie Page proved her mettle as an actress." Bettie also joined the Peabody Players radio guild, acting in fifteen-minute live radio dramas broadcast weekly from the college. She even wrote her own radio play, ponderously named *The Significance of an Urn*, a mystery about an ancient house with a spooky hidden chamber. It appealed to Bettie's darker side and her attraction to gothic ghost tales, a frequent source of fun reading for Bettie.

Bettie also took her first secretarial job in her freshman year, working for Dr. Alfred Leland Crabb, a well-known education professor and author of three Civil War mystery novels, *Breakfast at the Hermitage, Dinner at Belmont,* and *Supper at the Maxwell House,* the latter after the Tennessee landmark from which the famous coffee takes its name. He dictated all three books to Bettie, who typed the manuscripts for each. Bettie spent weekends with Crabb and his wife, who became a surrogate mother to her, and was certainly a more loving one than Edna. Bettie slept in their guest room on a huge four-poster feather bed. Mrs. Crabb took pleasure in doting on Bettie, running baths and fixing meals for her. The skills she learned as Dr. Crabb's gal Friday would serve her the rest of her life through many secretarial posts, some to captains of industry.

By the time the Japanese bombed Pearl Harbor on December 7, 1941, Billy, now twenty-two, was an A-1 draft choice. He worried constantly about what would happen to his relationship with Bettie if he were sent overseas. He was working blue-collar jobs and she was almost a college graduate, soon to be a school teacher, and was attracting more than her share of notice on campus with her bright smile, shiny black hair, long legs, and shapely body.

The air force cadets called her the Duchess and raised their swords as she walked by. At school dances, Billy would almost come to blows with the young college guys who tried to dance with her.

He badgered Bettie to marry him, pleading over and over, but she kept turning him down. "What if I'm killed over there?" he would plead.

One Saturday morning shortly after Valentine's Day in 1943, he talked Bettie into going on a day trip. She put on a black cotton jersey dress, and they hopped a bus about thirty miles north of Nashville to the town of Gallatin in Sumner County. It was the farthest they could get on the ticket they could afford.

The new brick courthouse in Gallatin was one of many built around the country during the end of the Depression by the WPA as part of Roosevelt's New Deal. It was a popular place to get married because of the mountain view, and the justice of the peace often hung around the courthouse to make some money doing weddings.

Billy and Bettie were wed in the office of the clerk of the court, Hubert "Hub" Perdue, a former pro baseball player turned politician who talked sports with Billy while he filled out the marriage application. Billy had obviously planned it all out: A civil ceremony required no waiting, and in Gallatin, where they didn't know anyone, no one could pick up the phone and warn their families.

Afterward, Bettie sat on the bus outside the courthouse and wondered to herself, "What have I done?"

4

···

Changes

In 1944 Bettie moved to the head of her class and took a student teaching job at George Peabody's demonstration high school, a college preparatory school for talented students. The newlyweds at first had lived with his parents, but soon moved into an apartment near Tennessee's Vanderbilt Hospital because of friction between Bettie, Billy, and her in-laws. Billy resented Bettie going to college as well as her aspirations to be a teacher, and he made frequent digs about her acting smarter than him. Billy's father clearly didn't think much of a woman getting an education, either, and derisively referred to Bettie as the "college girl." For her part, Bettie wasn't upset that Billy didn't want go to college, but she couldn't understand his small-minded attitude about her getting an education.

The argument wasn't fated to last long, though. Billy soon got his draft notice from the army and Bettie was looking at a career as an English teacher. However, fate decreed that Bettie would not be the Queen of Grade Curves. With Bettie in the classroom, teenage boys had a lot more on their minds than Shelley and Keats. Bettie recalled her student teaching as a disaster. She never had a hope of retaining control of a class full of the same kind of red-blooded American boys who would be buying her pinups a decade later. It's easy to imagine the boys overwhelming their shapely twenty-one-year-old teacher with wolf-whistles and catcalls. But to be fair, no alumni contacted from that period could remember Bettie, and they said that they had no recollection of any class being out of order or disrespectful to a teacher. Former students also said that student teachers from the college rarely led a class, so one must conclude that Bettie was either given preferential treatment as an honor student, or she simply made too much of her limited responsibilities in the classroom.

Whatever really happened to disillusion Bettie with teaching, she graduated from Peabody that spring with a bachelor's degree in education that she didn't plan on using. Bettie learned from the experience, however: Instead of viewing her beauty as a hindrance, she tried to cash in on it. When the Gene Kelly–Rita Hayworth musical *Cover Girl* premiered that year, a series of promotional beauty pageants were held across the country. Bettie entered Nashville's contest and came in second.

Meanwhile, Billy had been called to the 63rd Infantry army base in Mississippi, where he ended up spending more time in the stockade than on the training field. When Bettie would take a train down from Tennessee to spend the weekends with him, Billy would just sort of forget that a weekend pass lasted for only a weekend. Many men would have risked going AWOL for Bettie, but Billy went one better: He busted out of the stockade to see her—twice.

Up for a court martial, which in wartime was the kiss of death for anybody looking for a job, Billy could get off the hook only one way: by being sent into combat. Fortunately, a weary colonel, tired of Billy's antics, had him figured for a deserter and punished Billy with exactly what he wanted. Within a week Billy was stationed in San Francisco on a ship scheduled to shove off in a month for combat in the Pacific Theater.

Thrilled to be leaving Tennessee for the land of sunshine and movie stars after her beauty-pageant success, Bettie barely took time to pack before joining Billy in California. Billy, on the other hand, was a little less enthusiastic. He was under constant guard, living under house arrest, when he got the word that his ship would be leaving harbor two weeks early. Luckily for him, one of the officers on his new post, a guy named P.J., had been the equipment manager on one of Billy's high school football teams. Billy winked and grinned at P.J. every time he saw him, but the young officer just shook his head, telling Billy it wouldn't be good for him to let on that they were friends. Less than a week before Billy was scheduled to be shipped out, P.J. issued him a three-day pass. Billy ran for the apartment that Bettie was renting in San Francisco and made love to her with the gusto of a man facing months at sea. This time, when the pass was up, he went back to his post right away. Nevertheless, the army kept Billy under guard until his ship was three miles at sea.

The U.S. government obviously respected Bettie's powers.

As the months at sea piled up for Billy, things were looking up for Bettie. Even before his ship had left the harbor, she had taken back her maiden name and became more convinced than ever that their marriage had been a mistake. Rather than write Billy a Dear John letter, she figured it could wait until he returned. In the meantime, she made a life for herself in San Francisco, taking a job as a secretary to the sales manager of the Enterprise Engine and Foundry Company. It was a good job and the people were nice. She settled into her apartment and spent much of her time admiring the bay, wandering the streets among the thousands of sailors stationed in wartime San Francisco. At night she sewed, making form-fitting dresses to wear to work, patterning them after outfits she had seen in movies and magazines.

Not too long after Billy left, in 1945, Bettie was sitting at her desk when an older man who looked to be in his sixties introduced himself. His name was Art Grayson, and he had come to Enterprise Engine and Foundry looking to scare up new business for his window-washing company. But, as he told the starstruck Bettie, he had also once been a director of silent movies. He still ran a talent agency and an advertising production business on the side, Hollywood Commercial Motion Pictures. He told Bettie that he thought she would be perfect for some newspaper ads he was doing, as well as for a project at Twentieth Century–Fox he had heard about.

It didn't take much to convince the eager young woman. She posed for several still photos at Grayson's studio, and a couple of weeks later, she received a telegram from Twentieth Century–Fox asking her to come to Los Angeles for a screen test. At age twenty-two, Bettie had made it to Hollywood, but she almost didn't get there in one piece. As she and Art Grayson were preparing to board a plane for the audition,

Grayson's wife came running down the air field gateway, accusing him of running off with Bettie. He had never even so much as given Bettie a suggestive look, she tried to tell the older woman, but his wife wouldn't buy it. Grayson had to board the plane while running from his wife. Once at the studio, Bettie was escorted to makeup on the back lot, where she was made up to resemble Joan Crawford, her hair scrunched up on the sides, eyebrows magnified to Groucho Marx proportions, and lipstick smeared across the corners of her mouth. Dressed in a white sailing outfit, Bettie did a short screen test opposite John Russell, the actor who would later star on TV's *The Lawman*.

A week later, she was called in to view the results. She was mortified. Instead of the cute knockout girl-next-door the movie moguls had seen in Grayson's photos, Bettie was a whorish caricature of herself, caked with makeup. Her deep Southern accent didn't help matters, and Bettie wasn't willing to sway the producers' decision with a tumble on the casting couch. One of the studio executives had asked her to dinner, but Grayson had told her not to date anybody from the studio. Besides, Bettie didn't think he was good-looking. She turned him down and he told her, "You'll be sorry." The executives gave her a don't-call-us-we'll-call-you and Bettie returned to San Francisco, heartbroken at having been so close to her life's ambition, only to see it taken away. She was given a few negatives from the screen test to take home for a souvenir.

She spent a lot of time looking at those negatives in the following weeks. Deeply dismayed, she stuffed herself with a junk-food diet of doughnuts, ice cream, and chocolate. But after she gained almost forty pounds, Bettie decided that was enough. She sweated it out by exercising at the local YWCA and started eating health foods—habits that would follow her throughout her lifelong struggles with her weight. Back to a shapely 118 pounds, Bettie enrolled in a modeling course, figuring nobody could hear her voice in a photograph. She paid $100 to learn such secrets of the trade as how to balance a book on her head while walking. Pretty soon, through her contacts from modeling school, Bettie landed a job working as a full-time secretary and part-time runway model for Geary Furriers, where she quickly became accustomed to the silky, luxurious feel of ermine. She also entered another beauty pageant and placed second again, winning a $50 war bond. First prize in the contest at the Paramount Theater was a $100 war bond. Bettie thought a beautiful young woman in a blue bikini should have won. But the pageant was judged by a bunch of sailors who thought it would be funny to award the top prize to the contestant who wore the most clothing, and a girl clad in an evening gown was the winner. Bettie's successes there and at Geary Furriers soon led to a higher-paying job as a model and secretary for the Liliane Suit Company on Market Street.

One Saturday afternoon, as she was lying on her stomach on the beach, a young sailor named Joe walked by. He had just returned from a long stretch of duty, and while his ship was under repair, Joe and his fellow crewmates were on extended shore leave. This particular day, he had decided to take a walk down to the beach, but was stopped cold in his tracks by the hottest woman he had ever seen. Even from behind, Bettie was quite a sight! For some strange reason, there were so many sailors parking their towels around Bettie's that you'd have thought that corner of the beach was the only place the sun was shining.

Joe figured he had to outdo his competition. He raced down to the water's edge, scooping up a bit of the icy bay water in his hands, and ran to where Bettie lay, throwing it on her back. She looked up outraged, while the guys around her laughed. She took off after Joe with her fists swinging, chasing him down the beach. Fortunately for Joe, Bettie liked his handsome looks and didn't stay sore for long. After introductions, they were ready for their first date.

Bettie and Joe spent most of their time together haunting San Francisco's restaurants and movie houses. They'd walk along the bay at night, strolling in the moonlight to Bettie's apartment. Sometimes Bettie would tell Joe about her dreams of stardom, pulling out her photos and screen test negatives to show him. Soon after Joe and Bettie met, Bettie's sister Goldie came for an extended visit. She moved into Bettie's boardinghouse apartment at 1129 South Van Ness Street in the Mission District and took a job in the lingerie section of a local department store.

Not too long after Goldie moved in, Bettie got off work one night and found her sister sitting on the steps, a torrent of tears rushing down her face. Between sobs, Goldie told Bettie that she had been shaving her legs in the bathroom sink when it fell off the wall. Their fierce runt of an Italian landlord, Joseph Pace, had screamed and cussed at Goldie, saying she had pulled the sink off the wall, and he threatened to hit her. Furiously angry, Bettie rapped on the man's door and told him not to cuss at her sister again. The next morning, Pace came to the Page sisters' apartment, hammering his meaty fists on the door. When Bettie opened the door, he threw a punch. Goldie grabbed an empty milk bottle and smashed it over the landlord's head, cutting his face. Pace swore out a warrant against the two girls, and two detectives came by and dragged them to court. The newspapers had a field day with two young women accused of beating up their fifty-two-year-old male landlord, and Bettie's picture ended up in the *San Francisco Examiner* beside an article headlined, LANDLORD SAYS GIRLS BEAT HIM. On March 25, 1946, Bettie and Goldie stood trial for misdemeanor assault and battery. Pace claimed Bettie punched him in the eye and broke his glasses before Goldie hit him with the milk bottle. The girls said he was lying and pleaded not guilty. "He wasn't wearing glasses, and even if he had, I couldn't have broken them because I hit him on top of his head," Goldie told the judge. Bettie said she and Goldie acted in self-defense, adding, "He would have killed me if Goldie hadn't done something," but it was all to no avail. Municipal Judge Daniel Shoemaker gave the Page sisters thirty-day suspended sentences and ordered Bettie to pay Pace $10 for his glasses. This was the first of many run-ins Bettie had with the law.

Around the same time, Bettie's favorite little brother, the protective and pugnacious Jimmie, was also in the city on shore leave from the navy. (All of her brothers were in the service by then. Her older brother, Billy, was in the Army Corps of Engineers, building bridges in Europe, and her youngest brother, Jack, was cooking on a navy destroyer escort.) Jimmie, a gunner's mate on a Pacific destroyer, was a former Golden Gloves boxer whose career had ended with a broken jaw in a finals bout in Chicago. Later he earned a winning reputation as a fighter in navy matches. Jimmie was crazy about his sister, and he soon grew to like her boyfriend Joe, so he obviously must have agreed not to tell Billy Neal about Bettie's affair. The four of them—Joe, Jimmie, Bettie, and Goldie—went out together before Jimmie and Joe were shipped back overseas.

Joe returned once during 1945, and he and Bettie picked up where they had left off. But when he came back a year later, in April 1946, Bettie told him that she couldn't see him anymore. She said she had just met another sailor and they had gotten married. The "new" sailor was her husband, Billy. Recently discharged, the country boy had come back looking for his wife. Gaunt and wiry, Billy had shriveled away to just 84 pounds in a military hospital after being stricken with a severe case of dysentery in the Pacific. When he returned to Bettie, he weighed about 117 pounds, still some twenty pounds underweight. He argued with Bettie about her not using her married name and accused her—rightly—of having affairs with other sailors while he had been gone. Though she says she admitted the relationship to Billy, Bettie denied having sex with Joe. She and Billy stayed together for a month, and she got pregnant. Billy denied the child was his, saying he was told by army doctors that he was sterile, and that led to more accusations of Bettie sleeping around. Exasperated, Billy was ready to go back home to his family and purchased bus tickets for Nashville. Bettie told him to go without her.

In Nashville, Billy wrote to Bettie constantly. He worked out at the YMCA with Bettie's brother Jimmie, who liked him. "I don't blame Bettie for not coming home, the way you look," Jimmie would say, ribbing the downhearted Billy. Around this same time, perhaps in an effort to recruit her support in his bid to win Bettie back, Billy went to visit Bettie's mother, Edna, who had moved to Pittsburgh after marrying a Catholic army sergeant named Bill Darby. Unfortunately, Billy didn't know that Edna had lied to Darby to placate his devout family, telling him that she was unmarried and had no children. The deception lasted until Billy showed up at their front door, and the marriage lasted for only a few years more. Edna and Bill Darby divorced in 1953. Bettie was incensed at her mother's denial of her children.

However, things were looking up for Billy. After some cajoling from Jimmie, Bettie returned to Nashville a month later, and moved in with Billy at his parents' house. In California she left behind an offer for a second screen test, this time from Warner Brothers. Art Grayson had forwarded the telegram to her, but to her eternal regret, she didn't answer it, choosing instead to try to save her marriage in view of her pregnancy. It was a bad decision, no matter how she looked at it. From the moment she moved in with Billy, the arguing was ceaseless. He was jealous of everyone, including her brother Jimmie, and wouldn't allow her to go out to the movies or even skating. Not too long after, Bettie miscarried. The baby had been the only thing holding her to Billy, she realized, and so she squirreled away her money for five months, working as a secretary in the state Office of Price Administration, and left him in the fall of 1946.

This started years of footloose drifting for Bettie, who early in 1947 went to Miami, not because she knew anyone or had any prospects there, but simply because she had always wanted to see the Atlantic Ocean. In later years, Florida would become Bettie's only sanctuary and she returned to it again and again. During her first stay in Miami, Bettie filed for divorce from Billy, admitting failure and feeling somewhat guilty—perhaps not about hurting Billy's feelings, but instead about the fact that she had fallen prey to the same amatory desires that had destroyed her parents' marriage and driven away her father.

Not long after leaving Billy, Bettie was walking along Miami Beach, when she met a furniture importer who owned a mahogany furniture manufacturing firm in Haiti. He was being forced out of business by mounting political tensions between the island nation and the United States and needed a secretary and stenographer to accompany him on a trip to close out his affairs in Haiti. He offered Bettie a salary and additional money for plane fare and expenses. The man's wife, who owned a hat shop, was staying behind to manage their businesses stateside.

Bettie lived and worked in the poor Caribbean nation for four months. It was an experience that stayed with her the rest of her life, purging the lingering racial prejudices she kept from her childhood in the South. She recalled ashamedly how, when she was a girl in Nashville, she had hurled racial epithets at an older black girl who had thrown her to the pavement and stolen cigarette trading cards from her. Bettie made many friends in Haiti, both black and white, and got as much out of the tiny island as she could, immersing herself in its culture and history. She climbed the three-thousand-foot summit of a mountaintop fortress by mule, dismounting and creeping on her stomach to get the best view over the edge of the fort built by the Haitian slave-turned-king Henri Christophe. Soon, she found love again. This time it was a steamy affair with a man who turned out to be married. Bettie says that she refused to see him after she found out, but recalls with a thrill the time he led her in darkness through the thick Haitian woods to eavesdrop on a Haitian voodoo ceremony. Bettie's heart raced in time with the drums in the darkness of the tropical jungle as natives in masks danced around a bonfire in a trancelike state to offer themselves to their gods. This encounter foreshadowed her later jungle photos, in which Bettie, looking very much like a brunette version of Sheena, Queen of the Jungle, pranced around in mock terror of "cannibalistic" tribesmen.

Bettie was a big hit with the American contingent in Haiti and dined frequently with the U.S. ambassador, who offered her a job as his secretary. But she never got the chance to take it. Like most of the good moments in Bettie's life, it was short-lived. She would have been glad to leave her present employer, and for more reasons than just better pay and a better title. For almost three months, the furniture importer had never said anything remotely suggestive to her, but one night he took her on a trip to Port-au-Prince and parked in a swamp forest. There, he tried to rape Bettie. She fought him off, crying her eyes out at his betrayal.

Bettie had filled out all the applications and was preparing to start her new job as the ambassador's secretary when civil unrest grew ugly in Haiti over President Truman's denial of key aid to that tiny nation. Haitian students rioted in the streets, threatening to pull Americans from their beds and kill them in their sleep. Under guard of U.S. military police, a frightened, shaken, and bleary-eyed Bettie boarded a plane along with the other Americans on the island and fled Haiti in the middle of the night, as crowds of hostile villagers threw rocks and bottles and yelled for them to go home.

Back in Miami, Bettie was without direction once again, but she met a famous comedian, Jackie Whalen, who enlisted her for his nightclub act. She sat in the audience and posed as Miss Tennessee when he introduced her as a celebrity. Maybe it was Bettie's beauty, her acting ability, Whalen's selling power, or just the alcohol, but no one ever saw through the ruse. Excited at having a show-business job, however marginal, Bettie was starting to return to her high school and college dreams. Restlessly wandering through the streets of Miami one night, she had seen a demonstration of a new gadget called a television. Drawn like a moth to its light, she now knew that Hollywood wasn't the only option for a would-be actress anymore. Ready for another try, she headed north to New York, the television signal's source, with $50 from Whalen in her pocket and his good wishes in her heart.

By fall 1947, Bettie was living in Manhattan and working as a secretary at the American Bread Company, whose office and bakery were close to Penn Station. Shortly after moving to the Big Apple, Bettie was approached by a good-looking man while she was window shopping on Broadway one night after work. Tall, lean, and sincere-looking, the young man introduced himself and hit it off with Bettie. He said he was going to go dancing that evening with a couple who were waiting to pick him up on Eighth Avenue and asked Bettie to come along. Bettie loved to dance, and with her dangerous combination of fearless derring-do and country girl naïveté, she accepted the stranger's invite right there on the spot. It proved to be one of the worst mistakes of her life. Bettie walked with him to the car, where another young man and his girlfriend were waiting. They stopped at a red light and picked up another two young guys who seemed to be friends of everyone else in the big sedan. Everything seemed innocuous enough, and Bettie was daydreaming of the dance floor and didn't dwell on the new passengers until two more young toughs jumped in the car a little bit down the road. As they crossed the Queensborough Bridge and left the city, Bettie had a sinking feeling that dancing wasn't on the agenda for the evening.

In fact, the driver pulled his large roadster behind a school in Queens. The other girl ran off with him, and Bettie was alone in the darkness with the other five men. They told Bettie they wanted sex. Terrified at the prospect of being gang-raped, Bettie thought quickly, and told them she couldn't because she was having her period. It bought her some time, but it didn't save her. Just when she thought she might make it out of the scary situation intact, one of the men said that if that was the case, then she would have to perform oral sex on all of them before they would let her go. Bettie has said in interviews that she was coerced into performing fellatio on each one of them before they finally drove her back home. They made her promise she would meet them the next Saturday.

Bettie didn't press charges, unfortunately, preferring to put the whole ugly business behind her, but as soon as she was back in her apartment, she phoned Billy and told him she was coming back to Nashville. The sobbing twenty-four-year-old wouldn't tell him or her family what was wrong. She just had to get out of New York, that's all.

Rushing back home, Bettie took a job near Centennial Park with the L&N Railroad's Coach, Paint, and Tank Shop. As usual Billy and Bettie's reunion was short-lived. Neither seemed to ever learn their lesson. Bettie wanted things to be like a fairy tale. Billy, overjoyed at Bettie's return, proceeded to treat her as a treasure—something either to be locked away or always kept within his sight. But Bettie was nothing to be possessed. Billy's jealousy was smothering and over-whelming to her. She would greet a male friend from high school in passing, and Billy would suspect they had been dating. Of course, after Joe, it wasn't a totally unfounded suspicion. Still, Billy took it to new heights of paranoia. He wouldn't even let Bettie go out with her own little brother—and his friend—Jimmie. Even the smallest thing set hard-headed Billy off on a tantrum, according to Bettie. By November, she had had enough. Bettie moved out, got a divorce lawyer again, and took up temporary residence at the same local YWCA where she had found her graduation gown after knocking on doors less than five years before. There was nothing comforting in the move, not even that memory. Not only did she still feel incredible guilt over ending her marriage, which she saw as putting her on the same path as her parents, but Billy wouldn't leave her alone. He'd show up at the YWCA and threaten her, she said. It wasn't a good way to talk her into coming back to him. With little fanfare, and a lot of bravery, Bettie sucked down her pain and fear and moved back to New York, a little wiser—but just a little.

5

....

Falling in Love

TODAY, his friends and family know him as Carl. But in January 1948, he was Carlos Garcia Arrese, the dark, dashing Peruvian engineer who was to become the only man Bettie Page says she ever truly loved.

Bettie had only been back in New York for a few months, and had just regained her courage and determination after her sexual assault in Queens six months earlier. She was renting a small apartment on 78th Street between Columbus and Amsterdam avenues from a sweet old Irish woman named Mrs. Murphy. Still in pursuit of a career in show business, Bettie had enrolled in tap-dancing classes and was supporting herself with a day secretarial job for an insurance salesman, J. H. Lehds, and a real estate developer, Joseph Sussman, who had joint offices at 10 Rockefeller Plaza in the Eastern Airlines Building.

It was there, at the next-door office of the Peruvian Consulate, that Bettie was spotted by a suave, tanned, clean-shaven young man with neatly combed dark brown hair and a thin, muscular build that showed under his tight, black business suit. He had a rogue's grin. His accent was soft and Spanish, his English impeccable. He introduced himself as Carlos Arrese, a twenty-one-year-old engineer. Bettie fell in love with him on the spot, and she never got over him.

"I could say the feeling was mutual. I was very much in love with her," Arrese, now seventy, said in December 1996 from his home in

East Williston, New York. "I was extremely fond of her. Unfortunately, at the time I was married to someone else."

Arrese, a native of Lima, Peru, had moved to the United States in 1943 to go to college at a polytechnic school in Troy, New York, and he later transferred to the Michigan College of Mining and Technology, where he earned a degree in civil engineering. In 1948 he was working for a now-defunct engineering firm on the twenty-eighth floor of the Woolworth Building on Broadway at Park Place. He was also married to a young American woman, who lived with their infant son at her parents' home in upstate New York. On the weekends, Arrese commuted to his in-laws' house in Albany, and during the week he worked in the city.

"We met quite accidentally," he recalled. "I had a brother, who has since passed away in a car accident. He used to be with the Peruvian Consulate in Rockefeller Plaza. Once in a while, I used to go see him. I saw Bettie standing next door to another office. I think she was applying for a job. She was leaning against the wall, standing out in the hallway, waiting for an interview, and I asked her if she would like to sit down. She was very gracious. I brought her into the Consulate, we talked awhile and I wished her all the luck, and she gave me her phone number, and that's how it all started.

"It was very innocent, very casual, and it lasted for a long, long time. A good six to eight months. We were very good friends. I thought I was older than she, but it turns out I was three years younger. At the time, I was twenty-one. She told me she was eighteen. She was actually twenty-four. I could care less. That has no importance whatsoever."

Carlos was smart, personable, and extremely capable, having been entrusted with important jobs early in his career. He did engineering work for the U.S. Army and Navy, and later helped design and build nuclear power plants, electric transmission lines, and a suspension bridge across Long Island Sound. He also helped develop mines in South America, extracting bulk metals such as aluminum from remote locations in Venezuela. Bettie found him both exotic and fascinating. When she got home that day, her landlady told her that Carlos had already been calling for an hour.

He recalled their first date. "We went to a nightclub in the village, a restaurant called El Chico. It was a very high society place, a Spanish restaurant, run by people from Spain." A Latin band played loudly on the bandstand, and Carlos passionately demonstrated his proficiency in the rhumba and other Spanish dances to Bettie. "We had a wonderful time," he said.

Maybe too wonderful a time, in fact. Their date was on a Wednesday or Thursday night, and he and Bettie stayed together for the next couple days. "I was supposed to show up at my in-laws on Friday, but I just stayed the weekend. I forgot about everything. That's the kind of effect Bettie had on me."

When he finally did remember to leave, Carlos met his brother at the train station on the way to Albany. "When I got there, my brother said, 'They know everything.'

"I had just gotten my paycheck. In those days, we got paid [in cash] on Friday, and my in-laws thought maybe I had been mugged, that maybe somebody robbed me and left me lying dead in the gutter." His in-laws had influential friends in New York, Arrese said, and these people called up friends they had at the New York Police Department, who in turn called detectives who tracked down where Carlos worked and lived.

"I used to live at 7 West 68th Street. A small, tiny apartment on the second floor with a balcony. The detectives got the landlady to open the door, and they found this luscious brunette sleeping peacefully on my bed stark naked, and they reported that to Albany. They told my in-laws, 'It's okay, he's keeping company with this brunette.' Bettie had to face the cops, and when I got to Albany, I had to face the music."

For the most part, Bettie took it well. She was "very congenial. We had a wonderful relationship, we really did. When she found out, when those detectives told her that I was married, she described everything we did together to them, and I mean everything! She was enraged, she was mad. She got mad at the detectives. She told them everything. When I got back Sunday night, what I did was, I got in touch with her again and patched things up, and everything was all right after that."

As Bettie has been wont to do, she tells a much different story of their relationship. Perhaps to appease her conscience, and make her role in the adulterous affair seem less sinful, she now says that she had no idea that Carlos was married until the day they broke up. She says that Arrese told her that the pictures of his wife and son in his wallet were really his sister and nephew. But Arrese said her account is "not at all accurate." He never showed Bettie pictures of his wife or his son, and he says, "After that episode, when the detectives found Bettie there in my place, I told her about my marriage. I told her my wife and I didn't get along that well, that we always argued."

In fact, he says that after that, "Sometimes when we went out, Bettie wanted to pay because she said I had a wife and child to support. Of course, I refused, but that's the kind of person she was, you can see. She was very thoughtful."

He and Bettie went out every day after that, meeting after work or at the Broadway dance studio where Bettie took her tap-dancing lessons. They often dined and danced until midnight and made love until daylight. Asked if the affair was a torrid one, Arrese replied smoothly, "It was that. Extremely so. You could put that in the superlative and you wouldn't be exaggerating."

He and Bettie talked a lot, about movies, current events, and sometimes her ambitions, but she never talked much about her past. "She showed me tons of pictures. She had a tremendous number of pictures. She was extremely photogenic, as you know. She had been to California. She had a suitcase full of pictures of her and famous actors and directors and producers. . . . She told me she didn't want any part of it because everyone wanted to get her in bed. She wasn't about to be exploited. She had been exposed to that Hollywood publicity and she didn't want any part of that."

After several months of uninterrupted bliss, a knock sounded on Carlos's apartment door one night in the middle of the week. It was his wife. "Bettie had a bad cold. I had purchased some medicine for her, nose drops, and I was just putting the drops in her nose when there was a knock on the door. I hid Bettie in the closet, but, unfortunately, my wife saw [Bettie's] pocketbook on the table and started screaming and yelling. I got between them and got Bettie out of there."

"Homewrecker!" his pretty blond wife screamed, tossing Bettie's belongings into the hall and slamming the door after her. Bettie didn't try to fight. It's hard to know if she was ashamed or just tired of sharing the man she loved.

Bettie says that was the end of it, but Arrese says there was a heartbreaking epilogue to their love affair. "The reason why Bettie and I got separated is my first wife threatened to take my son away from me. I didn't want to lose him, and I was having problems with her family," he said. Arrese says he has thought about Bettie all these years, and even tried unsuccessfully to look up her family as he passed through Nashville a few times, hoping to find her. "All these years, I just wanted to communicate with her and explain why I left so suddenly. She knew I was leaving. The night before I left, we made love. I left to go home in the morning, and she never saw me again."

Carl Arrese has been a naturalized citizen for many years. He's retired from engineering, and he dabbles in real estate. Like Bettie, he's been married three times. He has four sons, three daughters, and several grandchildren. All of them, even his current wife, know about Bettie. He's never forgotten her. He first saw her modeling pictures in magazines during the 1950s. He was happy for her and figured she had moved on with her life, so he never contacted her, though he always thought about it. In fact, he's written eight unpublished novels, and "She is in several of those books, just her first name. They're fictional, but there's a good deal of truth in them. That's what they say —the best fiction is the living you put in them. She has been in several of them. They're all different, some are romances."

Nearly fifty years later, Arrese has few mementos of his love affair. He and Bettie never thought to take photos together. But he gets *Playboy* in the mail and occasionally sees the photo tributes to her. His memories haven't faded.

"She was a wonderful person, warm, very sincere, very honest, and, needless to say, absolutely beautiful. I have a picture of Bettie in my head, all these years, it's never dissolved, never disappeared, never changed.

"There was something very unique about her. All I remember is those bangs, and the jet black hair straight down, those deep blue eyes, that light complexion, her turned-up nose, full lips, and she always had a smile, she always did." (Over time Carlos's memory of Bettie may have become influenced by her later modeling photos, because, according to family photos and snapshots taken during the time he and Bettie were dating, she still wore her hair parted in the middle and swept away from her forehead.)

He paused and added, "She said she had a hard time getting over me. Well, I never got over her, I never did, just between us boys."

After her affair with Carlos ended, Bettie left New York discouraged; she drifted south in 1950, visiting her sister Joyce in Coral Gables, Florida. While there, her ex-husband, Billy Neal, found out where she was and started writing, asking her for a reconciliation. Billy was living in Atlanta and working as a shoe-store clerk. Bettie visited him for a month, but as usual, they were more different than they remembered and fought nonstop. After an explosive argument, Bettie fled to the nearest bus station with $16 in her purse. She bought a $14.50 ticket to Washington, D.C., the farthest she could afford to go. With $1.50 left and no friends to call on there, Bettie was as good as homeless. She sought help from the Travelers' Aid Society, which obtained a room for her in a big boardinghouse and helped her get a job. She soon found work as a secretary for an insurance broker who was more interested in playing golf than signing new clients. Bettie spent several afternoons a week on the links, learning the game. Her swing was almost as good as her curves. It was the easiest job she ever had, she would say repeatedly.

By the summer of 1950, she had gotten over Carlos and had built up enough courage to give New York yet another try. After spotting a want ad in the newspapers for a summer theater apprentice's job, she applied and was accepted. She spent the summer acting as an understudy for a summer stock troupe at the Greenbush Summer Theater in Rockland County (New York) near Nyack. There she played occasional roles in *Gentlemen Prefer Blondes* and the regular role of loose lady Mabel in *Three Men on a Horse*. Mostly, however, she painted sets, lugged props, and learned the behind-the-stage business. When the playhouse closed for the summer, Bettie took a room in a house with a family in Spring Lake, New York, and went to work for an attorney. She played with the family's four boys and their puppies and strolled and splashed around the lake. There was also a late summer fling with a motorcycle-riding rebel named Tommy, who would zoom Bettie around the lake and serenade her at the end of their dates with "Good Night, Irene."

In September, Bettie took her savings and moved back to the city, into a small third-floor furnished apartment in the rear of a four-story walk-up on 46th Street next door to the Wentworth Hotel between

Fifth and Sixth avenues. For $46.29 a month (less than she would make in a night of modeling later), Bettie rented the small apartment, which had one sink (in the bathroom), a stove in the living room (which she kept covered with a drape), and a small alcove with a refrigerator and cabinets. Under the living-room window was a low wooden platform step speckled with a rainbow of paint splatters left behind by the previous tenant, an artist. Like her apartment in San Francisco, Bettie made the place hers. She added tile to the bathroom, upholstered the furniture, and stocked the little place with enough houseplants to start a greenhouse. A fishbowl full of angelfish and guppies kept her company.

One October day, not long after Bettie was settled in, she decided to get away from the city, and so she took a fateful stroll along the beach at Coney Island to watch the surf.

Dressed in a sweater and a pair of slacks to beat the brisk autumn chill, she walked slowly along the sandy boardwalk. Looking out onto the beach, she noticed a tall, well-built, light-skinned black man working out with weights. He had a long oval face, aquiline nose, and a friendly smile. After about an hour, he noticed her checking him out and walked over to introduce himself. He was Jerry Tibbs, a New York policeman who walked a beat in Harlem. His hobbies were weightlifting and photography. He asked Bettie if she had ever done any modeling; she lied and told him no.

As the conversation progressed, Betty confided to Jerry that she was an aspiring actress. Well, Jerry said, every model he knew had a portfolio of photos to take with her to auditions. Wouldn't Bettie agree to let him do hers? He'd even do it for free. He gave Bettie his card, and a few days later she met him at his studio in Brooklyn where he took several photos of her, including some shots of her in a bikini and in (and out) of lingerie. She was beautiful, even sultry, but Tibbs felt something was missing. First, much to Bettie's chagrin, he stuffed her bra with Kleenex. He fussed with her makeup and gave her luxuriant eyelashes, but still, it eluded him. Then he turned his attention to Bettie's hair, which, parted in the middle and away from her forehead, made her face look large and severe through his camera's viewfinder. "I know," he said, "Why don't you brush your bangs down?" And

Bettie Page, the black-banged Queen of Curves, was born. From that day forth, she would always style her hair that way. (The bangs style has now become so famous and synonymous with her that it has been featured in *Cosmopolitan* magazine and copied by modern actresses such as Patricia Arquette, Uma Thurman, and Debi Mazar.)

The photos from Bettie's first modeling shoot in New York were published in a small Harlem weekly newspaper. When Tibbs found out how popular the photos were, he sold the Harlem paper some shots of Bettie's "cousin," Laura Page—Bettie without the bangs. Bettie and Tibbs met for several more photo shoots and became friends. He'd phone now and again, seeing if she wanted work, or just to tell her about what he was working on. Their relationship was a strictly platonic one. He was married to a white Jewish woman, more of a social taboo at the time than a black man shooting nude photos of a white woman, as he did with Bettie.

The Tease From Tennessee also tried her luck at local beauty contests around this time. She was a second runner-up in the 1951 Miss New York pageant and she posed in several Long Island swimsuit competitions hosted by *See* magazine. Bettie never won any though, probably because she showed up to most of the contests tired and bleary-eyed from late nights out on the town. In 1953 she took seventh place in *See* magazine's Cover Girl beauty contest, mainly due to the fact, Bettie says, that she and her sister Goldie had been out on a double date the night before and Bettie was exhausted. Years later, the winner of the competition, Elaine Stewart, became an actress, starring in such films as *The Bad and the Beautiful* with Lana Turner and Kirk Douglas.

After meeting some of Jerry Tibbs's camera-buff friends, Bettie soon found lots of work modeling for amateur camera clubs, often in rented studio spaces or in remote outdoor locations such as on New York's Fire Island. Though she was usually at least a half hour late to every shoot, she quickly became quite popular with the photographers because of her cheerful willingness to work nude and to strike almost any pose with a down-home smile.

Bettie felt absolutely comfortable naked, and many of her photographers describe her as a true exhibitionist. In the super-moral era of the 1950s, Bettie broke taboo after taboo. Why was she able to do so? Some could say it was a rebellion against her strict religious upbringing, but others could point to the sexual abuse by her father and the sexual assault by the group of men in Queens. Though it's not a cheery idea to think that Bettie's sex appeal could be rooted in her pathology, experts on sexual abuse say that women often react that way. Victims of past assaults sometimes become sexually promiscuous or exhibitionistic in an effort to gain a sense of power, to gain control over their sexuality. Being sexually active also brings them special attention, which may be equated with the way they felt when their abusers treated them kindly in exchange for sexual favors.

Whatever the reasons behind Bettie's free sexuality, the attention did excite her. She worked overtime to fuel her career, sitting up late by the window of her small apartment, sewing her own bikinis and costumes for the shoots. Sometimes after a particularly long night, she would slip out to the all-night movie houses on 42nd Street, watching movies until dawn, and picturing herself as the leading lady in love scenes with Gregory Peck or James Dean. She drifted from theater to theater on the New York streets, dressed plainly and inconspicuously in a jacket, flannel shirt, and jeans, with a red bandanna tying back her famous black hair. She was also a big fan of horror and mystery, preferring Sir Arthur Conan Doyle's Sherlock Holmes tales and hardboiled crime novelist Raymond Chandler's private dick Philip Marlowe. A book called *Tales of Terror and the Supernatural* kept her awake and sewing for hours.

Once in the early fifties, Bettie was hired for a private photo session by a married couple who wanted to take pictures of her in the selfdesigned costumes and bathing suits they had heard she made. Bettie didn't find out until later what the photos would be used for. It turned out that the couple copied Bettie's outfits and used her picture in magazines to promote their catalog. Like so much of her work, Bettie made only a small modeling fee while someone else made a much larger profit from her image—and in this case, her original designs.

6

Camera Club Darling

ONE OF the photography groups Bettie posed for most often was the Concord Camera Circle, a private club led by Cass Carr, a Jamaican big-band leader turned photographer who used the DeLogue Studios on West 47th Street. Bettie had first started posing for Carr in Harlem, at the YMCA on West 132nd Street, when his club was called the Lens Art Camera Club. Some of the Concord photographers were factory managers, others executives, and some college students. Only a few were professional bread-and-butter photographers. The vast majority of them were men.

Bettie's regular clientele of photographers ranged from amateurs to more noteworthy contemporary shutterbugs like Weegee, the hard-boiled freelance crime photographer of the 1950s who was known for his stark and sarcastic photos of New York City street life. "I am often asked what kind of candid camera I use," he once wrote. "There really is no such thing. It's the photographer who must be candid."

Weegee, a.k.a. Arthur Fellig, took his nickname from the popular Ouija fortunetelling game. His uncanny ability to show up at the right time and place to get the best crime-scene pictures made him look like a psychic. In actuality, he started out listening to police radio calls on a scanner and became so well known that not only would the New York police call to tip him off about murders but so did the Mob. At least once, Weegee got to the crime scene while a couple of unlucky paisanos were still dying. A consummate professional, Weegee took their pictures, then called the cops.

Weegee's world ranged from bowery doorways to high-society affairs frequented by Hollywood luminaries like Montgomery Clift and Elizabeth Taylor, who admired his work. (Taylor reportedly once raised her skirt at a party to get Weegee's opinion of her legs.)

Weegee took dozens upon dozens of photos of Bettie and palled around with her frequently. But he also incurred her wrath on occasion by getting out of line. One time when the short, stocky, street-tough photographer was taking nude photos of Bettie in the bathtub at her apartment he took off his clothes, too, and climbed into the sudsy water with her—to get a better shot, he said. "Out, Weegee! Out!" Bettie screamed.

As for the camera club amateurs, Addison Yeaman Jr. is a good example. In 1951 he was a nineteen-year-old economics major at Yale University, but on the weekends he was one of the camera club guys, making the trek from New Haven, Connecticut, to New York to shoot nudes, seminudes, and lingerie pics of Bettie and the other ladies at Carr's studio on 47th Street.

"It was a very exciting moment for a nineteen-year-old," recalls a laughing Yeaman, who's now a sixty-five-year-old Justice Department attorney specializing in tax fraud. For about $4 or $5 admission each, Yeaman and his buddies would spend a weekend afternoon in Carr's long dark studio, feverishly snapping pictures of their favorite models. "That represented a fair amount of money in those days," he says. "The subway was a nickel and hot dogs were a dime."

Of the models, Yeaman says, "I liked Cocoa Brown, I liked June King, but I think Bettie was a standout. I think she enjoyed being photographed. She always made sure that all the fellas got the shots they wanted. She seemed to enjoy modeling."

Yeaman was a fan of another black-haired cheesecake model, Kevin Dailey. He first heard of Carr's studio after a Yale graduate told him about a new talent who resembled Dailey, named Bettie Page. The friend and another man, both amateur shutterbugs and vice presidents for big companies, took Yeaman along one afternoon when Bettie was posing there.

"It was on the second floor. It was a sort of long, narrow studio," Yeaman recalled. "A long, narrow room. To the right was the dressing room, and to the left, as I recall, was Cass's office, and [the studio] was, oh, I'd say about twelve to fifteen feet wide. On the far wall were the backdrops and lightbars and that sort of thing. And it was usually fairly dark, with the exception of the lights on the posing stand."

A dozen to fifteen photographers lined up in front of the stage where the models posed, though "it was not really crowded," Yeaman says. "There was enough room for people to move about and get the angle and shot they wanted."

After a while, Bettie became a habit. "Usually the word would go out that Bettie was going to be posing on a particular day, and my friends would call me and tell me that Bettie was going to be posing on Saturday and Sunday or something like that, and I would come down from New Haven," he says.

Most of the men there hoped for more than pictures of Bettie, but no one came close.

"I talked to her," Yeaman says. "Nobody dated Bettie. Of course, everybody tried, but the story was that she was engaged to an air force sergeant in North Africa and this was in the period of the Korean war, and in those days, men sort of honored a commitment. If a lady said she was engaged, or had a guy overseas, you sort of said, 'Oh, gee whiz, I'm sorry to hear that.'"

The soldier-fiancé may have been an invention of Bettie's, like the rumor that she kept a brick in her purse to discourage grabby photographers.

Either way, Yeaman says, "I never had that many conversations with her, because, if anything, I was the youngest photographer and I saw her only at Cass Carr's, and maybe one or two other camera clubs. I was just sort of a hanger-on. I didn't know her well. I doubt she would have recognized me if she saw me on the street. Certainly, I doubt she would recognize me now."

Yeaman had hundreds of pictures of Bettie, but threw most of them away over the years at the request of jealous wives and girlfriends. "It was an effort on my part to preserve the amenities. You don't keep a suitcase full of pictures of naked ladies with children around," he said. He has maybe forty or fifty Bettie photos left, and like many men who came in contact with Bettie, he protectively cherishes the memories and mementos he has of her, refusing all offers so far to publish or buy the valuable never-before-seen photographs he has of her.

"I think she was a very exciting model," Yeaman said. "Because, as I said previously, I think she enjoyed being photographed. I think she had a true exhibitionistic streak and I know she enjoyed modeling. And I think it showed in her pictures."

Aside from the indoor shoots that Yeaman attended on 47th Street, Cass Carr also organized massive weekend photo trips that would include four or five models and sometimes as many as sixty photographers, usually amateur middle-class hobbyists and more serious photography devotees. For $8 apiece—bigger money than the indoor shoots, an amount equaling maybe a week's groceries or more—the photographers would gather on Sunday and take hour-long road trips to upstate New York, shooting several models at a time on location, sometimes together and sometimes separately. If a "name" model like Bettie Page was going to be present, the price would jump to $10. Bettie herself earned $10 an hour indoors and $25 an hour when shooting outdoors. With the money she was making, she ditched her secretarial job and was able to make her monthly expenses through the once-a-week shoots alone.

It was at one of these shoots—at the South Salem Dairy in Westchester County—that the entire group was scooped into a paddy wagon by a bunch of local cops who threatened to charge Bettie and the photographers with creating pornography. They had, in fact, been taking outdoor nudes that probably would have been right at home in magazines like *Playboy*, or even the campy *Nude Volleyball Enthusiast*, for that matter.

If everyone agreed to plead guilty, the police said, they would reduce the charges to indecent exposure and disturbing the peace. But Bettie wouldn't play ball. She was steamed because she said a cop had spied on her while she was relieving herself in the bushes. "I am not indecent!" She yelled at the officers. "I will not plead guilty to it! You'll have to charge me with disturbing the peace, too!" Finally, the local justice of the peace fined everyone five dollars and Carr and his photographers signed an agreement pledging not to shoot in Westchester County again.

"The thing that impressed me about Cass Carr in those days that I went to his studio is that he was like a mother hen protecting his little girls," says Art Amsie, a Concord member from 1956 to 1957, whose photos of Bettie are considered to be among the best of the camera club genre.

"I have never seen somebody so prudish and protective," Amsie says, describing Carr. "That may have been an outcrop of the previous experience in upstate New York, where his group was pulled in for taking photographs of some nude models. Once burned, twice careful. In fact, if you rented one of his studios and rented one of his models and wanted to photograph them privately, he didn't allow any nudity or complete full frontal nudity.

"Some of the men were always complaining that Cass would have a reason to pick up some klieg lights or some camera equipment or a tripod so he could peek in and make sure you were not doing something that was illegal. Now, I used his [indoor] studio very seldom, two or three times, and I was not taking any full frontal nudity, but he impressed me as being a mother hen. Very protective of his girls, always telling them they shouldn't do anything naughty."

Amsie, who turned seventy in 1997, is a retired engineer who now runs the National Glamour Archives, in Alexandria, Virginia. The organization features a world-famous gallery of pinup art, including paintings and photography. Amsie's work has been published in a variety of books and magazines. In the early seventies, *Playboy* published a lingerie photo he took of a corseted Faye Dunaway, with whom he had acted in the Harvard Summer Players years earlier while Amsie was enrolled there. At thirty-three, Amsie was older than Dunaway, who, at nineteen, had come to Harvard's Loeb Summer Theater to perform in two plays. Amsie has also been featured on a variety of television programs, such as a show about Bettie on E! Entertainment Television, and an episode about beauty and glamour on the Learning Channel show *Neat Stuff*.

"Bettie Page had effervescence. She had a little-girl quality. She was pert and saucy," Amsie recalls. "You like perky? You like pert? That's the way she looked. Sometimes a little bit saucy, sometimes a little bit haughty. But unless it was an accident and she blinked, she never took a bad picture."

Amsie met Bettie on one of his first outings with Cass Carr's Concord club. At the time, Amsie was a twenty-nine-year-old amateur photographer and full-time student studying for his master's degree in math and physics at New York University.

A classic Jungle Bettie. Fans of the old bondage serials and the 1950s TV show *Sheena, Queen of the Jungle* appreciate this. Though this was taken in the studio, Bettie's jungle-girl look originated in outdoor photos taken in Florida by Bunny Yeager, who also shot Bettie's famous Christmas 1955 *Playboy* centerfold. This look spawned countless comics, statues, and posters, and remains a favorite among Bettie's fans. (*Movie Star News*)

In this photos from Irvin Klaw's Movie Star News studio, Bettie makes even 1950s street clothes look sexy. (*Movie Star News*)

One of the many faces of Bettie. Photographers valued Bettie's range of expression, which could go from humorous to sexy or even intimidating. (*Movie Star News*)

Bettie with self-styled Pin-Up King and entrepreneur extraordinaire Irving Klaw, who started his Manhattan-based mail order pinup photo empire from a struggling used book store and newsstand, after he noticed kids were ripping photos from movie magazines. (*Movie Star News*)

With friend and sympathetic confidante, Paula Klaw, Irving's sister and partner. (*Movie Star News*)

Tamer examples of the Klaw studio's bondage and sadomasochistic photos. Here Bettie paddles an unidentified model with a hairbrush. (*Movie Star News*)

Some of the photos that got Bettie and the Klaws subpoenaed by a Senate subcommittee looking into corruption of juveniles. It was believed that photos like these prompted the bondage-style suicide of a Florida Eagle Scout. (*Movie Star News*)

Still photos from one of Bettie's dancing-girl silents for the Klaws. During a single session, photographers would shoot stills and film, selling both to their customers. (*Movie Star News*)

Bettie relaxing at "home": note the trappings and furniture of the fifties, especially the television. Though TV was still a novelty in many homes, Bettie took advantage of the medium, accepting small speaking roles in commercials, talk shows, and dramas. (*Movie Star News*)

Most of the Klaw photos were taken indoors on a low budget, often using old furniture as props. Displaying the smile— and little else—that made her famous, Bettie's work led to appearances on everything from magazines and record covers to postcards and playing cards. (*Movie Star News*)

In her shoots at the Klaw studio, Bettie switched facial expression quickly, from an innocent country girl in one instant to sultry mistress with a dangerous look the next, as in this shot. (*Movie Star News*)

"I said 'Hi.' She said 'Hi.' How mundane, right? It was at the Cass Carr shoot. She was standing out on the sidewalk. Bettie Page walks up, and I told Cass, 'You want to use my Lincoln, right?' He said, 'Yeah, we don't have a bus.' So I said, 'Put Bettie in the front seat next to me and I'll put a whole bunch of guys in the backseat.' That's how I met Bettie."

Amsie took almost all his pictures in 3-D color-stereo slide film—a popular but expensive 1950s photographic novelty that allowed the viewer to see the image in three dimensions when viewed through a stereo viewer that was sort of a sophisticated version of a child's Viewmaster. He also stuck almost exclusively to photographing Bettie. "A lot of people would come up with the group to photograph Bettie but would end up taking pictures of other models," he explains. "I would go over sometimes to see the new models to see what they were like, but more often than not, I drifted back to Bettie. Why stick with a Chevy when you've got a Rolls-Royce? You may want to see what the new Chevy looks like, but after the quick peremptory glance, you'll want to go back to the Rolls. Why drink André Champagne when you can get Dom Perignon?"

His photos of Bettie are almost all outdoor shots. Bettie often complained about the lack of variety at Carr's indoor studio, as well as the boring backdrops he selected. "Bettie was happier outdoors," Amsie said. "You look at the faces of Bettie. All the faces she's presented, indoors and outdoors. Outdoors, she's absolutely having a good time. It's not a forced smile, just a standard smile. Indoors, she didn't show any exhilaration, effervescence, effusiveness, as she did when she photographed outside with me. She was really having a good time."

Eventually Amsie and about ten other photographers split off from Cass Carr's group, finding Carr's rules too restrictive. They formed the Associated Photographers' Club, which met on Cedar Street in New York, near the site where the World Trade Center now rises. Amsie says his sessions with Bettie furthered his education and developed his present philosophy on pinup art. "Without appearing to be immodest, I was a photographer, as opposed to 99.9 percent of the people who owned cameras in this country. You know what they are? They are snapshooters. I do not take snapshots."

There are three criteria for creating a top-notch pinup, rather than just another picture of a pretty girl, Amsie says. He calls his system

CPE—Clothes, Pose, and Expression. And he says Bettie Page instinctively understood it.

"Once she knew what I wanted, I would give her maybe three or four or five suggestions. She'd say, 'I know just what you want. How's this?' I'd say, 'Bring your head up. Fine. Give me pert. Give me saucy. Give me haughty. Give me this. Give me that.' And then she'd say, 'Okay, how about trying this?' She knew about Clothes, Pose, and Expression. She knew what I wanted."

Unlike the other camera club guys who stood by in quiet awe of Bettie, Amsie became fast friends with her, recognizing in Bettie not just one of the world's most beautiful women, but a fellow intellectual.

"Bettie and I, we're simpatico," he says. "In fact, I proposed to her." When she sent him a copy of her biography recently, Amsie recalled, "She wrote all sorts of nice things, and she said, 'P.S. You wanted to marry me? I'm still waiting for that proposal.' Who knows? Maybe I'll just marry Bettie. Michael, my son, needs a mother."

Amsie describes his affection for Bettie as not just the love an artist has for his subject, but rather on the scale of Henry Higgins's love for Eliza Doolittle in *Pygmalion*.

"I found Bettie so easy to talk to. That was one of the things that attracted me to her. We were having such a good time. I was torn between my desire to date her and the great photographs I was obtaining and I didn't want to hit upon her," he says, especially since Bettie already had a boyfriend, and he was dating other women.

"If I had the opportunity, I would have probably started to date her, and she would have married me, and we would have had a great, great career together," Amsie said wistfully. "She would have been married to this brilliant electrical engineer who is also a great photographer and admires her brains. Smart and sexy scares most men. I have a fetish for women who are beautiful and smart."

Nevertheless, Amsie says, his and Bettie's relationship was a platonic one, limited to long conversations on location and during the drives to and from photo shoots. They talked politics, flying, movies, just about anything except pinup modeling or Bettie's past. "With Bettie, I could go anywhere [intellectually]," he said. "If you were to tape our conversations on the one-hour trip to Fire Island, maybe a psychologist or psychiatrist would be able to spot some indication that she was interested in metaphysical concepts, the intangible, the ethereal. Bettie and I were usually on the second floor in our conversations.

"The only thing I regret about Bettie is my relation with her was too brief," Amsie says. "I would have liked to have known her better. I would have liked to be able to meet her in the early fifties, rather than those two years. Those two years were very rewarding, but those two years went by too quickly for me, as far as Bettie is concerned." Amsie adds, "I got her at the peak and at the end, at the finale of her career. The longer you work at any endeavor, the better you become. In fifty-seven, she was at the apex of her career. People were crazy about her."

One of the last amateur photographers to snap photos of Bettie was Don Whitney, who, at the time, was a manager in charge of lens development with American Optical Company. A New Englander, he traveled to New York on business every six weeks or so and usually carted his camera along in case a good shot presented itself.

In 1957 he decided to try his hand at photographing a figure model, so he called up a couple of studios, looking for a reference. To his surprise, he ended up in a dream private photo session with Bettie Page.

"I had heard her name," Whitney says. "I had not realized she had been in *Playboy*. I did not realize that until sometime later, but her name was familiar enough to know she was one of the better known models and I was lucky to get her."

Over the one-hour session, using a Kodak Retina III-C handheld camera, Whitney took a series of twenty fully nude photos of Bettie on Ektachrome color slide film.

"I was amazed how easy it was to photograph Bettie," Whitney says. "She always had a good expression, she never seemed to blink. She always seemed to assume a graceful pose. She was very photogenic. A very nice person and obviously very intelligent."

Choosing color film for his nudes of Bettie presented problems for Whitney in a day when publishing photos of pubic hair was illegal (the offending hair was *usually* "removed" in the developing process). "I did a lot of color photography. I usually used Kodachrome, but that had to be processed by Kodak in Rochester at that time, and they would not process nudes, nor was it legal to send nude photographs back and forth through the mails. I knew that was not a suitable option, so I used a film I could develop myself." Whitney processed the film in his cellar, mounted the slides, bravely showed them to his wife, and promptly forgot about them for nearly forty years.

Then one day he saw a picture of Bettie in *Playboy*. "The minute I saw her picture, I knew it was Bettie, of course. When I read that article, I said, 'My God, I've got to find those slides.' " He looked all over for them, but to no avail. Then a couple of months later, when his water heater went on the fritz, Whitney went down into his cellar to move some boxes around so he could put in the new heater. In the course of doing that, he noticed a familiar little green steel box. Inside was a smaller plastic box with twenty faded photos of Bettie Page, all never before seen by the public. "I was delighted to have them," Whitney says, "And now I was able to demonstrate to my son and my grandkids and so forth that in effect I had taken those photographs."

Whitney's last memories of the photo session are these: "We had the studio to ourselves. After it was over, we turned off the lights and locked up the studio and then I walked with Bettie along West 56th Street and then down Broadway for several blocks, when we reached a point where Bettie turned off to go to her apartment. I remember feeling quite something walking along with this very glamorous girl. It's something I won't ever forget."

In December 1951, Bettie's ex-husband Billy Neal again crashed back into her life, briefly and boisterously. Hoping to win Bettie back, Billy had come to New York City, where he rented an apartment and found work as a welder at an auto body shop. But, unfortunately for him, his country-boy rowdiness jinxed the deal.

Late on the first night he arrived in the city, he walked up to Bettie's building with a cardboard box full of some of the things she had left behind in Tennessee. As he neared her apartment, two city police detectives pulled their car over and asked what he was carrying in the box. They jumped out and made Billy spread himself out on the car. Billy offered to call home so his dad would okay his alibi. The cops agreed and drove Billy over to a restaurant, where he made the collect call home. One of the detectives talked to his dad, who may or may not have been surprised by the call. A couple of minutes later, the cops arrested Billy anyway. According to Billy's version, he was just minding his own business and was nabbed for virtually no reason. However, given his wartime struggles with authority in the military, he probably wasn't the embodiment of civic cooperation when questioned by police.

Early the next morning, unshaven and dirty from a night spent in a New York City jail cell, Billy returned to Bettie's place and knocked on her door. He didn't get an answer so he knocked louder. According to Bettie, who said the incident took place a couple of years earlier than this, she was inside and didn't want Billy to know she was home. He threatened to kill himself if she didn't let him in. Awakened by the noise, an irritated tenant down the hall came out of his apartment wearing only his pajama bottoms to see what was going on.

"He said something smart to me and he was a bigger guy than me," Billy recalled later in an interview published in *The Betty Pages*. "I thought to myself, Well that ol' boy ain't walking down here to talk to me, so when he got into arm's reach, I knocked the hell out of him."

The man fell down a few steps and tried to get his footing, but before he could, Billy pushed himself off the rail and kicked the man in the chest, sending him over the railing and down to the next landing. Billy jumped down onto him and the two men wrestled, rolling down the remaining two flights of stairs, out the front door, and onto the snowy sidewalk. Once outside, the man ran. "I just couldn't figure out why he run, because he had the advantage on me," Billy said in the same interview. "And then I looked down on the snow and saw blood. Well, that scared me—I felt all over myself and didn't find any on me, so I just figured he had cut himself on a nail or something when we were fighting on them steps."

Two nights later, the cops were back for Billy—this time at his front door, and lined up and down the hallway with their guns drawn. They confiscated a small pocket knife stuck in a piece of cheese on Billy's dresser. He said he used it to clean his fingernails "and stuff." Billy was hauled back into court. The tenant he had fought, whose face was slashed pretty badly from mouth to ear, claimed that Billy cut him with the pocket knife. Billy denied it and the case was thrown out for lack of evidence. Bettie was mortified at the whole incident. The neighbor, a man in his fifties, was a friend of hers, and she figured Billy really did cut him. Bettie made another phone call to Billy's father and asked him to fetch his son. She finally relented and agreed to visit her ex-husband at his place, though it was probably just an effort to get him to go away. But if Billy ever had any chance of rekindling the old sparks, they were definitely extinguished three days later when he got into a brawl at a local bar. Everybody else but Billy had the presence of mind to flee from the bar before the cops arrived.

Dragged before the same judge for the third time in less than two weeks, Billy knew he was in for it. The exasperated old judge told him, in words Billy could understand, "Boy, I ain't going to put you in jail. You're going home or I'm going to pick this jail up and set it on top of you and never let you out." Billy took the next bus back to Nashville.

As for Bettie, she barely noticed Billy was gone. She was too busy modeling.

Her impromptu career had really taken off after a camera club photographer, looking to sell some pictures, showed Bettie's smiling face and curvaceous body to magazine publisher Robert Harrison. Harrison, an ex-newspaper man, had built a small empire of cheese-cake mags with titles such as *Wink, Flirt, Beauty Parade, Titter,* and *Eyeful* during the 1940s and early 1950s. His models were busty, his magazines overflowing with cleavage. And for good reason: Harrison taped their breasts together. Bettie quickly became in demand for featured spreads in all his titles. She posed in elaborate prop-heavy burlesque comic-strip-like photo stories such as "What the French Maid Saw"—in which French maid Bettie spies on a shapely woman through a keyhole—and "Pretty Larceny"—in which jailbird Bettie, dressed only in bikini briefs with a numbered sign hanging over her chest, attempts to escape from a sexy, short-haired female guard in hot pants. Other notable photoplays included Bettie as a near-sighted woman driver and as a shapely beauty with a boyfriend who's a real beast—a gorilla! From 1951 to 1956, Bettie made more than seventy-five appearances in the Harrison magazines.

Bettie clearly enjoyed posing for Harrison. It allowed her to employ some of her little-used acting skills from college. Most of the Harrison spreads show a clowning and expressive Bettie demonstrating a never-before-seen comic side. She pouts, she gapes in mock amazement, she sticks her tongue to the corner of her mouth in concentration. The shots are more cute than sexy, more cartoon than portrait, but they're classics, and firmly representative of the innocent pinup days before modeling for men's magazines became more gynecological than anatomical. The only thing Bettie didn't like about posing for Harrison was his habit of enhancing his model's breasts. Bettie's bust was smaller than many other models of the day, but she didn't think she needed the boost. Besides, the duct tape was uncomfortable to wear and intensely painful to remove. Moreover, Bettie thought the tape made her breasts look strange and artificial when she was shot in profile.

Bettie's appearances in Harrison's magazines marked the first time her name had been seen widely in print as a model—and it was also the origin of the misspelling of her first name as *Betty*, which continued until the 1990s. Overnight, she became a "name" covergirl. Outtakes from the dozens and dozens of shots from the Harrison magazines and her camera club shoots soon appeared on the covers of everything from tabloid magazines to record albums and matchbooks. By the mid-fifties, topless photos of Bettie by camera club snapshooters were appearing on some newstands in costly magazines devoted solely to Bettie. Local commercial artists used her as a model for figure drawing books, automobile ads, and the covers of trashy romance novels and sleazy hard-boiled true-crime mags. She never would have been considered for the type of magazine that today's trendy fashion models grace. Bettie wasn't uptown enough, and her pinup reputation had preceded her. Through most of the 1950s, it wasn't unusual to see Bettie's face smiling back at you on newsstands from magazines with captions like "Forbidden Sex Rites of the Tropics!" and "How We Licked the Teenage Sin Clubs."

Harrison made his big money and infamous reputation for his series of *Confidential* magazines, similar to today's *National Enquirer* or *Star*, for which his reporters wrote juicy and scandalous exposés of Hollywood stars. His contacts in the entertainment business and his newspaper background forged other important opportunities for Bettie. He knew the press and, more important, knew how to get space in local columns. With publicity in mind, he took his new star model out on the town in 1951 to the Beaux Arts Ball at New York's Waldorf Astoria Hotel. Bettie's high-society debut was a "coming out" in more than the usual sense—at Harrison's suggestion, she appeared at the costume ball clad only in a pair of black fishnet stockings, high heels, and twin telephone dials over her breasts. A box advertising the next month's cover of Harrison's *Dare* magazine covered Bettie's lower extremities. Bettie was a hit—her number got dialed more times that night than Grand Central Station's did in a week! At the close of the evening, she was crowned Queen of the Ball. Though the title was fleeting, it came with a full set of Revere cookware pots and pans.

7

Movie Star News—
Of Pinups and Bondage

THE HARDEST-working model in 1950s New York became a lot busier after an anonymous camera club photographer decided to show her picture to Irving Klaw, the self-styled Pin-Up King.

All the book and magazine and record covers and even Robert Harrison's pinups couldn't come close to gathering the following Bettie would earn as a Klaw girl. For better or worse, Bettie's fledgling career became much more profitable under Klaw's tutelage, though she was unknowingly about to enter a shadowy world of bondage and leather and become its Dark Angel. To many Bettie fans, her hundreds of Klaw pictures epitomize the essence of Bettie Page, her yin and yang. In some, she is smiling, laughing, clowning—the teasing girl-next-door without a care, the eternal Queen of Curves. In others, she's all business—sultry and serious, dominant and firm; the Kitten With a Whip.

Irving Klaw was a short, balding man who always wore a shirt and tie and usually had a smile on his lips and an eye locked on the ladies. Already a failure in the fur business by age twenty-eight, he opened a struggling used bookstore in 1939 at 209 East 14th Street in Manhattan. His partner was his aloof younger sister Paula, a tall, thin, slightly homely girl with brown hair that she wore in a pompadour style long after the cut had faded from fashion. They were born-and-bred Brooklyners from a family of six siblings.

Irving didn't gamble everything he had on the bookstore, though: He also opened a mail-order magic trick business, the Nutrix Novelty Company. But by all accounts, neither the magic venture nor the used book trade brought him much in the way of financial rewards. However, by the time Irving Klaw turned thirty in 1941, he had started on a path that would transform both his unsuccessful bookstore and mail-order business into a lucrative pinup empire. It all happened after he started to notice that photographs were being torn out of many of the movie magazines on his store's newsstands. With a little surveillance, he discovered the culprits to be neighborhood kids with a penchant for photos of Hollywood stars. One day, after hearing the distinctive sound of ripped paper, he snuck around his bookcases, and cornered a little girl, catching her in the act with a stack of Clark Gable pictures. She pleaded with him: "Please, mister, all the kids do it." In fact, the kids did it with precision. Some used razor blades, and a Katharine Hepburn fan even employed a ruler to give her pirated photos a straighter edge.

A savvy businessman, Klaw let the little girl go and decided to give the public what it wanted. When many stores would simply have moved the magazines closer to the front counter or installed mirrors to end the vandalism, Klaw decided to capitalize on it. He ordered movie stills and surplus lobby photo cards from the big movie studios and was amazed at how quickly they sold. Adding to his good fortune was a steady stream of movie fans coming from the plush Jefferson Theater across 14th Street. His business rapidly outgrew the cramped confines of his basement store, and he soon relocated into the storefront upstairs. He renamed the store Irving Klaw Pin Ups and proclaimed himself Irving Klaw, Pin-Up King. It would soon be known by its more famous name—Movie Star News. Eventually, the store was nothing but file cabinets and boxes of photos from floor to ceiling.

"They were tearing out the pictures in the books. After a while Irving said, 'Why sell books? Let's sell pictures,'" recalls Paula Klaw's son, Ira Kramer, who took over the business after his mother's death in December 1996. "A lot of these studios at that point, they were just throwing this stuff out, but Irving was paying for it."

Irving Klaw's patrons included the full spectrum of movie fans. He got gangster and B-movie fans; he got little boys who collected pictures of the cowboy and serial adventure stars like Buster Crabbe; he got old women who remembered silent film stars; and he got swooning, moon-eyed teenage girls, much like Bettie herself had been in Nashville. She must have enjoyed the store quite a bit, finding it reminiscent of her dimestore days when she would post pictures of the stars on her bedroom wall and use their world as an escape from her own unhappy childhood. As the store gained popularity, some of the actors and actresses even came there for brief appearances to sign their photos, and Paula Klaw captured them on film, posting the proof on the wall.

During World War II, Irving Klaw had started a brisk international mail-order business, largely providing cheesecake photos of movie stars to servicemen stationed overseas. At one point he was getting more than three hundred orders a day. "At times, when the least doubt comes to my mind as to whether anything or anyone is worth fighting for, or perhaps dying for, I have but to think of Lana [Turner], and all doubts vanish from my mind!" a soldier once wrote to Klaw.

But Klaw also received some unusual requests, which, because of their growing frequency, ended up becoming not so unusual after all. "Damsel-in-distress" photos of bound-and-gagged starlets and rarer pictures of name actresses spanking other actresses and getting spanked themselves became a budding business for Klaw, who even offered standing subscriptions, automatically shipping pictures such as these to customers as soon as he found them. But that was the problem—Klaw had to wait for a Hollywood movie that included such a scene before he could get the pictures. And nobody in the Frank Capra-esque forties was shooting bondage photos for movie release, let alone publication. A lawyer known to Bettie researchers only as Little John was a regular customer of Klaw's at the time, and he suggested that Klaw shoot his own models. That one idea forged a million memories for men who grew up in the fifties with the Klaw pictures of Bettie Page. Little John, a bondage devotee, funded the photo shoots and let Klaw have the rights to resell the pictures. Most of the girls were either striptease dancers or models for Robert Harrison's magazines.

The photos were posed to meet specific customer demands, which ranged from girls dressed in bikinis to photos of girls with bare feet, or girls wrestling, getting spanked, and tying each other up. Ultimately, after Little John's untimely death in a house fire, Klaw took over the financial responsibility for the shoots.

The Klaws took many photos and short films of each of the many individual models they employed. Their images were posted for sale in the Klaws' biannual mail-order catalog, *Cartoon and Model Parade*, which featured cartoons such as "The Duchess of the Bastille" and photos of a cavalcade of voluptuous beauties and female impersonators clad in high heels, thigh-high boots, satin lingerie, and rubber and leather. Often they carried whips or were bound by ropes and chains. For Irving Klaw, no fetish was too weird as long as it didn't involve nudity, sexual acts, or physical harm to one of his models. As far as he was concerned, he was not a pornographer, he dealt in cheesecake.

"This stuff was G-rated," Klaw's nephew Ira Kramer says. "If a woman came in with a run in her stocking, Irving wouldn't let them work. He wouldn't let them work with a run in their stocking. There was no skin, no nothing, nothing at all. It was basically G-rated stuff. And, truthfully, that's more sexy than a woman taking all her clothes off. Just as she's about to take the last piece off, boom, it's gone, end of the movie. In my opinion, that leaves more to the imagination and it's sexier than having a woman walk around naked."

Movie Star News was a true family business. Ira Kramer's father, Jack Kramer, even worked in the Movie Star News warehouse in Jersey City, filling mail orders for his brother-in-law. "A lot of the furniture that you see in the pictures, we bought a new chair, and we brought the old ones in. It became a prop," Kramer says. "All the stepladders, and stuff like that, that's all it was."

As far as the Movie Star News bondage and pinup business went, "This was not something we discussed," recounts Kramer, who has worked in the store since 1976, when he turned sixteen. "We were your basic American family. They came home from work, and that was it. 'How was your day?' We didn't go into detail. It was just selling pictures, just like selling pictures of Clark Gable or anybody else. It was another day at the office for them."

Irving Klaw's studios were low-budget operations, set up in big, old lofts. The first was upstairs from the Movie Star News store. "He had two or three different locations, but only one at a time," recalls Jack

Bradley, who was one of Klaw's photographers. "In New York in those days, there were literally hundreds of second-floor lofts, especially down in the twenties and thirties streets and in the Village, and they were cheap to rent."

Bradley, now seventy-nine and retired, lives in Atlantic City, New Jersey, where he has served as an official photographer for the Miss America Pageant. In the 1950s he was married to the late showgirl and occasional Klaw model, Joan Rydell. "I was hired like a model," Bradley recalls. "I was paid by the day. I was the photographer but I used his equipment at his studio and he owned everything that I shot. I was paid a fee for the day. I got $75 a day, believe it or not. We didn't shoot that often. Maybe once every couple weeks. When I worked for Irving it was on that basis. He supplied everything, film, camera, and so on down the line."

Bradley describes the Klaws in this way: "He was a portly guy, a little overweight. He wasn't a glamour guy or anything like that. Paula was just an average-looking woman, not a raging beauty or anything, but a nice person and a good businesswoman."

Bradley remembers that among "his girls," Klaw was known as a kind boss. "He was nice to them, but it was all business. After a shoot on a Saturday, maybe, we shot on Saturday afternoon, he would take everybody who wanted to go up to a nice restaurant for dinner like the Press Box. He would take everybody out to dinner and pick up the tab, but he never made any moves on anybody. He was all business."

The Klaws found their models by word of mouth. "It wasn't something you could advertise in 1953 or 1954," Kramer said. "They would ask each model, 'If you think you have a friend who wants to work, send her down.' So they didn't even get to choose their models, they had to take what they got." Sometimes it showed. Not all of Klaw's models were knockout Bettie Page types. But then again, some customers wanted that, too.

Before long, Klaw's business moved again, this time to 212 East 14th Street, the location most familiar to the majority of his customers still alive today. Those customers, most of whom were working guys ranging from middle-class retailers to U.N. diplomats, would have to ask for Irving Klaw to pull out his cheesecake and bondage catalogs at Movie Star News. They'd come in the store at all hours (Klaw opened at 10:00 A.M. and closed at 11:00 P.M. or later), sitting along the long counter, three and four at a time, flipping through the books with pencils and pads in hand to write down the catalog numbers of the photographs they wanted to order. "I'd like this number, that number, and this number," they'd say. It was an unending litany in the Klaw shop.

The bondage and S & M photos were by far the most popular and profitable of Klaw's offerings. Art Amsie says: "I remember the first time [Klaw] came over and said, 'How's everything going?' I said, 'What are all those weird things over there that the other guys are looking at?' He admonished me very quickly, saying, 'Shhh, those are my best customers. Don't scare them away.'"

Before Amsie himself ever photographed Bettie, he says, "I knew of Bettie because I had seen her photographs in Irving Klaw's shop, which I visited from time to time, and she did some real great pinups then. I bought the pinups, mostly 3-D slides and they were in color. The visit to Irving Klaw caused me to proceed into new areas—Bettie Page and stereo photography."

Bettie Page fan Richard Merkin, a New York artist and illustrator and former columnist for *GQ* magazine, went to Movie Star News as a boy to buy keepsake pictures of cowboy stars like Lash LaRue. He recalled, "There was this rotund man up there and the whole place had a kind of wonderful sort of enthralling sleaziness to it. I was a little boy, maybe nine or ten or eleven or twelve, and I would see these things. I'd see these pictures of women with strange high heels spanking each other, and although I didn't understand why they were interesting, I certainly knew they were interesting."

Klaw sold four-by-five black-and-white bondage and S & M snapshots for forty cents apiece, a hefty price at the time for one picture, Amsie recalled. Sets of eight photos were $2. "The four-by-five cheesecake photos, which were just girls in bathing suits and lingerie posing on a chair or a couch, they were only fifteen cents. So I would be over there going over his cheesecake books. I used to buy the four-by-five cheesecake slides plus the stereo slides, which were very expensive. They were a dollar and a half. That would probably be $10 or $15 today." Klaw also sold short movie reels of his models, called "loops," which were shot at the same time as the still photos.

"We had certain people who would make requests," Kramer said. "One guy wanted black rubber, one wanted white underwear. They would pay for the models, they would pay for the film, and they would get a set of pictures, and they were happy. This was 1953 and you couldn't go to 42nd Street and get pictures at the newsstand. It was a lot different back then."

Bettie's home movie shoots for the Klaws ranged from benign lingerie and striptease shoots such as *Pretty Betty Dances Again, Betty's Fireplace Dance*, and *Dominant Betty Dances With Whip* (Bettie danced all of these without music, which was dubbed in later) to the more intense and sometimes creepier stuff like *Hobbled in Kid Leather Harness* and *Jungle Girl Tied to Trees*, in which Bettie, dressed in a leopard-skin bikini, is roped between two trees while another woman dressed in a leather skirt and high heels lashes her from behind with a bullwhip. In the Klaw film *Betty Gets Bound and Kidnapped*, two female models slip her a mickey, abduct her, and tie her up in her underwear. Among the stranger fetish photographs Bettie posed for was a set in which she wears a pony costume, and the odd fetish piece *Betty's Clown Dance Parts I and II*, in which she dances seductively with a little stuffed clown. Other shots from this period include photos of a lingerie-clad Bettie spread-eagled, gagged, and bound by ropes and pulleys in what appears to be an empty, starkly lit warehouse. Her eyes are widened, and her eyebrows furrowed in a mock expression of melodramatic fear. These are the pictures that earned the Queen of Curves another appellation: the Dark Angel.

"I bought some of the bondage photos," Amsie says. "I guess I must have purchased six or seven Bettie Page bondage shots, but that was because she was so good at that and she had a cute little outfit and she wasn't tied up, but the others were. She was sort of dominating.

"She was cute as a dominatrix, which seems to be a contradiction in terms, but to me, she was cute, so what are you going to do?"

Jack Bradley photographed many of the bondage pictures. "I just shot it, I didn't give a shit about what the people thought that tied them up, who were friends of Irving's. They more or less knew what they were doing. It was something that I never understood, but there are people who like that sort of thing. It takes all types to make a world."

Bettie took most of her bondage and fetish work in good humor. "She said it was just a job, a good-paying job," says publisher J. B.

Rund, who was one of Bettie's agents in recent years. "She made more money working for Klaw on a Saturday than she did working in a week, Monday through Friday, as a secretary."

Bettie and the other Klaw models found a good friend in the down-to-earth Paula Klaw, who always had a sympathetic ear to lend to the Klaw girls and shooed the men out of their dressing rooms. They'd laugh with her about some of the odd photo requests and privately complain about the sore ankles they'd get from spending inordinate amounts of time in the stiletto heels favored by most of the Movie Star News customers.

"They were very good friends. It wasn't just a working thing, they were pals," Kramer says of Paula Klaw and Bettie. "There was only one complaint my mother had about Bettie. She would take an hour to brush her hair. Paula would say, 'Come on already. Let's go.' Bettie would stay in her dressing room combing and combing her hair, for a long time."

Bettie was almost never on time, whether it was at the camera clubs or the Klaw shoots, her friends say. "Bettie was notoriously late for shoots because she had to put on makeup. She didn't think she was attractive just to walk out the door," says Rund. "She was always late. But if you had to work overtime, Bettie would do it. She was a hard worker and a good model. Everybody liked her."

The Klaws liked her so much, in fact, that Bettie was virtually the only model they saw socially. Many of the Klaw studio outtakes show her clowning around with Irving or hugging Paula, who were like older siblings to Bettie. Sometimes after photo shoots, she and the Klaws and their spouses would meet at the Morocco restaurant, and everyone would walk Bettie home afterward. They were like any close-knit family of coworkers, albeit with much more unconventional jobs.

Interviewed in 1993, Paula Klaw said, "I love her and I know her. She is one of the nicest people I've ever met; congenial, beautiful body, one of the best models we ever had." She called Bettie just "a plain country girl."

It didn't take long for Bettie to become the most requested model that the Klaws had. In fact, the Klaws were so enthusiastic about the first photos that Bettie took for them in 1952 that they rushed one of her pictures into print on the cover of *Cartoon and Model Parade* even though they didn't have any photos of her to actually offer for sale to customers yet.

"It was difficult to take a bad picture of her. She was a good model," Bradley says. And maybe with good reason: Bettie has said that she tried to view the camera as a potential lover. "She was easy to get along with, [but] very fussy about the fact that she wanted her hair just right. She was forever messing with her hair and she was always late, sometimes hours late."

Because Klaw didn't do nudes, Bradley occasionally shot sexier pictures of Bettie outside the Klaw studio at the apartment of a model buddy, Jonni Wilson. Like his Klaw material, he sold all the rights to it, however. Most of it appeared in magazines and figure-drawing books, like a series he did of Bettie with Wilson's canary perched on her hand and shoulders.

"It's hard to really describe her," Bradley says. "She was an attractive girl, a very small bust, but they didn't go for the big busts in those days that they do today. Today some of them are grotesque, especially when they have had them supplemented. When you see the words natural attributes, they were true in those days. What you had was yours. The only thing I remember about Bettie is if you wanted to shoot figure stuff of her, she wanted you to do it right before her period, because she thought her bust looked bigger."

Eventually Irving Klaw became the money man and store manager at Movie Star News. Paula Klaw took over the modeling side of the business, picking out costumes for the models and learning from Bradley how to take pictures. She ended up as a more-than-capable photographer in her own right, snapping thousands of the Movie Star News cheesecake photos and many of the short films with her Speed Graphic four-by-five camera and 16mm Bolex movie camera.

"She was basically easy-going," Kramer says of his mother. "Whatever turns you on, as long as you don't hurt anybody, that's okay." In fact, Paula Klaw was often the one who tied the knots in the ropes binding her models in the bondage shots. The customers taught her how to do it because they were "kind of afraid of the women," Kramer says. "They would show her how to do the knots, saying, don't make them too tight. My mother was just like, 'You want it? That's fine. Get the picture. Just don't hurt anybody.' Laugh and go, that's all she did. That was her motto."

Photo shoots were almost exclusively done on Saturdays, and the girls would work for up to six hours at a time. They made $50 a day, during which time Paula took as many as three hundred photos and shot at least one film loop.

During one of Paula's films, a girl wrestling movie that Bettie was filming one Friday night with the redhead June King, another of Klaw's hottest and most popular models, King landed on Bettie's knee with a loud cracking sound. Wincing in pain, and bleeding from a cut inflicted by King's sharp high heel, Bettie was unable to extend her leg. By the time she got home that night, Bettie could hardly make it up the stairs to her third-floor apartment. Her leg was stuck in a bent position. She was taken to the doctor and booked into a hospital. An operation was scheduled for Monday morning.

But that weekend, as she was lying on her bed in pain and with nothing to do, a loud voice cried out to her, echoing in her head with a reverberating tenor according to an interview in *The Betty Pages*. "Bettie, you can straighten your leg," it said. Sure enough, when she tried, her leg straightened out effortlessly and without pain. In awe, Bettie decided it had been the Lord who had spoken to her and healed her, she has said in numerous interviews. She never had the operation. The episode reaffirmed her childhood faith, and most Sunday mornings after that, a bleary-eyed Queen of Curves could be found at her local church.

8

Sunshine and Shadows

WHILE Bettie had quickly earned a reputation as the hottest pinup model in town, in her heart she still saw herself as an actress. Much of the money she made modeling was spent on the acting classes she enrolled in at the Dramarena Studio on West 55th Street, and she toiled for many hours, practicing her lines and delivery, while struggling to overcome her molasses-thick Tennessee drawl. But that, she found out, wouldn't be the only impediment to landing the film and television roles for which she longed.

Bettie's standards were high. When a prominent gay businessman she knew reportedly offered to pay her room and board and other expenses if she would pose as his girlfriend, she firmly declined. She didn't love him, and she didn't feel right taking the money.

Among the men she posed for, Bettie was known as a pretty straight flyer. She never smoked, drank, or took drugs. In fact, today she can't stand one of her most famous early "Bad-Bettie" photographs taken by the Klaw studio, because it pictures her with a cigarette in her mouth. It was out of character for the real Bettie. She didn't date the photographers who clamored for her attention—mainly because she wasn't attracted to them—and she was rumored to carry a brick in her purse for protection, which discouraged all but the truly hardy suitor. But that reputation hadn't reached many directors and producers, and the casting couch system became a frequent frustration for Bettie, who did not mind getting attention for her looks, but who drew the line at sleeping with someone to get a job.

Early in her career, Bettie was offered a starring part in a Columbia Pictures Western which was to be filmed in South Dakota. The producer of the movie told Bettie that if she was "nice" to him, the role was hers. But he wasn't even close to good-looking, and Bettie couldn't stomach the thought of his touch. Moreover, Bettie was outraged. She turned him down and walked out of his office, never looking back. He yelled after her that she was making a mistake and there were plenty of women who wouldn't pass up a chance at a movie role.

"God knows it happened a lot," says Hillard "Hillie" Elkins, who was an agent at the William Morris Agency in the early 1950s and sent Bettie to some auditions.

Bettie had contacted the William Morris Agency, looking for representation, and was taken on as a "pocket client," an actor or actress who shows promise and potential but perhaps isn't ready for a full-fledged contract yet. "I knew her as a pinup gal, so I agreed to meet with her and found her absolutely the antithesis of her look—a sweet, warm, charming Southern girl," Elkins says. "She was warm and sweet and a very straight-ahead kid, totally belying her look."

"She was no fool," he says. Bettie knew what many directors and producers were after, but she also knew that some of them weren't that way, so she asked Elkins to tell her who could be trusted, and who couldn't, as she searched for acting jobs. He says, "Some people had a reputation for that kind of thing, and I shared that with her."

But, Elkins says, Bettie wasn't entirely just-off-the-bus naive, either. She knew her star was rising and was trying to find a way to ride it to the top. "She was recognized, I don't know [if it was] by name, [but] you couldn't pick up a cheesecake magazine without seeing her. Back then, hot sex was bra and panties. It was not Larry Flynt time, or even Hugh Hefner time yet. You couldn't walk by a newsstand [without] seeing a picture of this gal on one magazine or another. You thought that was real hot stuff in those days, and whatever went along with that in the puritanical fifties."

Hillie Elkins met with Bettie about four or five times and sent her to three, or maybe four auditions, he thinks. He doesn't remember her getting any of the parts, but he definitely recalls the brief times he spent talking with her—just talking, he remembers, almost mournfully. "I had my own little fantasies," he acknowledges. "I didn't act on them, and I enjoyed her. She was quite charming, quite naive, quite direct, very clear, and she didn't bullshit, a real straight-shooting lady." After a couple of meetings, Elkins and Bettie moved from his office to the less formal atmosphere of the coffee shop in the talent agency's lobby, where they would grab a cup of joe and talk over her prospects. And once Elkins met Bettie at her apartment, after a teary and de-feated Bettie phoned him, upset after a couple of theatrical agents called her for an audition but really used it as a front to hit on her. "It was not an unexpected situation," he says. Elkins remembers Bettie's apartment as "tumultuous," with "a lot of stuff heaped over," yet well-kept.

For the casting directors who weren't interested in getting Bettie in bed, her country accent wasn't a help. It "kind of breaks the image," her former agent acknowledges. "But on the other hand, it's another kind of sensuality. It would have limited her, but some places looked for that image." Bettie's main problem may have been that she some-times viewed her greatest strength—her looks—as a weakness. "She would have loved to have had, I think, at that time, some kind of acting career," Elkins says. "Her attitude in my short and very spo-radic relationship with her was, very simply, that she did not consider what she did anything but modeling work. She was not stupid, she was aware of the fact that she was a very sensual lady, but that was her day job."

Still, Elkins adds, "Let's be real. She could wear a fucking sheet and look sexy. There was no way with that shape, those eyes, those bangs, and that body that she was going to look demure."

Now an entertainment manager and Broadway producer best known for staging the nude musical *Oh! Calcutta!*, Elkins considers himself a Bettie fan, perhaps one of the luckiest, and certainly among the first. In fact, he talks glowingly about a recent prize: a hardcover French comic book about Bettie he bought while on a business trip in Belgium. But Elkins's memories of Bettie are not just those of the coquettish nude playmate or the leather-clad bondage angel pictured so often these days. To him, she was a lady, "a lady who happened to look very sexy, but a lady."

In 1952 Bettie took a vacation from New York and her growing modeling career to go to Miami—where she ended up modeling again. Some of her most famous shots came out of this period; in the fresh light of sunshine, Bettie lost some of the dark quality often found in the all-indoor Klaw photos, in which she appeared so wan and malevolent.

No sooner had she hit the beaches of Miami than she was spotted by a television casting director looking for an actress for a cigarette commercial. Bettie jumped at the chance to be on TV. Her first role was hardly larger than life. She stood around looking sexy for thirty seconds in front of a cheap, painted backdrop while the commercial's leading man eyed her up and down suggestively and asked, "How did they get so much into one little package?"

When the commercial finally aired, though, it was all worth it. In small, grainy black and white, Bettie was on television! And she didn't even have to go to New York to do it! Bettie was overjoyed.

In Miami, Bettie hung out in Matheson Hammock Park, a palmy oasis primarily frequented by University of Miami students. Bettie would often challenge her athletic skill by swimming across a boat canal, dodging water traffic, to reach an island dotted with sweet mango trees. Soon she was listed with a Miami modeling agency, and Florida's top pinup photographers—well-known talents such as Hans Hannau, Jan Caldwell, and Benno Correa—were clamoring to photograph her. Many of their swimsuit photos of Bettie became popular postcards that could still be bought at East Coast beach resorts twenty years later. One of the most famous, a Hannau shot, has Bettie flashing that famous teasing smile as a stuffed alligator attempts to make off with her briefs, à la the Coppertone suntan lotion ad. It reads: "Wow! We alligators do have fun in Florida!" Still, Bettie found Hannau a demanding boss, recalling how he once suggested she climb some rocky outcroppings—barefooted—for a shot.

Bettie returned to New York rejuvenated by her success and more determined than ever to succeed as an actress. She made several friends who were either in show business or trying to get in. Robert Culp, who later starred in TV's *I Spy* with Bill Cosby, taught some of Bettie's drama classes and attended other classes with her. He also performed opposite her in a one-act play, *The Dark Lady of the Sonnets*. Another acquaintance was Buck Henry, the comedian who would write the screenplay for the Oscar-winning film *The Graduate* (1967) and co-create the campy 1960s TV series *Get Smart* with fellow funnyman Mel Brooks before earning real fame on *Saturday Night Live* as a host and the straight man to John Belushi's samurai-of-all-trades.

In the mid fifties, Henry was dating "a nice Jewish girl from Brooklyn" who also happened to be a Klaw model. He also went on many of Cass Carr's photo outings where he, too, photographed Bettie.

In an essay written for the December 1992 issue of *Playboy*, Henry recalled bumping into Bettie at an all-hours diner in Greenwich Village: "At four in the morning, the place would be jammed with the determinably Beat and the desperately hip, crouched on stools at the curving counter, stoking their (usually) marijuana-induced feeding frenzies with jelly doughnuts and double-orders of corned beef hash. Confirmed junkies drank endless cups of coffee into which, for that added lift, they would stir the contents of Benzedrine inhalers.

"She came in with some guy whom we all immediately hated, sat down, smiled, and ordered something. Oatmeal, I think. Even the severely stoned sat up straight, stopped giggling, and watched the spoon going in and out of her mouth."

Almost forty-five years later, those men who were lucky enough to have had a brush with Bettie may not remember all the minute details that Buck Henry can, but they sure can remember Bettie. Pioneering television talk show host, musician, comedian, and author Steve Allen got a letter from a Bettie researcher in 1990 or 1991, and at first couldn't recalled meeting her. But when he saw a few photographs of her, it all came back.

"I remember somehow our paths had crossed, I don't know how, maybe she appeared briefly on one of the television shows I hosted," Allen says. "I remember her look, that brunette hair in that distinctive style, certainly, and the fact that she was beautiful, but that's all that's in the memory banks."

Well, not exactly all. After a moment, Allen also recalled a fond memory shared by many other men in the 1950s who were not fortunate enough to actually make Bettie's acquaintance in person, as he did. "Now that we're talking, I can also remember [seeing] a photograph of her in a natural setting. It was a nude photograph, but not of the vulgar sort that's common today. It was more of an artistic photo, common to Europeans, and there was nothing suggestive in the pose. But that's really all that's in the memory banks."

Bettie's biggest television spot was a small performance on the

Jackie Gleason Show, though she says that, off-camera, the comedian was an overbearing despot who verbally abused his crew. Bettie rubbed shoulders with many other famous entertainers at the New York nightclubs she frequented, sometimes catching a meal or dancing with them, or, as she once did with Sammy Davis Jr., sharing a cab.

The more time she spent around television and movie stars, the more focused she became on becoming one herself. Bettie swore off junk food and joined the Park Sheridan Hotel's health club. There she took calisthenics and swam six hours a week, conditioning herself.

Her first job acting in the movies came in 1953, though it still wasn't the type of role she dreamed of during her youth in Nashville. Ironically, Bettie found that the "adult" filmmakers of the day didn't have the same intentions of making moves on her that the mainstream studio execs did. Hired by New York theater operator and film producer Martin Lewis, Bettie performed a short and sudsy bathtub scene for a B-movie burlesque revue called *Strip-O-Rama.* The picture included elaborate strip routines, including one in which trained Hawaiian pigeons made off with a stripper's clothes. The film was a phenomenal commercial success, bringing in $80,000 in box office sales in nine weeks—an amazing sum for the time.

Impressed, and fearing the loss of his crown as Pin-Up King, Irving Klaw decided to venture into the movie business. Although he had already produced a few successful 8mm and 16mm loops of Bettie that he sold through his catalogs, now he was thinking big. *Varietease* (1954) and *Teaserama* (1955)—feature-film-length Klaw productions shot in Eastman color and starring Bettie—soon premiered. Dressed in a sequined harem girl's outfit for *Varietease,* Bettie danced a particularly sexy but amateurish Dance of the Seven Veils. In *Teaserama* she stripped down to her black silk underwear and stockings. Klaw's movies also featured a variety of burlesque talent including world-famous strippers Lili St. Cyr (billed as the Most Beautiful Woman in the World) and Tempest Storm, comedian Joe E. Ross (Toody from television's *Car 54—Where are You?*), and female impersonator Vickie Lynn.

Jack Bradley made the stage for *Teaserama,* which was shot in one of Klaw's lofts. He recalls the origins of the film's odd pairing of Bettie and Vickie Lynn: "There was a club in New York I used to go to in the Village called the 82 Club; it was on Second Avenue over in the East

Village. It was a gay club. The customers were straight, but the show was female impersonators doing fabulous production numbers in this little joint, and all the waitresses were lesbians. I used to take people to see the show, because they put on a terrific show, and Irving at that time was wanting to photograph some of them, so I brought a few of them to him and we in turn photographed them. That was another area of sales for [Movie Star News]—men dressing as women, cross dressers."

Irving Klaw, who liked Vickie Lynn's look, asked if Lynn would be interested in being in *Teaserama*. The day of the shooting, they still weren't sure what to do with the sultry transvestite, so Bradley suggested, "Why don't we make it a contest between Vickie and Bettie, of this harem girl dance?"

"We dressed them alike. Vickie did her dance and then Bettie said, 'Oh, I think I can do it better than that.' It was just a reason to get them both in the same picture, a flimsy reason. There were no writers for these movies, okay? They were put together with spit and chewing gum, shall we say. However there was a professional photographic crew that didn't put together any schlock deals. They were union people. Big union photographers with big union cameras."

At the time, the Lewis and Klaw feature films were hot stuff, with their footage of Bettie and various big-chested models strutting their stuff in black brassieres, high heels, and garters, but today, both features would probably merit a solid PG rating.

By spring 1954, Bettie was ready for another Florida "vacation."

She reactivated her listing at the modeling agency in Miami, and soon, through Miami newspaper columnist Herb Rau, met Bunny Yeager. Bunny, tall, blond, and a former model herself, taught a modeling class at the agency but yearned to get on the other side of the camera. She had achieved some modest successes with nudes and cheesecake photos of her friends published in magazines like *Chicks and Chuckles* (billed as the magazine of dirty jokes and even dirtier girls). But Bunny hadn't experienced anything like the magic when Bettie Page fell into her viewfinder. From the moment they met until the end of Bettie's month-long stay, Bunny kept a virtual monopoly on her new friend and model. She took photos of Bettie romping nude on the beach and rolling in the surf, and walking outdoors at Miami's Africa USA wildlife park leading twin leopards on a leash.

Some of Bettie's sexiest and most memorable pictures were taken as she cavorted for Bunny at Africa USA in a handmade jungle costume she sewed herself, reminiscent of Sheena, Queen of the Jungle. Though probably unconsciously on Bunny's part, the photos are reminiscent of Harlem beauty queen Josephine Baker. In the photos, Bettie has a dreamy, faraway, almost distracted expression. It could have been due to the Florida sun, but probably it had more to do with the fact that the night before the photo shoot, a large man had tried to break in through her bedroom window while she was undressing for bed.

Bettie was living in a small house on a private estate on Miami's Sixth Street. Spending the evening in the estate's mansion, she had just put the finishing touches on her jungle-girl costume and walked back to the guest house where she was staying. By midnight, she was getting ready to go to sleep when she heard a scratching sound at the window. She stood still, frightened. Then she cut the light. As her eyes adjusted to the darkness, she could make out the black silhouette of a large man removing the window screen. Bettie summoned up her last bit of courage and yelled for the man to move away or she'd gun him down. Her bluff worked. He ran, she yelled for help, and when she saw it was safe, bolted for the night watchman's cottage down by the river. After talking with him for a couple of hours, she spent the rest of the night before the Africa USA shoot awake and huddled inside the mansion's screened-in porch, too rattled to sleep. Bunny came to pick up Bettie at 7:30 that morning. Bettie tried to beg off, but Bunny already had set up the props—including a black actor dressed in a tribal outfit. Bettie had to do the shoot. Later she said she thought the photos made her look haggard and hung over. If they do, her fans haven't noticed. The Africa USA shots are some of Bettie's most popular pictures.

At first Bettie posed for Bunny in what she had with her: the black nylons, stiletto heels, and leather gear from her Klaw shoots. Slowly Bunny persuaded Bettie to pose for softer nudes—draped in fur, wearing stockings, dressed in a see-through negligee by candlelight, donning a devil costume. Bunny just couldn't get enough of Bettie.

"What I wouldn't give to find another model like Bettie! We had a very good relationship. I still believe she was the best pinup-glamour model that ever lived," Bunny said years later. "I was so lucky in my beginning days of learning how to be a photographer that Bettie came along. We made a good team. She seemed to know just what I wanted. Our sessions were fun for both of us.

"I was impressed by her professionalism as a model. Every hair in place, but natural-looking; makeup well done but not too much. Perfect tan skin, healthy hair. Creative in her posing and her facial expressions, exuberant."

Bunny would lug her elaborate lighting equipment onto the beach and into parks for her shoots with Bettie, dragging her two cameras, rolls of extension cords, and up to four floodlights to give Bettie's skin that perfect creamy, unblemished, air-brushed look.

"Bettie was a Vargas girl come to life. She was like a drawing—a perfect woman; unreal, fun, fantasy. Bettie always portrayed a woman that hinted she would be lots of fun to be with, someone who would never have a headache or a bad mood. Sure she'd pout . . . but you always knew she was playing with you."

Bunny and Bettie found they had a lot in common. When Bettie had danced the hula at the orphanage as a girl, Bunny and her childhood friends had photographed themselves wearing hula skirts made of iris leaves from her mother's flowerbed. Both she and Bettie were also fiercely driven women who didn't put up with the notion that they were second-class citizens in a man's world.

In a moment of whimsy early in their shoots together, Bunny decided to pose Bettie in a Santa hat, a wink, and a smile, hanging a Christmas ornament on a miniature tree. The sassy photo became Bettie's famous January 1955 *Playboy* centerfold. It earned Bettie $20 and Bunny $100—and a reputation as a talented photographer. The original issue in which it ran now fetches hundreds of dollars—reportedly the second-most valuable issue of *Playboy* among collectors, next in price only to the first issue with its Marilyn Monroe centerfold. Bunny's other shots of Bettie would show up on the covers of everything from gossip magazines to Fats Waller albums. From the 1950s until the mid-sixties, Bunny took seven more *Playboy* centerfold shots, sold three hundred non-Bettie cheesecake photo sets to men's magazines worldwide, and authored eleven books of photography. Bunny even appeared on the *Tonight Show* with Johnny Carson in 1964 to promote one of the books, *How I Photograph Myself.*

As for Bettie, she seemed totally recharged by her time in Florida with Bunny, as if she were powered by solar cells. Not only did she have great fun and success modeling, she also had a brief but enjoyable romance with a young man from Key West. Bettie was strolling White Street, the longest street in Key West, one day, when she saw Armond Walterson, wearing a white shirt and bathing trunks, and staring out to sea. Thirteen years Bettie's junior, the eighteen-year-old Armond spent most of his time on the beaches, playing volleyball and soaking up sun. Though he was younger, the dark-skinned, black-haired Armond was taller than Bettie and looked old for his age. The two met when Bettie traveled to Key West for a day trip and suddenly got an urge to have a picture of herself taken at the southernmost point of the United States. She asked the handsome young man standing by a wall to take the picture. It came out blurry because his hands shook from nervousness; Bettie thought that was pretty cute.

Bettie went swimming with Armond and his friends. The buddies showed off, goofing around, trying anything to swing Bettie's attentions their way. It was to no avail—she was captivated by the shy, silent Armond. By the time one of his brothers came by to pick him up, and Armond started to enter the car, Bettie panicked at the thought of not getting a chance at romance with him. She asked where he was going, and he said, simply, "home." So Bettie took the offensive: She asked him out. Armond was relieved—he told her that he thought she wanted to go out with his friends. No, Bettie told him, she wanted him. They went on a date to a drive-in movie the following weekend and didn't get home until early the next morning.

The older, experienced Bettie tutored the lucky young man in the art of love like only Bettie Page could. Armond was a virgin. He didn't even know how to French kiss. Bettie remedied that quickly. Soon Armond was making love to Bettie with gusto. The two were inseparable for weeks, going to the movies, making love, sunning on the beaches, and playing in the surf. He even accompanied Bettie to some of the shoots with Bunny at Africa USA, staying off to the side while Bunny and Bettie worked. But Bettie was too focused on her career to let the romance develop into anything but a summer fling.

Returning to New York, Bettie took her new-found energy and

enrolled in acting classes at the renowned Herbert Berghof Studios at 120 Bank Street in Manhattan. Berghof was a well-known actor and director, respected for his teaching of Stanislavsky method acting. In his declining years, he was probably best known for his occasional roles on TV's *Kojak* and a starring role in the 1985 film *Target* with former student Gene Hackman. Berghof's wife, Uta Hagen, who starred in the 1990 film *Reversal of Fortune* with Jeremy Irons, still runs the school.

Berghof found Bettie anxious to please, as she rehearsed her scenes and sought ways to make her acting more convincing and realistic. He was especially pleased with Bettie's performance opposite fellow student Robert Culp in *The Dark Lady of the Sonnets*. In the role, Bettie was to play a servant who had been caught making love to Queen Elizabeth's paramour, and so would have her head cut off. Her rendition of the part was mournful and filled with remorse. When Berghof asked how Bettie had accomplished it, she told him that she had imagined how God would punish her for her many sins. That anecdote in particular reveals something very telling about Bettie's psyche in later years and the internal conflict that was already building inside her between her free spirit and her strict religious upbringing and the guilt Edna Page made her feel over her budding sexuality as a teenager.

Besides inner contemplation, the Berghof studios also brought contacts and legitimate work for Bettie as an actress, though Bettie didn't always pursue it. "She had very serious aspirations to be an actress," says J. B. Rund, one of Bettie's agents in recent years. "I'm certain she would have been successful, but I don't think she believed in herself."

When the Broadway auditions opened up for *Li'l Abner*, Berghof urged Bettie to try out for the part of Moonbeam McSwine, thinking her Southern belle air would help, but Bettie chickened out. "He believed in me," she said of Berghof in a December 1995 article in *Playboy* magazine. "But I didn't believe I could do it. I really lacked ambition in those days. I did nothing to promote myself."

Maybe so, but before coming to Berghof, she had already starred in television commercials and off-Broadway plays, and with the help of Irving Klaw, she made an appearance on former newspaper columnist Earl Wilson's live variety show, where she was crowned Pinup Girl of the World. As a student of the Berghof and Dramarena studios, Bettie started taking occasional dramatic roles in off-Broadway shows as well as on television. She acted in *Time Is a Thief* at the Finch Playhouse in Manhattan with Darnay Pierre and Richard Kennan, as well as in *3* at the Playhouse on 78th Street, and in a Greenwich Village production of the comedy *Sunday Costs Five Pesos*. On television she had roles on shows such as the *Eyewitness Show*, a half-hour mystery anthology series broadcast live from the NBC Studios in New York, and on the *U.S. Steel Hour*, a dramatic series that aired at 10:00 P.M. Wednesdays on CBS and which featured new young talents such as Andy Griffith, Paul Newman, Richard Kiley, and Johnny Carson. Her part on *U.S. Steel* was that of a jailed illegal alien from Mexico named Carmelita. Her dark hair and tan may have won her the role.

The summer before she started at Berghof's studio, Bettie had also given summer stock another whirl, apprenticing at Long Island's Sea Cliff Theater, where she brushed shoulders with groundbreaking black actress Ethel Waters who starred in *At Home With Ethel Waters* that summer and reprised her role in a playhouse production of the 1943 film *Cabin in the Sky*. Though Bettie was primarily relegated to the grunt work of an apprentice, working backstage on productions such as *Bell, Book, and Candle*, which starred Hollywood stars Alexis Smith and Victor Jory, Bettie also landed a couple of bit parts herself. She played a hooker in *Camino Real* by Tennessee Williams, and had a small role in *Gentlemen Prefer Blondes*.

Around this time, Bettie began dating Marvin Greene, a fellow acting student at the Berghof studios who aspired to be a director. The two had an almost-three-year romance, taking occasional summer camping trips to Canada, upstate New York, New England, and Nova Scotia. Not much is known about Greene, who people say was a patient, if somewhat moody man. Bettie says he was blond, and hints that he might have been short, because she says he was insecure about his height. He would always find a way to make himself look taller than she was, no matter where they were, even while tanning. He also had a wonderful singing voice and would often croon, "On the Street Where You Live" to Bettie from the alley below her apartment window. The relationship was serious, but not overly so, and the two spent time together only around Bettie's busier schedule.

It was also around this time that Bettie attracted the attentions of another man— industrialist Howard Hughes. Known for his philandering, Hughes would pick girls out of men's magazines like a hungry man ordering from a menu at a steakhouse. And when Hughes's call came, so too came stardom . . . after the casting couch.

A popular story about Bettie and Hughes relates that she was turned down for a film role when she slapped Hughes in the face, rejecting his advances. The truth is close but a bit more mundane.

"About Howard Hughes—I never met the man," Bettie said in her 1992 letter to the author. "Bunny Yeager, the Miami photographer, sent me a magazine article with my picture and five other models and actresses, claiming we were girlfriends of Mr. Hughes. [But] my only involvement with him was through his right-hand man who contacted Irving Klaw, advising him that Howard Hughes wanted to meet me. I talked to this man on the phone and told him that I was not interested in meeting Mr. Hughes. They made a screen test of me, but nothing ever came of it."

Hughes's right-hand man had arranged for her to come out to California on Hughes's dime for a screen test at Hughes's RKO Studios. While there, Bettie made a few test photos—headshots, profiles, and such. Eventually the assistant told Bettie that Hughes still wanted to meet with her, but Bettie said she wasn't interested. Knowing what Hughes was after and unwilling to pay the price, she returned to New York. RKO never called her back.

For Bettie, it was another lost chance at stardom. But unbeknownst to her, she was soon to receive lots of publicity. Her work, in fact, would become a leading topic of conversation in homes everywhere, as the United States of America prepared to take on Irving Klaw.

9

....

Trials and Tribulations

ALTHOUGH Senator Joseph McCarthy's witch hunt for communists was over, there was still plenty for politicians to be paranoid about in 1955.

Senator Estes Kefauver—a Tennessee Democrat who ran unsuccessfully for vice president as Adlai Stevenson's running mate in 1956—made a name for himself in the early fifties chairing a subcommittee investigating organized crime. (Ironically, John Russell, the actor with whom Bettie shot her Twentieth Century–Fox screen test, starred in a 1952 film, *Hoodlum Empire*, loosely based on Kefauver's hearings.)

The crime hearings helped Kefauver defeat besieged President Harry Truman in the 1952 Democratic primary in New Hampshire. Although Kefauver ultimately lost the nomination, he became one of the first politicians who learned how to turn a new medium—television—into votes. A gaunt, balding man with appalling dental work and an affinity for coonskin hats, Kefauver wasn't much to look at, but his televised hearings, in the words of one contemporary reporter, revived the Middle Ages morality play. And Americans watched.

By late April 1954, Kefauver had turned his attentions to the evils of juvenile delinquency. His Senate subcommittee hearings about violence in comic books (with the help of child psychologist Fredric Wertham's book *Seduction of the Innocent*) nearly shut down the comics industry, writing an end to the career of many Golden Age superheroes and their publishing companies. Horror titles such as

Rare outdoor photo taken by Art Amsie, considered one of the best camera-club photographers who shot Bettie. She posed for dozens of shutterbugs at a time on weekends in remote locations. Outdoors, Bettie presents a fresh-faced quality not seen in her wan and slightly malevolent Klaw photos. (© *Art Amsie*)

"Bettie was happier outdoors," observes photographers Art Aimsie of these outstanding camera-club beach photos. (© *Art Amsie*)

Amsie found in Bettie not just another beautiful model but a friend and a fellow intellectual. "We're simpatico," he says. (© *Art Amsie*)

These impromptu photos, taken in Fort Lauderdale, Florida, in December 1957 by lifeguard Ellsworth Boyd, are from Bettie's last modeling session and mark the end of a relatively carefree era in her life. (Boyd and a friend introduced themselves to the famous model on the beach and took her skin diving; she loved the experience and happily posed.) (*Ellsworth Boyd*)

The happy boss poses with Bettie, *right,* and an unidentified model. The fetishwear favored by Klaw's customers later influenced performers such as Madonna, whose designers reportedly appropriated some of Bettie's look for the Material Girl's infamous cone bras. (*Movie Star News*)

New and Naughty! Bettie's third feature film, Klaw's burlesque movie *Teaserama*, featured Bettie in a harem-girl dance contest versus sultry transvestite Vickie Lynn. Even though Bettie's face had graced hundreds of magazine covers, stripper Tempest Storm was the film's headline performer. (*Movie Star News*)

Two scenes from *Teaserama*.
(*Movie Star News*)

Another scene from *Teaserama*. (*Movie Star News*)

Tales From the Crypt and *Vault of Horror* disappeared from drugstore shelves. Bonfires were started in towns across the nation and countless four-color heroes played Joan of Arc at the whim of angry mobs.

A year after the comic book hearings, Kefauver put Irving Klaw under his microscope. Klaw had been under scrutiny by the Federal Bureau of Investigation for the bondage pictures in *Cartoon and Model Parade* since 1950, when a mother had found an issue of the magazine in her teenage son's bedroom drawer and registered a complaint. It wasn't the first time a protest had been registered over Klaw's catalogs—the FBI had also received complaints in 1942, 1944, and 1945—but U.S. Postal authorities in New York were also investigating Klaw, because they believed his photographs and advertising were getting bolder.

FBI agents surreptitiously bought photos from Klaw, hoping for him to slip up and sell them something explicit. Of course, he didn't, because he didn't have anything like that. Still, Klaw's legal bills mounted as his lawyers wrangled with the FBI and postal inspectors, arguing that his photographs weren't pornographic. Eventually the FBI agreed—for a while, anyway. The 1950 incident with *Cartoon* and *Model Parade* was put to bed after the investigating agent concluded in a batch of Jack Webb–style reports that Klaw "is too smart to deal with or handle strictly obscene material . . . [his photos are] all performed by females, and . . . Klaw has kept males out of the pictures so as to cunningly avoid what may possibly appear to be obscene."

But after Kefauver set his hawkish nose to sniffing around Movie Star News, the Feds started another investigation, this time in cooperation with postal investigators. FBI director and reputed cross-dresser J. Edgar Hoover even got involved with the case this time, personally reviewing the reports.

"They had it in for Klaw, but they couldn't really get him because what he did wasn't pornographic," comments writer and artist Richard Merkin. "It was just these funny-looking second-rate chorus girls wearing heels and riding each other. It was weird, but they couldn't arrest him for it."

Irving Klaw evaded arrest under a legal loophole for determining obscenity. Obscene material had to arouse or excite the "normal" person. Klaw's stuff, the Feds finally said, was appealing only to "certain types of sex perverts."

"It was in the late fifties. [The Klaws] were worried about going to jail," Paula Klaw's son, Ira Kramer, says of the moralist atmosphere that prevailed at the time. "They had these religious nuts, here they are good religious people, they won't let you look at a dirty picture, but they're hanging black people and Jews."

Though the FBI ruled that Klaw's material didn't count as pornography per se, it was just the kind of juicy stuff that Kefauver knew would get the voters' attention. He scheduled nationwide hearings into pornography's impact upon juvenile delinquency. Not coincidentally, the cross-country hearings, which were held in Texas and Florida and New York, also allowed Kefauver to get an early start on his campaign for the 1956 Democratic nomination for president. In May 1955, Kefauver came to New York City with a fistful of subpoenas, looking for corrupters of youth and innocence. Bettie Page and Irving Klaw were at the top of his list.

Bettie and the Klaws sweated out unwanted attention from the Senate and the *New York Times* and *New York Mirror* for more than two weeks between the time they were subpoenaed and May 24, 1955, the day of the hearings. Newsreels carried their pictures and angry ministers railed against them in their pulpits. Kefauver charged that because Klaw's customer lists included little girls (who were only buying pictures of movie stars, a fact Kefauver conveniently chose to ignore), that meant Klaw was pushing obscene materials on minors. Two of Kefauver's assistants even went to Bettie's apartment and tried to get her to testify against Klaw. They wanted her to rat on him for producing pornography, but Bettie told them, truthfully, that Irving Klaw had never even shot a topless picture in his studio, let alone anything pornographic. She was deeply offended and a little frightened by the visit.

When the hearings finally started at the United States Courthouse at Foley Square, Kefauver tried unsuccessfully to link Klaw's photos with the recent bondage death of seventeen-year-old Eagle Scout Kenneth Grimm in Coral Gables, Florida. His body, trussed up much like some of the Klaw models, was discovered by his father. The boy may have been engaged in autoerotic strangulation or asphyxiation. There was no proof that Kenneth Grimm had ever seen the Klaw pictures, but Kefauver made Irving Klaw out to be his murderer.

Holding two of Klaw's ads for short movies—*Chris Strips for Bed* and *Lounging around in Lingerie*—one of the subcommittee members questioned Dr. George Henry, a clinical psychiatrist at Cornell University's School of Medicine. "Doctor, might I ask you, as a father of five children, and as many parents around the nation have wondered from time to time, if we have read about the senseless killings by teenagers during the past few years, would you say that it is a fair statement that many of these killings are the direct result of some sort of erotic stimuli that have been given to these teenagers, these children, which resulted in their taking part in gang violence, torture, and so on?"

"Yes, I expect that entered into a large portion of such killings," the doctor replied. When asked about *Cartoon and Model Parade*, the same psychiatrist testified that it was intended to "stimulate people erotically in an abnormal way." Clearly the subcommittee was playing hardball.

Kefauver himself said Klaw's material fell into "a twilight zone of obscene material . . . and deals particularly in fetishes, masochism, sadism, and other forms of perversion." Interestingly, Kefauver's report to the subcommittee completely misrepresented the scope of Klaw's operation, making him out to be a pornography kingpin. Not only did it say that Klaw was making more than $500,000 a year—an outrageously high estimate—but it stated that Klaw dealt "exclusively in fetish, bondage, whipping, torture, and related pornographic material." While the bondage and pinup pictures were a lucrative enterprise for Klaw, he still made much of his money selling pictures of movie stars, sports stars, and other entertainers out of his 14th Street storefront.

Using dubious logic, Kefauver maintained that, FBI rulings to the contrary, Klaw's photos were obscene. "It's rather difficult, unless one has an understanding of the particular perversion involved, for the average person to completely understand and notice the pornographic nature of Klaw's material," Kefauver wrote in the subcommittee report.

A popular tale holds that Bettie appeared before the subcommittee and, when asked by Kefauver what she thought of the bondage photos, she replied, "Why, Senator honey, I think they're cute!"

In reality, she arrived at 9:00 A.M. on a Saturday and nervously waited for sixteen hours in a witness room outside the chamber, but was never asked to testify.

"Bettie was scared shitless she was going to be called," Jack Bradley, the Klaw photographer, says. "I know it scared her because she called me on the phone, and she was scared. I told her, 'I don't think you're going to be called. They have nothing to gain from talking to you. They've already talked to Irving and they didn't get anything,' but she was scared and I think that's what made her mind up to get out of New York."

Irving Klaw pleaded the Fifth at the hearing on the advice of his attorneys, Joseph E. Brill and Coleman Gangel. Kefauver grilled Klaw furiously, driven to rage by Klaw's adamant refusal to answer any question except those that didn't deal with issues of pornography and obscenity. Kefauver asked many suggestive questions, asking if Klaw hired teenage models, asking if his models were posing for pornographers, and if so, who. Klaw didn't crack. No obscenity charges were brought against him, though he was nearly cited for contempt.

"This was a federal case, and we beat the United States," Kramer said. "I think Larry Flynt learned from us. Of course, he was a little bit of a pig there, and you certainly can't compare those pictures to ours, but he went up against the government, too."

Irving Klaw's victory was short-lived, however, and it became evident that he had won only a Pyrrhic victory. The pressure had made Klaw infamous, and his associates, no matter how fleeting their relationships with him, were catching heat for it. The photo lab that printed his pictures also did some jobs for the Walt Disney Company, and Uncle Walt's people weren't happy. Disney officials told the photo shop owner to terminate his dealings with Klaw or lose their lucrative and prestigious account. Immediately after the hearings, Klaw closed up his New York-based Nutrix novelty mail-order business, through which he had been distributing his bondage photos. His sister Paula and her husband, Jack Kramer, reopened the Klaw mail-order business in Jersey City under a new name, Ikay Productions. Irving Klaw had hoped he would escape further trouble by moving his catalog business away from New York, where he was a known man, to a warehouse in New Jersey where he was technically not involved with the day-to-day operations. Paula and Jack had been there a week when the local police stormed the place, seizing inventory samples.

The case was tied up in the courts for another year and a half, during which time the conservative United States Congress instituted change in the postal laws, making it more difficult for Klaw to distribute his catalogs and photos. The postal authorities confiscated all his orders on July 16, 1956. Klaw tried to appeal his case to the U.S. Supreme Court, but they saw no compelling reason to consider overturning the law.

By 1957 Klaw had stopped shooting any new photos, for fear of federal prosecutors pursuing his models and photographers. He had even called Bettie to apologize, telling her that it was nothing personal. In 1960 he began releasing specialty compilation books of his bondage and pinup photos, like *Bettie Page in Bondage*, through the mail-order business in Jersey City. But not long after, the Feds were breathing down his neck again. U.S. Attorney General Robert Kennedy was on the warpath against "smut," and so the FBI busted the Klaws again, once more invading their Jersey City warehouse and seizing cartons of photos.

"My father was working at the warehouse that particular day, and the FBI agents came in and arrested him because he was the only one there," Ira Kramer recalls. "I think he spent the night in jail. They should have arrested Irving instead, but my father was the one filling the orders."

Eventually, though, Klaw was arrested. He and Jack Kramer both faced federal charges of felony conspiracy to distribute obscene material through the U.S. mail. They were indicted on June 27, 1963, and were later freed on $10,000 bail. Facing a five-year prison sentence, Irving Klaw offered to destroy his bondage and pinup negatives in a bid to gain his freedom. It worked and he escaped conviction. Klaw never spent time in a federal prison. A Freedom of Information Act search of the U.S. Department of Justice's Federal Bureau of Prisons database came up blank on his name.

Despite Klaw's victory in earning his liberation from a prison sentence, his livelihood was badly damaged. Many of his original Movie Star News photographs and negatives were shredded, never to be seen again. Luckily, however, Paula Klaw hid several sheaths of the negatives away, many of which were the photos of Bettie. Even that was not enough to turn the tide for her brother, though. By the mid-sixties, tired of fighting the Feds, a beaten and stressed Irving Klaw turned control of Movie Star News over to Paula, then made arrangements to retire in Florida. Unfortunately, his story does not have a happy ending. Shortly before he was to leave, Irving Klaw fell ill, but his doctors didn't catch his burst appendix. He died in New York in 1966 at age fifty-nine. The official cause of death was an abdominal inflammation, but those close to him said it was more likely the endless defense of his pinup business that did him in. He was survived by his sister, his wife, and their two sons.

"Larry Flynt, he made no bones about what he was putting out, but Klaw never did show anything. There was no nudity at all in Klaw's stuff. He never showed a boob ever," Jack Bradley says passionately in defense of his former boss. "However, you have to go with the climate of the times. At the time, that was considered very risqué. By today's standards, that would be nothing. You can go on the beach and see more in the thongs than with the pinup outfits they were wearing in the forties, fifties, and sixties."

In fact, Irving Klaw was so neurotic about avoiding nudity in his photos that he sometimes made his models wear two pairs of panties under their stockings, just to make sure no pubic hair showed.

"Klaw was very careful. He didn't want to do anything that smacked of being pornographic," says publisher J. B. Rund, Bettie's former agent and a self-styled expert on pornography. "When he was being persecuted by the postal authorities, he was writing letters . . . saying, 'You can see these same things in movies and on magazine covers, so why are they after me?' "

Klaw didn't understand the power of the bondage pictures, Rund believes. Because he himself wasn't an S & M aficionado, he couldn't see why the photos were any different from his standard cheesecake fare.

As for Bettie, after the Kefauver obscenity hearings, she had hastily retreated from New York to the safe haven of Miami for the summer, modeling on the beaches, far from the attention of being a formerly subpoenaed bondage model. Bettie returned to posing for her friend, Bunny Yeager, and for a while at least, the negative attention surrounding her seemed very distant.

"People ask me if I knew of any trouble Bettie had with the

Kefauver committee or the FBI," Yeager says. "I knew of nothing. I never heard any rumors of any type, or problems, until later. And I still don't know what it was all about. In those days, you were not allowed to take photos or publish photos showing pubic hair. The rumor was that Bettie had done that and it got her in trouble. That was all I heard."

Bettie has said in recent interviews that she enjoyed all her modeling work, including the leather, fetish, and bondage shoots, and that if she could relive it, she'd do it again. It was just part of the job if you worked for Irving Klaw—you did an hour of bondage each shoot or you didn't get a paycheck.

Nevertheless, Bettie's photographer pal Art Amsie recalls that when he first met Bettie in 1956, he asked how she and Irving Klaw were getting along, and her reply was less than glowing. "She said, 'Don't ever mention his name again. If you want to be my friend, don't ever talk to me about bondage or Irving Klaw ever again.' " Amsie says, "I quickly figured out that was a topic I wouldn't broach with Bettie."

Kramer said Paula Klaw and Bettie "used to correspond with each other until the Kefauver days and that's when they stopped. I heard my mother say a lot about Kefauver. It wasn't anything you could print, though."

Bettie said her final good-byes to the Klaws sometime in late 1956 or early 1957, when she started seriously looking for more mainstream work as an actress. She played the leading role in a small off-Broadway play in 1956 and continued to do some private modeling and cheese-cake photos. Small roles in nationally televised drama shows were also starting to come, but faced with the continuing strain of being reminded of the Senate ordeal and the humiliation of being confronted at auditions with questions about the seamier underside of her work, Bettie began to have problems.

One night in 1957, after finishing dinner with boyfriend, Marvin Greene, Bettie felt like flying—literally. She tried to take a leap from the third-story window of her New York City apartment house, but Greene stopped her, according to a source very close to Bettie. If the story's true, it would be another harbinger of Bettie's paranoid schizophrenia later in life, just like the time she says she heard a voice talking to her after she hurt her leg while making the wrestling movie at the Klaw studio.

During this time, the same source says, Bettie would also become hostile and confrontational, blaming friends for sabotaging her success. Greene, perhaps hoping to ease her turmoil, was pressing Bettie to marry him, to settle down and get out of the business, but it only made matters worse. She didn't love him and his proposals just pushed her farther away from him. Months later, Greene's father called Bettie to tell her that Marvin had been in a head-on car crash. Marvin's brother, who was riding in the passenger seat, had been killed. Bettie believed that Marvin had probably been drinking and that his father was suggesting she was the reason for it. No one's sure what happened to Marvin. Few people associated with Bettie recall him as much more than the boyfriend who picked her up or dropped her off at shoots.

By this time, Bettie's emotions were crumbling and every hardship was magnified. One problem was that her apartment building was going to be demolished and replaced with a parking lot. She wasn't sure where else she would go. Another more serious problem was a stalker who had been harassing her. Years earlier, she had been followed for weeks by a mysterious man, but that stopped after a while. In 1957 she began to be barraged with threatening typewritten letters from an obsessed fan. The author of the frightening missives threatened to twist Bettie's nipples off with pliers, among other horrors. After reporting the notes, Bettie was in for a bigger scare: The FBI thought her stalker might be a wanted serial killer. With the possibility of a dangerous criminal after her instead of an annoying crank, Bettie went along with the Feds, who wanted her to be the bait in a sting to capture the suspect. In one of the letters, her harasser ordered her to bring a package of photos of herself to the corner of 116th and Amsterdam, and to come alone. If she didn't comply, something bad would happen, the creepy writer told her. Six FBI agents staked out the block, waiting to see if he would show. After a half hour, a group of teenage boys walked out of a tenement building briefly and glanced around suspiciously. An agent questioned them. Bettie's stalker turned out to be an obsessed sixteen-year-old boy.

Life in New York was building to a crescendo for Bettie, and she wanted out. Years later, her younger brother Jack would tell interviewers that he thought her problems stemmed from shame over some faked magazine photos, purporting to show her engaged in hard-core sex acts. However, Bettie herself later said that she had posed for uncharacteristically explicit photos at a party with some camera club guys where she had a couple glasses of wine. Normally a teetotaler, Bettie was a health-food and fitness nut who never even smoked. Her tolerance for alcohol was reportedly extremely low, and one night she lost control. She could remember posing, but not exactly how she posed. It came back to haunt her, she has said, when police showed up at her door in 1957, holding a copy of the pictures, bought under the counter at a local store. Bettie says she later found out the cameraman had sold them to pay off a gambling debt. She was furious. She never expected the photos would be seen by anyone but the photographer. And after all, she says, it was a one-time thing.

Some longtime Bettie fans and associates say the Queen of Curves doth protest too much, however. It was actually fairly common for Bettie and other pinup girls to pose for explicit spread-eagle shots in private settings, they say.

"This kind of party line that all of this happened in some terrible eight hours one night, that's bullshit," says artist-writer Richard Merkin, who claims to own dozens of the more-revealing Bettie photos bought from a private collector, including "four or five pictures which genuinely would have been considered pornographic under any circumstances."

Jack Bradley recalls that he first heard about Bettie posing for more than simple nudes one day in the fifties when "a guy called me who had a store. He said, 'You'll never guess what I just saw, what I was just offered.' He showed me, and I said, 'I'll be damned.' I never confronted Bettie about them, because I had no reason to."

As far as photos revealing Bettie's pubic hair, there are several, but shots of Bettie showing much more are practically nonexistent nowadays. Most, if they do exist, must have stayed in the private possessions of the photographers who shot them. Merkin explains, "You could pose for these illicit pictures because you knew there was no way they were ever going to get published." Most of the time, anyway.

"We, as professionals, could not shoot them because if we were found with them, we'd go to jail," Bradley says. However, he adds, "There was another tribe of photographers that hired Bettie and hired June King and so on down the line. These were amateurs, but they were amateurs with money. Now, they would go to these camera club shootings where Bettie or June King, the models, were, and they'd get on talking to them privately. The person running the enterprise didn't want the models to mingle with the guys and get any phone numbers because it would be the end of their business, but some of these guys were smart enough to slip a phone number to the girls and ask for a private session.

"What would happen, a guy or two guys, the money guys, had an apartment and they would hire Bettie or June King and maybe the first couple shootings, they'd give them a lot more than what they were earning at the [camera club] studios, and they began to become friendly with them to the point that they'd say, 'You want a drink? I've ordered steaks,' you know what I mean?

"And eventually, what would happen? They'd say, 'How about showing the thing?' And shots were made: wide-open shots with dresses pulled up and big smiles on their face. I never saw a man in the shot with them. I saw shots where Bettie or June King would be sitting in a chair with their legs wide open. These people, whoever took them, they probably told Bettie, 'They're just for us, after all, we're big-shot businessmen, we wouldn't do anything to bring attention to ourselves,' but all they have to do is give a single print to somebody and a copy negative could be made and run off. In some ways, [the pictures] began to find their way to the Times Square area, and a guy might say to a good customer, 'I have something special for you under the counter.' "

J. B. Rund, however, who published some copies of the disputed photos in his *Private Peeks* magazines, thinks they were a one-time thing. He's talked to Bettie in person and he believes the story about the drunken party. Bettie just could not hold her alcohol, he says, and she slipped up.

Merkin says the whole debate about whether or not Bettie posed for explicit photos, and how many if she did, is a bit of a tempest in a teapot, anyway. "Nowadays, they're really quite mild. Nobody has ever seen what anybody would call a truly pornographic picture of Bettie Page, like something that would show penetration. To my knowledge, it doesn't exist."

Whatever her inner demons, at the height of her career and on the brink of success in television and probably greater fame, Bettie Page left New York City quietly at the age of thirty-four, shortly before Christmas 1957, never to return to acting or modeling again.

"I quit modeling in December 1957 when I left New York for good. I was tired of my life as it was and wanted to try something else," Bettie said in her 1992 letter to the author.

10

···

Salvation

ELLSWORTH BOYD had just come back from lunch and was about to start his afternoon shift as a lifeguard on the beach at Fort Lauderdale in December 1957, when the word was passed down to him: Bettie Page is on the beach!

More than predictably, Bettie had drifted from her fear and shame and disappointments in New York back to Florida, where her life could be bleached clean like a dirty bone left in the sun. She had spent a sandy, lonely Christmas in 1957 in her cottage at Fort Lauderdale, staying to herself, and not seeking modeling work to keep her busy. She was there nearly two weeks before she went down to the beach on the day twenty-six-year-old lifeguard Boyd happened to be on duty.

"I had been to lunch and one of the lifeguards at the main station, Dave Gentry was his name, he told me that Bettie Page is on the beach," recounts Boyd, now sixty-five years old and a retired professor from Towson University's College of Education in Baltimore, Maryland.

Bettie was down near the main stand, the lifeguard station perched on the roof of the beach restrooms where Fort Lauderdale's primary artery and drag strip, Las Olas Boulevard, meets the beach. Boyd had been living in Fort Lauderdale for over a year and was studying to be an elementary school teacher.

"Word had spread that Bettie Page was on the beach and it was late in the afternoon and she was alone, so I said, 'I think I'll walk over to talk to her,' " recalls Boyd, who was already a fan of hers and knew Bettie's pinups from her various magazine layouts.

"Fortunately it was late in the day, because the captain [of the lifeguards] would drive up and down the beach because we weren't supposed to get down from the stand and talk to people. We could get down and stretch our legs, but I was taking a big chance getting down from the stand and walking down to the water's edge to talk to Bettie," he says. "You can flip a coin from the beach to the road, and the lifeguard chairs were on the high end of the beach and it was easy for the captain to go by and see if you were there. He could check up on you real easy by driving up and down the beach highway. It's still that way today. . . . If he caught you off the stand, you could get fired. I got a chance to slip off the lifeguard stand and go down by the water and see her go by and start casually talking to her."

Strolling on the edge of the surf, Bettie was wearing a green bikini and had on a light-colored jacket for a top. "She was quite well-known," Boyd says. "I struck up a conversation with her and I was impressed how nice she was. She was very cordial for someone with such a big name, very down-to-earth, and very easy to talk to; the girl-next-door type, very pretty." Boyd told her that one of his hobbies was skin diving and snorkeling, and he told Bettie that he and his friend Jim Kelly taught skin diving and were, in fact, going on an underwater expedition the next day. "I mentioned how we would dive up there in the shallow water with the tropical fish, and she said, 'Oh, I'd love to see that.' And I said, 'Have you ever tried it?' "

Fortunately for Boyd, Bettie's adventurous spirit prevailed that day. The next afternoon, he and Kelly picked her up at the cottage she was renting and took her to Lauderdale-by-the-Sea, a coastal town about ten minutes north, between Fort Lauderdale and Pompano Beach off U.S. Route 1. "The reason we went there is because of the coral reef. There's a whole north-south reef. It swings in close to Lauderdale-by-the-Sea, so close that you can throw a stone from the beach to that reef we took her to. It's shallow, and there's a lot of growth, hard coral, soft coral, and all kinds of tropical fish: parrot fish, tiger fish, clam fish, small groupers, and small snappers. . . . There's a terrific variety of fish on that reef. She was crazy about the fish, the bright-colored fish.

A couple times she dived down and held her breath. She said, 'I'd like to stay down there and play with the fish.' She was wild about it."

Boyd and his friend stayed down at the coral reef, teaching Bettie the fine art of skin diving for about four hours. He didn't think to ask Bettie out, because he assumed she had a boyfriend, and she said she was going to Miami the next day to visit someone. Besides, "My ego wasn't that big," he says, with a hearty laugh.

But Boyd did commemorate the day by taking a half dozen snap-shots of Bettie playing in the surf in her homemade pink, white-flow-ered bikini. Most haven't been published in nearly two decades. "I said, 'Could we take some pictures of you?' and she said, 'Oh sure.' We had some equipment with us. We put a [scuba] mask on her head and gave her a three-point trident—we used to gig lobsters with it—and she posed with that trident in a couple real cute poses. I guess I got half a dozen poses of her before we ran out of film."

Unbeknownst to Boyd or Bettie, the informal beach "photo ses-sion" would be the last pinup modeling Bettie would ever do. Later, thinking back on the day after his photos came back from the devel-oper, Boyd thought it would make a good short article—and it did. He published the tale of his day with Bettie along with one of the pictures in the June 1958 issue of *Skin Diver* magazine under the title, "The Latest Rage With Bettie Page." Interesting to note is the fact that Boyd knew the correct spelling of Bettie's name. The photo that ran with the article shows a tall, skinny, crew-cutted Boyd, looking at first glance not a little like the "Before" in the old Charles Atlas fitness ads, until you notice his trim muscled legs and biceps, a byproduct of his lifeguard swimmers' training. He's handing a spear gun to the bikini-clad Bettie, who is holding the trident and wearing a scuba mask propped on her head. A pair of black swim flippers rest on the sand at her feet, as the edge of the Florida surf laps close behind at her heels.

Ellsworth Boyd's account in the magazine of his day with Bettie is, for obvious reasons, filled with much more vivid details then his recol-lections forty years later. His magazine article reads as follows:

It's not every day that our Ft. Lauderdale skin diving school has the opportunity to instruct one of America's top pinup mod-els—the lovely Miss Bettie Page.

Miss Page expressed sincere interest in learning the funda-
mentals of diving and yearned to visit the coral reef.

She took to the water like a fish. In no time at all, the dark-
haired beauty was accompanying Jim Kelly and me on a swim to
the coral reef, a quarter of a mile from our sunny Florida shore.

It was difficult for Kelly and me to keep our eyes on the reef
with a lovely mermaid like Bettie along.

Bettie was fascinated with the silent world of the fish and
coral. In twenty feet of water, she dived like a veteran.

She was especially enthused with the multicolored Queen Angel fish and a pesty Trigger fish which followed us all over the
reef. Bettie liked him so much, she wanted to dive down and find
some food for him!

Once Bettie exclaimed, "If I could only get down there and
walk on the ocean floor and breathe underwater!"

"That," we explained, "would come in the next lesson with the
lung."

After two hours of exploring the wonders of the deep, Kelly
and I felt a chill, but not a complaint did we hear from our lovely
mermaid.

The weather prevented us from returning to the reef the rest
of that week and Bettie's vacation ended.

She did, however, promise to return and go diving with us
again.

[Bettie] was enchanted with the beauty of the reef and we
were enchanted with the beauty of outdoor gal Bettie Page.

The article started a side career for Boyd, whose other hobby besides skin diving was writing. He now writes for a string of publications, including *Sport Diver* magazine, for which he scribes a monthly
column, "Wreck Facts," about shipwrecks and divers.

Bettie never made good on her promise to go diving with Boyd
again. He didn't hear from her again until 1996, when, with the help
of Bettie Page fan club president Steve Brewster, Boyd sent a letter to
Bettie, and she replied, thanking him for teaching her to skin dive.
They've since written each other two or three times.

Bettie left Fort Lauderdale in December 1957, not for Miami, as
Boyd had recalled, but for Key West. Shortly before she met Boyd—

lonely and running out of money—Bettie had called Armond Carlyle Walterson, the young man from Key West with whom she had had a summer fling three years earlier. Armond invited her to come live with him in his place on Elizabeth Street in Key West. For Bettie, the invitation to move to the island couldn't have come at a better time. She hopped the next bus to Key West, and Armond was waiting for her at the depot when she got off it. The two picked right up where they left off, making love and hitting the town. Of course, there was the small matter of Armond's girlfriend, a spicy blonde named Margaret. She was history when the thirty-four-year-old Bettie came back into twenty-one-year-old Armond's life, but Margaret wouldn't be jilted so easily—she literally tailed Bettie and Armond on their car dates, riding their bumper threateningly.

While Armond took odd jobs during the day, Bettie looked for work. At night they would go to the drive-in movies, escaping into their private fantasies, then living them out, sometimes by moonlight on the warm beaches of Key West. Bettie soon made close friends with Armond's extended family of eleven brothers and sisters. They reminded her of all-too-brief, happier days in Nashville when she was among her own siblings. Armond's family was a friendly, wholesome group that went on large picnics together at Boca Chica and had sack races and jumprope competitions on the beach. His mother would even join in the events, which Bettie thought was fantastic.

In February Bettie was playing volleyball on the beach with Armond when she jumped for the ball and a sickening crack could be heard in her lower back. She plummeted to the ground, paralyzed with pain. The doctors told her she had severely sprained the left joint of her sacrum, the bottom-most vertebrae in the back. Though she was fortunate the accident didn't have permanent repercussions, it left her wheelchair bound for four months, during which time money became tight and tensions rose between her and Armond. After a few months of depending on her rapidly depleting savings for shelter, groceries, and other necessaries, Bettie was unable to pay the rent on her storage shed in New Jersey and the owners evicted her, selling everything she owned, from family mementos to her entire modeling portfolio. Somewhere, maybe someone still has rare Bettie Page screen-test photos now thought lost to time, or unpublished snapshots of Bettie bought on a whim at that auction. The only thing certain is that

Bettie no longer has them, and never even had the chance to bid or stop the sale, a crushing event in her life, and one that perhaps made her exit from her modeling life seem so much more final.

While she was recuperating, in desperation for money, she decided to give teaching another try. On June 4, 1958, she filled out an application with the Monroe County public school system to teach elementary school in Key West. She listed her previous job experience as "secretarial and theatrical." Apparently no one checked her references. Somehow, after a ten-year absence from teaching, she got the job. Bettie began teaching a class of fifth graders at Harris Elementary School on August 15. She resigned just shy of three months later.

"I lasted just one term. I had a very rowdy bunch of students in my class and I could not control them," Bettie said years later. "I was very disappointed in my teaching experience and didn't care to pursue it any further." For all her experience with bondage and spanking on film, Bettie was not much of a disciplinarian. Her downfall ended up being the teenage son of a naval officer who had failed so many times he was still in the fifth grade. His acting out made the classroom so chaotic that, in retrospect, it may be a no-brainer as to why there was an opening in the fifth grade that year and why the school system was so eager to hire Bettie.

After that, Bettie took a civil service exam and worked for nine months at the Key West Naval Base as secretary to the public works director there, J. S. Meggs. Contacted by the author in 1993, Meggs's daughter said her father, then extremely elderly and ill, had looked at pictures sent by the author, but could not recall the lovely Bettie. One can only surmise that Mr. Meggs must have been an extremely diligent public servant, indeed, to have no memory of the Queen of Curves sitting at the next desk.

On November twenty-sixth, Bettie and Armond married at the First Methodist Church in Key West, in what was Bettie's first church wedding. She walked down the aisle past Armond's family wearing her own handmade beige silk wedding gown. Bettie says very little about Armond or her life with him, but others close to her have said it was a stormy relationship, complicated by her mood swings, his lack of ambition, and money problems. Armond, by this time, was working as a civilian shipping manager at the naval station, a good job for someone so young to land, and it was enough for him. He was a simple man, who, unlike Bettie, wasn't interested in travel and wasn't driven by ambition or dreams of greater success. He was content to hang out on the beach, fish, and eat hamburgers; and most of the time, that's all he wanted to do. But for Bettie, who was accustomed to fine dining and traveling the country whenever she wished, life with the younger, less experienced Armond was stagnating.

The two also had bitter fights over a business loss: They had pooled their money to come up with the $2,000 they needed to buy a twenty-six-foot fishing boat with which they had hoped to catch seafood to sell to local restaurants. They built more than one hundred wire lobster traps over nights and weekends, working around their day jobs. At daybreak they would lay out the traps and return in the evening to reap the harvest. Unfortunately, most nights the sparring lovers would come home from a hard day of work to find their lobster traps hanging empty, raided by a bunch of local kids. Bettie and Armond ditched the boat at a $1,400 loss. Their marriage ended after a month and a half, on New Year's Eve 1958. After a particularly nasty argument, Armond refused to take Bettie dancing for New Year's, mainly because he didn't know how and was afraid to try. Bettie changed out of her party dress into her street clothes and fled into the night, frustrated, tearful, and angry.

On that warm, windy New Year's Eve, Bettie ran down White Street, the two-mile strip of road that runs the length of Key West, where she had met Armond just three summers before. Her hands frantically brushed away the tears that streamed from her eyes, making blurs of the stars overhead. A slight mist hung in the wind, adding to the salty taste of her tears. Once again, she felt alone in the world. She slowed to a shuffle, her sobs coming in dry heaves.

Then, a bright light appeared on the ground. Bettie raised her head and faltered forward, unsteady. Illuminating the darkness, a large white cross glowed above her.

"I was walking alone down White Street at twenty minutes to midnight on New Years' Eve [1958] with my head hanging low. I was very lonely and blue and intended to go down to the beach and look up at the stars," Bettie recalled. "All of a sudden I felt a hand in mine, leading me across the street to a small church with a bright white neon cross on top. The door was wide open and a New Year's service was in progress."

Bettie stumbled into the open door of the church and stood in back of the congregation watching a tall, muscular, charismatic preacher who stood in the midst of his crowded flock, imploring them to put Jesus above all else. It was a night watch service, designed so parishioners could see the end of the old year and the beginning of the New Year in church. Electric fans hummed from the alcoves as the worshippers raised their arms upward in prayer, sweat making their shirts stick to their backs. The minister's message of salvation seemed to be directed to Bettie alone. As she listened, the tears flowed from her eyes, streaming down her face. All the emotion from her argument with Armond, from the loss of her acting career, the loss of their business, all of it spilled out. Singing rose around her. She knew she had found a purpose, a place where she belonged.

"I walked in and stood at the back of the room and cried as the preacher delivered his sermon," she said. "I could hardly wait till Sunday to go back to the Latin American Baptist Temple and listen to Pastor Wright again."

She found an apartment that week, and the next Sunday morning she was waiting at the door of the church. The same charismatic pastor was there. This time, when he gave the invitation to accept Jesus Christ, Bettie walked forward, entranced. The young reverend held her hand and welcomed her to the congregation. "When he gave the invitation, I went forward and received the Lord Jesus Christ as my personal savior," Bettie said. "I turned my life over to the Lord, and God led me to go to Bible schools for three years."

The young pastor's name was Morris Wright, though he went by M. O. Wright, using his name to tell people he was "mo' right" about religion. A part-time preacher and full-time roofer, the twenty-seven-year-old Wright was a fire-and-brimstone kind of guy who warned the unrepentant of the dangers awaiting them on Doomsday.

Born and raised the son of a sharecropper in Mississippi, Wright got his start preaching in a Key West jail. A construction worker by trade, he joined the navy at the end of World War II and served in the Korean War. Working his way to the rank of a chief petty officer, he was stationed in Key West in the early 1950s when he killed a man in a car wreck and was sentenced to a year in jail. While there he became a Christian and preached the gospel to his cellmates.

"I appeal to the down-and-outer, the person who's down on their luck. I don't appeal to people who have a whole lot of money or even know what money is," Wright said in a 1993 interview. "They call me a dinosaur. I'm the old school. They call me Hellfire and Damnation real quick. I started preaching when I was in jail to the men in the cell with me. When I started to win them over to Christ, it just came natural to me."

Soon after his release from jail in 1958, Wright began preaching as a lay pastor to the English-speaking congregation at the Latin American Baptist Temple. The temple was the brainchild of the Rev. Dr. Ishmael Negrin, a Cuban missionary who had a vision that he would unite the Spanish and English cultures in the United States through Christianity. He had preached in Cuba for more than thirty years before coming to America to build his temple, a 140-person gothic-style church in the middle of a quiet Key West neighborhood about eight blocks from the beach and across the way from the elementary school where Bettie had taught.

Once his temple was built, Negrin realized he had a problem: He couldn't speak English well enough for any of the Americans in his congregation to understand him. Then came Wright. Negrin and Wright took turns preaching the same sermon, but as the church grew, they started separate services, one in English, the other in Spanish. When Wright joined the church in summer 1958, there were sixty Spanish-speaking parishioners and thirty-five English-speaking ones. By 1959 Negrin still had the same sixty parishioners, but Wright had 180. That summer the English speakers split off into their own church, the Key West Independent Baptist Temple, ending Negrin's dreams of greater unity between the two cultures.

Still its leader today and now a fully ordained minister, Wright claims to have personally saved more than eight thousand people— one of whom was Bettie Page.

11

....

Servant of God

LIKE MANY other people, Bettie entered the 1960s searching for her identity. She had found a purpose serving God and now she needed to know how to fulfill it. In the summer of 1959 she left the growing Latin American Baptist Temple and traveled back home to Nashville, leaving a crying Armond behind at the bus station, begging her to give it another try. He made the trek from Key West to Nashville a few weeks later, hoping to talk her into coming back with him, but Bettie's mother told the downhearted young man that Bettie had already left. She and Armond never crossed paths again.

Bettie had moved in with her brother Jimmie, who now lived in Gardena, California. To her, the climate and atmosphere of southern California was close enough to her sunny haven in Florida to feel familiar and comforting. Soon after she arrived in Gardena, Bettie was on her way back from an unsuccessful interview for a job downtown as a church secretary at the First Methodist Church when she heard gospel music playing on a speaker in a building down the street. Two girls were leaving the building, their arms loaded with books. Bettie found herself compelled to know what the place was, so she asked the girls. They told her it was BIOLA, the Bible Institute of Los Angeles. When she was still at the Latin American Baptist Temple, Bettie had grown interested in Bible studies through conversations with a Sunday School teacher from Ohio. After finding BIOLA, Bettie arose early the next day and enrolled. Because she was virtually penniless, the school showed Bettie some Christian faith, hope, and charity and gave her a no-interest loan for tuition and living expenses.

Founded in 1913, BIOLA is a leading worldwide institute for Christian learning that offers a curriculum ranging from art to nursing to psychology. Bettie arrived in time for the first semester at the college's new location. BIOLA had outgrown its old campus in Los Angeles after merging with another religious college, and so the newer, larger BIOLA had relocated to La Mirada, about a half-hour's drive away, near Laguna and Huntington beaches and Disneyland.

Bettie attended night classes at BIOLA for a year, renting an apartment in the Hollywood Hills close to Hollywood Boulevard on Vista del Mar. She supported herself by returning to an old love: radio. She became the secretary for the president of BIOLA's Christian radio station, where she probably contemplated more than once going before the microphone, as she had in her college years as a radio dramatist at George Peabody. Four months later, not being able to make tuition payments, she took a better-paying job working as a secretary for the contracts administrator at the Lockheed Aircraft International headquarters on Sixth Street in downtown Los Angeles.

By the end of the spring semester, Bettie was feeling restless. In June 1961, on the advice of friends, she went to Chicago and enrolled in summer school at the Moody Bible Institute, a college founded in 1886 by evangelist and boot salesman Dwight Lyman Moody. The school's curriculum included aviation, science, and broadcasting. BIOLA's first dean had been a president of Moody and the two schools had strong ties.

While at Moody, Bettie lived in student housing on Chicago's LaSalle Avenue and took classes in personal evangelism and Bible synthesis. The school application she filled out confirmed her employment history: secretarial work, some teaching experience, and theatrical jobs.

As the summer neared its end, Bettie wanted to stay at Moody, but her savings were running out. She couldn't afford tuition or rent, so she took a day job working as a secretary at F. E. Compton & Company, the publishers of Compton's Encyclopedia. During the fall and spring semesters, she audited evening classes at Moody. On the weekends she could be found walking in Lincoln Park handing out religious pamphlets with her friend Bob, a fellow evangelist. Bettie liked the summers in Chicago, and spent many afternoons sunbathing at Lake Michigan.

Early in her stay at Moody, in June 1961, one of the most profound and memorable events in Bettie's life occurred: Billy Graham came to town. Reverend Graham started his evangelical Christian Crusades in 1949, traveling from Los Angeles to New York and from Scotland to India. In stadiums around the world, he has preached to more than fifty million people in person, and millions more through television. He has been an insider to presidents from Kennedy to Clinton. In the summer of 1961, Graham came to Chicago's McCormick Place stadium, where he filled forty thousand seats every night for three weeks. During his final rally, which was being taped for television, he collapsed from the 110-degree heat in the outdoor stadium. Hours later, he completed the broadcast in the vacant stadium, preaching that without an audience, the stadium was as empty as a heart without Jesus Christ. What could have been a disaster instead cemented his reputation as the keeper of America's faith.

His crusades also sponsored one-month evangelism schools and often provided scholarships to local Bible students. Bettie worked for nineteen consecutive nights that summer as a counselor for the Billy Graham Crusade, spreading Graham's message to local city women. It was a fulfilling and joyful experience that made her decide that she wanted to work toward being a missionary and preach the gospel to those who hadn't heard it. As his Chicago crusade came to an end, Graham shook hands with local volunteers to thank them for their help, just as he did at the end of every crusade. It's easy to picture Bettie Page, the former *Playboy* playmate, the Queen of Curves, with tears in her eyes, coming face-to-face with Billy Graham and clasping her hands tightly around his, as if to absorb his goodness.

The next year Bettie took the money she had saved from her secretarial work and signed up for a thirty-day Bible retreat at Winona Lake in Indiana. There she heard influential and persuasive speakers with exciting new theories of Bible interpretation. Enriching the spiritual experience were the outside sermons delivered on the forested shores of the clear lake. Bettie sought out the peace of the Winona Lake retreat repeatedly, returning there for the next four years.

After Winona Lake, Bettie enrolled full-time at Multnomah School of the Bible in Portland, Oregon. Sitting near the junction of the Columbia and Willamette rivers near a nine-acre city park, Multnomah was founded in 1936 by local ministers and businessmen. Dr. Willard Aldritch, who was the school's president when Bettie attended, was famous for saying, "If it's the Bible you want, then you want Multnomah." He couldn't have been speaking more literally. Unlike the other colleges Bettie had attended, Multnomah taught one thing and one thing only: the Bible. The school was a cloistered campus for seriously devout students who favored an ascetic lifestyle. Bettie lived in the Doris Coffin Aldritch Memorial Dormitory on the northwest campus and attended graduate classes in Bible study. Bettie, now nearly forty, was probably the oldest of her classmates, the majority of whom were at least ten years younger. There wasn't much for the outdoors-inclined like Bettie to do—it rained more or less constantly for the nine months she attended the school. Still, that didn't deter Bettie, who, umbrella in hand, went on nature strolls and grew to appreciate the mammoth Northwestern trees. Most of her nights at Multnomah were spent alone in quiet contemplation, sitting by the radio and sewing. Embracing the Bible school's strict, chaste lifestyle is another example of Bettie trying to gain control over her life, while looking for stability.

"Those were the happiest years of my life," Bettie said. "All three of them were very strict schools. I didn't have any problem with their no smoking, no drinking, no drugs rules—I have never indulged in any of these—but it was hard for me to give up going to the movies. I had been a movie fan ever since I was a little girl."

Bettie later moved into the former home of a Multnomah teacher, high above the valley, where she could look down onto the breathtaking city lights of Portland. Earning course credits through volunteer work, Bettie helped out at the nearby Louise Home, a center for pregnant and unmarried teens. Among the unwed mothers whom Bettie counseled there were two thirteen-year-old girls. Bettie took the girls along with her to church for services that she led with another student and friend at Multnomah, Sharon Reed.

Perhaps reflecting the tumult she had been through in her life, Bettie chose Philippians 3:10 as the quote to accompany her yearbook photo: "That I may know Him and the power of His resurrection, and the fellowship of His sufferings, being made comformable unto His

Death." Bettie's inner turmoil was evident to some of her classmates, who found her mysterious and seemingly haunted by a past she didn't want to talk about. "We knew very little about her background other than she seemed like she had been through a rather rough time," says classmate Arden D. Patefield, who now lives in Washington.

"It seemed to me she had been saved fairly recently. She had a real fervor for other lost people," Patefield says. But, he adds, "It seemed like perhaps we felt like her fervor got the best of her sometimes, that it controlled her emotions." In fact, Bettie's ardent fanaticism about Christianity and her gruff way with others made some students suspect she was unbalanced. Her age and background may have isolated her from other students, but Bettie also so wanted to make up for her past mistakes and what she saw as the evil way of life she had led that she probably overcompensated and became paranoid, not believing others to be as good as she now saw herself to be, or wanted to be.

"Rudeness involved her fervor," Patefield recalls. "There was a time when she seemed to be frustrated with the progress of school and lashed out against a teacher, and most of us felt for the teacher. It was in Bible study methods, where we were supposed to be learning techniques and approaches. [Bettie] got off on a subject about whether they were concerned enough about winning the lost [souls] and then she got very emotional about it, and the teacher and all the other people just kind of let her go until she had vented. There wasn't any [physical] altercation."

Bettie also knocked heads with the school faculty after she suggested an unusual proposal for bringing wayward souls to God. As Patefield recalls, "I think there was one thing that the school was concerned about. She wanted to work down on skid row because she felt like she drew men, and they were concerned that that was the wrong way to bring men to God. That's why she ended up in the Louise Home."

As far as drawing men to her at Multnomah, Bettie apparently didn't have the same appeal as she had in the past. Patefield couldn't remember any of the single men asking her out. "I didn't recall that she was that pretty. I can see, yes, that she probably had been, but it seemed like she had been through a rough time."

In class meetings with the other grad students, Bettie "would be quite vocal, but so were others," Patefield recalls. He also remembered that one time Bettie "was concerned about something and we went to the chapel and prayed about it. I don't really remember what the problem was."

"She's in just one small chapter of my life," Patefield says, summing up his brush with a Bettie Page quite different from the playful model her fans today know. "I almost knew nothing about her, where she came from, or where she went after that."

When the spring semester was over, Bettie decided through prayer that missionary work was still the path God intended her to take, but she was turned down by the mission board. "I had wanted to be a missionary, but no mission board would take me since I had been divorced," she explained. (She had told them only about Billy, not mentioning Armond, because she wasn't certain she was divorced from him.)

Heartbroken that her dream of being a missionary was denied, and hearing from her stepmother, Lulu, that her father was seriously ill, Bettie, now forty years old, returned home to live in Nashville for the first time in almost twenty years. Once there, she settled in with her family and for a year and a half taught a Sunday School class composed of thirteen-year-old girls at a Baptist mission church in a poor neighborhood in South Nashville. Bettie would load up the girls and their mothers in her station wagon and take them for outings to Nashville's Old Hickory Lake. It remains a very pleasant memory for Bettie.

Keeping herself afloat, Bettie found a job for several months working as a secretary to the office manager at Benson Printing Company, a publisher of high school yearbooks. Bettie visited Roy Page at the hospital almost every night. Her former abuser was now ravaged by diabetes, which, in his stubborn and headstrong way, he had let go untreated because he didn't want to be bothered with going to a doctor. Both his legs had been amputated, and the doctors at the hospital now gave him no more than a few months to live.

Roy had undergone a radical and significant transformation in his later years. He had found salvation during the fifties and studied at the Nazarene Bible College to become a preacher. Though he had no education to speak of as a boy, Roy was scholarly when it came to the Bible. Even Bettie was impressed with his knowledge and interpretations. Bettie had seen Roy preach on several occasions and believed that his conversion was genuine. She even felt pity for him. Roy was a preacher on the order of M. O. Wright or maybe even Jimmy Swaggart, driving his congregation to seek Jesus as, with tears streaming down his face, he confessed his own past sins and told of the past infractions he had committed against his wife and children. Most of them, anyway.

Even though Bettie had tried in front of Lulu to get Roy to apologize for sexually molesting her as a child, Roy insisted it had never happened. He said Bettie made the whole thing up, and he refused to acknowledge it, even on his deathbed.

Dying of diabetes, Roy was angry and bitter at God, forever asking why He was forsaking him. Lulu wanted Bettie to help bring comfort to Roy. Alone, at his bedside, Bettie made her peace with Roy and brought *him* peace, forgiving him his sins without asking him to seek forgiveness. It was probably the most Christ-like thing Bettie would ever do.

In the meantime, Bettie still hadn't given up on her goal of being a foreign missionary. On November 22, 1963, the day President John F. Kennedy was assassinated, Bettie came up with the answer. She called Billy Neal and invited him to her new apartment. Billy had been working for the post office for seven years and had been married and divorced from another woman named Betty (which was helpful since he still had a tattoo with the first Bettie's name on his arm). He had a six-year-old daughter from his second marriage. Bettie made it brief: She asked Billy to marry her again. Billy was taken aback, but first loves die hard. He said yes, and they made plans to remarry at the courthouse in Gallatin where they had first married twenty years before. While stopped in a Gallatin drugstore for lunch, Bettie told Billy about her marriage to Armond, who had called her around the same time to tell her that his girlfriend was pregnant and he needed a divorce. Bettie had agreed to finance it, but wasn't sure if the papers had been finalized. It was apparently the last time Bettie heard from Armond, who passed away in the 1970s, according to a cousin still living in Key West.

Billy refused to marry Bettie until she found out if she was divorced from Armond. He wasn't going to be a party to bigamy, even for Bettie. From a pay phone in the drugstore, Bettie called Armond's lawyer in Key West and found out that she and Armond were indeed divorced. Billy wasn't convinced. He asked for the papers to be sent, and he and Bettie headed back to Nashville to wait.

Not long after the divorce papers arrived, Billy and Bettie drove back to the Gallatin courthouse and were married again. Bettie moved into Billy's house on the Cumberland River. The majority of her belongings consisted of religious books and Bible texts. She filled a whole room of the tidy house with them. Almost immediately after they were settled in, she demanded that Billy quit his job and become a missionary with her. It was part of a dream that had been congealing in Bettie's head for years. Upon finding out that she was divorced from Billy, many of her teachers and mentors at her Bible colleges had counseled that if she were able to bring Billy over to God, He would see to it that they remarried. Bettie remarried first, and waited for Billy's conversion to come later, so sure was she that she could bring the formerly wild and woolly country boy to God.

Billy loved Bettie and would've done almost anything for her, but when he discussed her missionary idea with his father, he was reminded that he wasn't getting any younger and if he left the post office, he'd lose his pension. Billy refused Bettie, but she didn't give up. She lectured to him about the Bible at night and took him to almost every church in Nashville on the weekends, trying to persuade him. And she was somewhat successful: On a trip to Old Hickory Lane in Billy's car, Billy prayed with Bettie and said he wanted to find Jesus.

In January 1964, Roy Page died at age sixty-eight. He had been in a coma for more than six months, after his rapidly deteriorating health had left him wasted and senile. By the time Roy died, things between Billy and Bettie had worsened considerably. They began to have fights that were fierce, frequent, random, and often puzzling to Billy, who may have found himself in the same position with Bettie that Marvin Greene had years earlier.

"She had a split personality, I think," Billy said in an interview with *The Betty Pages*. "She could be so loving one day, and the next day— and it wouldn't be me that was making her mad, it would be something else a lot of times. When she was mad, she was mad at everybody." For her part, Bettie said Billy was also strange, refusing to have sex with her, because he falsely believed she had caught a venereal disease while she was a model in New York.

Still determined to be a missionary, Bettie snagged a federal loan from the National Department of Education, because she was the daughter of a wounded war veteran. In the fall semester of 1964, she enrolled again at the George Peabody College for Teachers to work on her master's degree, in hopes that it would make her more attractive to the missionary board.

Billy disagreed with her going back to school and thought she should stay at home. Their final fight took place only a month after they married for the second time. Billy had brought his little girl for a visit from her mother's house in Mississippi. Bettie told him when he got home that she was going to the second part of a Bible lecture she was attending about the Book of Ephesians. According to Bettie, Billy flipped out. Billy won't say anything about it, but chances are Bettie may have let her passion for God get in the way of her relationships here on Earth, something that would be a significant problem later in her life. Still, there was no excuse for what followed, if it really happened as Bettie claims it did.

She says Billy told her she wasn't going to the lecture and ordered her to stay at home with his daughter. Bettie said she had fixed dinner and would be home soon, but Billy took her by throat and began strangling her on the spot, with his six-year-old daughter watching. Bettie tried to fight him but was losing consciousness. She finally squeaked out to Billy that he would go to Hell if he killed her, that God wouldn't forgive him for this. Billy was rattled and let her go. The incident was a strange and violent harbinger of a later time in Bettie's life when she would become the unreasonable attacker and others would be begging *her* for *their* lives. She has said that she spent that night awake and seething that Billy would do that to her, especially with his own child there. Bettie fantasized about killing him, considered it in her head. Perhaps the final fight between her and Billy didn't really happen the way she told it, and it's her way of trying to relate to her own victims of violence. Perhaps nearly twenty years later, when she picked up a knife in the dark to wreak terrible violence upon someone smaller and weaker than herself, she was thinking of Billy. Maybe she even saw his face.

Bettie left Billy the next day, once again calling her brother Jack to help her gather her things and take her away. She moved into an apartment near the Peabody school campus in 1965, never speaking to Billy again. He has said in interviews that he's still not certain if their second marriage was ever legally dissolved because he never filed for divorce, but Bettie claims she received an annulment because she and Billy never had sex during their second marriage. As for Bettie, she studied for a year and a half, but didn't complete two history courses and wasn't recommended for a master's degree. She had intended to get a job as a teacher again but discarded the notion, and apparently her desire to be a missionary went with it.

Frustrated and directionless yet again, she moved like a magnet to the only safe haven she had known over the years—Miami.

12

....

Disintegration

"STRANGERS in the night . . ."

The orchestra played velvety smooth across the dance floor as Harry Lear stood in the entrance of Miami's Palace Ballroom on Biscayne Boulevard on a warm August night in 1966, scratching at the collar of his cotton sport jacket and brushing the bristly, freshly cut hair at the nape of his neck.

The Palace was the last of a dying breed, a post–World War II dance hall with a bandstand and shiny black-and-white marble floors. It was a dreamland for Americans who still longed for sultry film noir nightclubs, and a reminder of home for Miami's growing contingent of Cuban expatriates. The orchestras who called the Palace home reflected the eclectic nature of its clientele—one band was American, the other Latino.

Well-dressed middle-aged divorcées spun by on the dance floor, looking for love. Cigarette smoke rose in thin plumes from the tables in the alcoves like wisps of gray cotton.

"Exchanging glances . . ."

From the other end of the room, Harry locked eyes with the most beautiful woman he had ever seen. Harry was a little on the short side, with close-cropped, receding hair brushed to the side. He was new to the singles scene, and he had never been to the Palace before. He had also never seen this black-haired beauty before but . . . she looked almost familiar. He smiled.

She smiled demurely, teasingly, back at him. Her black hair was cut in bangs and she looked to be in her mid-thirties, late thirties at most. Her figure was dynamite—great hips, long shapely legs and round, firm breasts.

"Wondering in the night, what were the chances . . ."

Harry's eyes were hungry. He was lonely and a little embarrassed. The forty-three-year-old World War II veteran and father of three had left his wife months earlier when he caught her having an affair with a neighborhood fireman. She got the house and the kids. Harry got the street.

A telephone lineman for Florida Bell by day, he found work at nights driving the body van for a local funeral home. Having served in Europe and North Africa, he was used to a no-frills life. He would catnap in between calls, sleeping on the funeral home's leather sofa and awakening occasionally to phone calls telling him to go out and get a body to bring to the embalmer. It was easy work and paid enough to take away a little of the sting of alimony. Besides, if nothing else, the funeral home was a quiet place to sleep.

"We'd be making love . . ."

Harry stood there, shifting his weight from foot to foot. People entered and exited the ballroom like a tide, pushing past his thin, broad-shouldered frame. Harry looked out into the crowd, seeing only the black-haired woman who was now driving her sexy curves across the dance floor toward him. A touch insecure, Harry noticed that he wasn't the only one watching her. Matter of fact, it was hard to find any guys who *weren't* watching her, slicking back their hair and popping breath mints in anticipation.

"Before the night was through . . ."

But she walked straight up to Harry and said, "Would you like to dance?" The syrupy thickness of her Tennessee drawl at once startled him, because it seemed alien to that cosmopolitan body. But at the same time, it put him at ease, because it was a homey voice, a comforting voice that was not a part of this aging pickup scene.

"Uh . . . I'm Harry." He fumbled through an introduction, wondering how stupid he must've sounded. "Oh, really?" she laughed in an intoxicating southern giggle. "You don't look it. I'm Bettie."

"Come on, let's dance!" Before he knew what was happening, the black-haired woman had grabbed his hand and yanked him out onto the dance floor. He moved his arms around her soft curves and they glided away, oblivious to the world. Harry didn't think he could dance, but Bettie convinced him otherwise.

These days, Harry has said he was practically "stalking" Bettie and that he was the one who asked her to dance, but Bettie recalls it differently. "He was very shy and I had to practically drag him onto the dance floor," she said in her letter to the author. "I fell in love with him while we were dancing. The band kept playing 'Strangers in the Night.' It became our theme song."

They danced and talked into the early hours before dawn. Bettie told Harry she was divorced, working as a secretary, and living with her sister.

Bettie had made a beeline for Florida to get over her most recent and last break-up with Billy. She was close to finishing her master's degree, and was contemplating taking some historic research classes at the University of Miami. More than anything, she just wanted some time in the sun and surf. She talked about growing up in Tennessee, Harry about growing up in Pennsylvania. They talked music (they both enjoyed what's now called easy listening) and movies (one of Bettie's favorite topics).

Surprisingly, Harry found out that the attractive "younger woman" was actually forty-three and (could he be this lucky?) a retired model.

Thinking back, Harry thought he remembered some postcards he had seen while on a vacation with his family of a beautiful woman on a beach with an alligator pulling at her bikini bottom. He had to put them back when his wife caught him looking at them. What would the children think, after all?

Now all Harry could think about was Bettie. They kissed goodnight.

She and Harry began seeing each other almost constantly. Harry worked every other night at the funeral home, and, in between, he and Bettie went out. Some weekends they'd find themselves at the beach ("Even the dogs would turn their heads when she went by in a bikini, and she was in her forties then," Harry recalled years later.) Other times they would take picnics to nearby Cramden Park. Harry preferred drive-in movies and indoor pursuits, mostly to get a chance at making love with Bettie, but partly because he had spent all day climbing telephone poles in the hot Florida sun.

Rejuvenated by that same Florida sun, Bettie was back to her old self, dancing, teasing, living life. For a while, at least, she seemed to shrug off her religious fervor. Jesus took a back burner to her passion for Harry.

Within a couple of months, Bettie and Harry were engaged. On Valentine's Day 1967, about six months after they met at the Palace Ballroom, they were married by a justice of the peace in Miami. Bettie became Bettie Page Lear. She and Harry moved into a three-bedroom suburban ranch house at 161 W. 17th Street in Hialeah, a Miami bedroom community known for its racetracks and balmy climate.

Now that he was remarried and settled into a new home, Harry sought shared custody of his three children: Larry, eleven; Brad, nine; and Linda, seven. During his courtship of Bettie, he had had visitation rights, but he and Bettie had never spent a lot of time with the children.

Bettie was excited at the idea of having a ready-made family. She had always wanted children, and here she thought God have given her the chance. Harry had a home again, he had his children, and he had a beautiful new wife.

For all outward appearances, the new Lear family was a handsome, happy suburban clan like any other. Behind closed doors, it was a different story.

Married life started off quietly for Bettie and Harry. They spent lots of time together at home, listening to records, watching movies on TV, and planting a garden in the backyard. Later, they put in a small in-ground swimming pool. On Saturdays they bowled or went to the beach, and on Sundays the family all went to church. At first, about the only thing Bettie and Harry disagreed about was their eating habits. Bettie ate a lot of fruit and vegetables and not a lot of the meat that Harry preferred.

It was exactly what Bettie had been searching for her whole gypsy life—a safe, stable environment; a sense of family; and a place where she belonged and was clearly important.

Harry's sons shared a room at the house and Harry's daughter had her own room. "I couldn't have children, yet I wanted to have a family. I was very fond of these three children, but they wouldn't accept me as a mother substitute; they wanted to live with their mother and father," Bettie told the author. "Their mother, Pat, caused me continuing trouble over the kids throughout the five years that I was married to Harry."

The boys were tow-haired, tall, and sported shaggy bangs. They seemed to adjust slowly to the marriage, Harry recalls, and even called Bettie "Mommy," but little Linda, who had brown hair, never accepted Bettie's friendship. Much of that was the influence of Harry's ex-wife, Pat, who didn't care for Bettie.

Pat wouldn't talk to Bettie about discipline troubles, and sometimes would call up Bettie after she had turned in for the night and tell her to go to hell, Bettie has said. Bettie also claims that the kids would often wait for Pat to pick them up and Pat wouldn't show up or even telephone. It's difficult to say how true that is. The kids clearly loved their real mother, and in many ways may have resented Bettie's almost obsessive overtures for their love.

In the spring, when Harry decided to enroll the family in scuba diving lessons to bring them closer together, Linda refused to go. Harry bought tanks for the rest of the family and they went to Crystal River, swimming alongside the manatees that migrated to the river from Florida's coast. In fact, years later in a 1996 letter to lifeguard Ellsworth Boyd, whom Bettie had hung out with in Fort Lauderdale in 1957, she told him, "Thanks to you, when I went to Miami, I met a fellow who I eventually married." She learned to scuba dive as a result of that early skin-diving expedition, she said.

Bettie began carrying a little Kodak camera on almost every trip the Lear family took, snapping hundreds of pictures of Harry, the children, and landscapes. It was apparent from her expertise behind the lens that she had learned to do more than smile prettily when she was a model.

"The happiest times the five of us had were the trips we took," Bettie remembered fondly. In the summer of 1968, the new Lear family took a month-long cross-country trip to attend the World's Fair in San Antonio, Texas. Called the Hemisfair, the 1968 World's Fair marked San Antonio's 250th anniversary and celebrated the cultures of North and South America. After that, Harry, Bettie, and the three kids took the family station wagon east on U.S. 10 to New Mexico's Carlsbad Caverns, a network of labyrinthine caverns, the deepest of which descends 1,013 feet. Bettie and Harry took turns driving, and talked quietly while the kids slept in the backseat.

They later drove up the California coast to San Francisco, where Bettie pointed out landmarks, including the house where she once lived. After that they visited Redwood National Park and hiked up the coast to watch the sea lions and seals. The vacation was topped off with a trip to Disneyland. For Harry, Bettie, and the kids, it was one of the happiest times of their marriage.

When they came home, however, the honeymoon had ended. Bettie was discouraged by the children's lack of acceptance of her as a surrogate mother. The rivalry between Linda and Bettie heated up when Harry bought Linda a blond baby grand piano for her birthday and Bettie took lessons to learn how to play it, apparently reviving the interest she had in the piano as a child when she studied it at the community center. Linda eventually lost interest and Bettie continued to play, though she couldn't play very well. "She was not an accomplished piano player, that's for sure," Harry said. "But she would try hard and she put a lot of time in on it."

Bettie was very firm with the children and began to demand that they pray before dinner and keep their rooms fastidiously clean. Harry's ex-wife, Pat, had been complaining for some time to Harry that Bettie was too strict. "[Bettie] made problems that didn't really exist in some ways, you know? She was very orderly and very neat and very slow and very methodical," Harry said. Meanwhile, Bettie began to renew her faith. She put up pictures of Jesus around the house and prayed fervently. The Lear family attended church three times a week at Bettie's urging—twice on Sunday, morning and evening, and again for prayer meetings on Wednesday night.

"She's devoted to the Lord's work, and that's always been a struggle for her," said Harry, who, at the time, tried to take everything in stride, hoping that things would eventually settle down.

In 1969 the family took another summer trip, this time up the East Coast to Canada. Harry bought a new pickup truck and a travel trailer. The kids rode in the trailer and Harry and Bettie again took turns driving. They stopped in Virginia to visit Colonial Williamsburg and Richmond, then toured the Smithsonian Institute in Washington, D.C.

Later they visited Radio City Music Hall in New York City, a stop that may have provided some conflict for Bettie, confronted with memories of the city and the turbulent past she had left behind more than a decade before. After that, the Lears went to the Old Man in the Mountain, a rock ledge in New Hampshire that resembles a man's face and that was the inspiration for Nathaniel Hawthorne's short story, "The Great Stone Face." Finally they made their way through the beaches of Cape Cod to Niagara Falls and Quebec. Tensions mounted between Bettie and the children as she became more demanding, and the trip was not very pleasant.

After returning home, Bettie's behavior became increasingly erratic and bizarre. She would stay up all night in the backyard, gardening. Her relationship with Harry deteriorated as he tried to defend his children from her increasing barrage of verbal attacks. She had developed strange ideas about Christianity, including that there was not one, but seven gods, and she declared herself their prophet.

By the early 1970s, Harry was ready to concede that Bettie was mentally ill. He was also ready to admit that their marriage was over. In October 1971, Bettie left Harry, seeking the only stable thing she knew anymore: religion. She moved about fifty miles east of Hialeah to the conference motel at Bible Town Community Church in Boca Raton near the Florida coast.

Established in 1950 as the Boca Raton Bible Grounds by the Rev. Dr. Ira L. Eschleman, Bible Town still operates as an interdenominational ministry retreat center and runs Bible lectures about five months a year during the winter. In the 1970s, participants like Bettie paid a small fee for room and board at the conference motel and attended free morning and evening Bible lectures and classes given by well-known ministers and professors such as the Rev. Torrey Johnson, who was in charge of Bible Town at the time Bettie stayed there. ("A big phony," Harry calls him these days, with more than a touch of resentment.) Teachers back then included Dr. Gerald Stanton, a published Bible expert, and his wife, Mary, a biblical archaeologist who taught at Palm Beach College and was known for discovering mastodon bones in North America years before.

Bettie found a closely knit intellectual and religious community at Bible Town that probably reminded her of Multnomah or even Winona Lake in Indiana. She stayed mostly to herself at Bible Town, taking her meals in her motel room, which had a small television, a bath, a double bed, and a tile floor. The only telephone was a pay phone in the lobby. She phoned Harry a few times and mentioned that she was writing a book about herself and her prophecies. Most of her spare time was spent in the hotel room, in quiet meditation and prayer, asking God if it was His will that her marriage should fail.

Harry filed for divorce in December 1971, citing separation and irreconcilable differences. On January 17, 1972, the divorce was granted. Bettie, who had been absent from all the proceedings, signed the final judgment and mailed it from Boca Raton. She turned over all interest in the house in Hialeah to Harry. In turn, the circuit court judge awarded her $5,000 in alimony, most of it to be paid in small monthly installments of about $50. Harry kept his 1970 Ford pickup and his 1969 camper. Bettie was awarded the family's 1961 Ford Falcon station wagon, which she had taken to Boca Raton.

She didn't take the news of the divorce well.

George Strickland, Bible Town's business manager, was in a meeting one evening in January when he heard a commotion in the hallway. He recalled that a staff member burst in, interrupting the meeting. "There's a woman running around with a gun at the motel!" the staffer yelled.

Sure enough, Bettie was running through the motel complex, waving a .22–caliber pistol and shouting about the retribution of God. Residents fled and locked themselves in their rooms as she ran by. Strickland saw her briefly and ran for a phone to call the police. Fearing Bettie might bring harm to herself or one of the guests, another Bible Town staffer ran behind Bettie and tackled her, knocking the gun from her hand and taking it away from her.

It was late in the evening when Harry got the call from the Boca Raton police. Harry and his son Larry, now sixteen, jumped into the family pickup truck and headed for the Boca Raton police headquarters. Harry explained to the desk sergeant that Bettie was upset over the recent divorce and that he had given her the gun for protection. After some discussion, the sergeant nodded understandingly and released Bettie into Harry's custody. Harry left the gun there.

Harry felt sorry for his ex-wife and knew she had no other place to go, so, after taking her back to Bible Town to gather her things, he invited Bettie back to the house in Hialeah. She stayed in Linda's room for a while and then slept on the sofa. As the weather warmed, Harry decided to add another bedroom onto the back of the house for Bettie. It was still under construction on April 13, 1972, when Bettie called Harry and the children into the living room. Harry had just gotten off work. She asked them all to stand before a picture of Jesus hanging on the wall. Then, standing behind them, she pulled out a large kitchen paring knife and told them to pray.

"If you take your eyes off this picture, I'll cut your guts out!" she threatened.

No one moved.

The children stood looking at the wall, wide-eyed, not believing this was happening. Harry looked over his shoulder at Bettie. She was too close to twelve-year-old Linda for him to make a try for the knife. Linda began to shake. They all stood in front of the picture.

Time dragged. How long had they been standing there? Minutes? Hours?

Finally Harry told Bettie he had to use the bathroom. "I'll be right back to pray," he said smiling through clenched teeth and wondering if he had made the right choice to leave his children alone with her. It was chancy gambit to be sure, especially in light of Bettie's violent later years.

Sneaking out the bathroom window, he ran to the house of his neighbor, Howard Harchberger. While Harchberger phoned the police, Harry returned to the house through the bathroom window and went back to standing in front of the picture of Jesus, this time standing closer to Bettie. Soon after, Harchberger came to the front door and distracted Bettie while Harry wrestled the knife from her. She cursed, fighting him, yelling loudly about God's will.

A police car pulled up while Bettie was still screaming at the top of her lungs. She was charged with breach of peace by an officer identified in reports only as Sikorski, and she was committed to Jackson Memorial Hospital, a state mental care facility.

Bettie stayed at Jackson Memorial for about four months before being discharged into Harry's care. By then, the addition on the house had been finished. Bettie had her own bedroom, bathroom, a small area for cooking, and a separate entrance. She seemed calmer after her stay at the hospital, but it was just the calm before another storm.

Bettie still had trouble dealing with her divorce from Harry. Getting into another argument with him over religion and the divorce, she started tearing apart his house early in the afternoon on October 28, 1972, throwing anything she could pick up. When police answered a call placed by Harry, they found Harry and Bettie in front of the house. Bettie was hitting Harry repeatedly with her fists and venemously cursing him. A rookie Hialeah police officer, Tom Fitzpatrick, pulled Bettie away and put her in the back of his squad car while he took a statement from Harry. Harry told the officer about Bettie's mental history and said he thought she might need more help.

According to police records, when Fitzpatrick returned to the car, he saw Bettie in the backseat, with her dress pulled up, panties around her knees, and hands cuffed, masturbating with a coat hanger that the officer had left on the backseat of the squad car. He grabbed the hanger from her. "Defendant psycho," he summed up in his report before driving Bettie to Jackson Memorial's emergency ward, where she was treated for cuts from the coat hanger.

"I remember it happening," says Fitzpatrick, who's now retired, in a 1994 interview. "She was just out of her mind, completely berserk. . . . I caught her in time. She didn't hurt herself."

Charges of disorderly conduct and assault and battery filed against Bettie were dismissed after she voluntarily recommitted herself to Jackson Memorial's care.

Arrest records accurately describe her, from her date of birth down to the dime-sized scar on her left hand from a cooking accident as a teen. The mug shot of Bettie following this arrest shows an exhausted, sad-eyed woman staring hollowly into the camera. Her hair is short, graying, and disheveled. At forty-nine years old, she looked her age for the first time in her life.

Fitzpatrick's final arrest report gave this account of the events: "Defendant was striking Mr. Harry Lear of 161 W. 17th Street, Hialeah, and attempted to do bodily harm to herself with a coat hanger. . . . Defendant has undergone psychiatric treatment at Jackson [State]. Had been all right for past three months. Defendant was striking her husband when unit arrived on scene, and when placed in police car, started masturbating with a coat hanger. Defendant was taken to Ward D for possible cuts. Defendant was out of her mind."

Bettie would stay at Jackson Memorial six months this time, spending some of it under suicide watch for fear she would harm herself. Occasionally the faithful and sympathetic Harry would visit, reassuring her that she would have a place to go after she was better.

No one but Bettie knows what happened to her during her stay at the hospital, but she was markedly changed. She returned to the house on West 17th Street in Hialeah, a quiet, withdrawn woman who stayed relatively isolated from the outside world. She bought two dogs: Po, a white poodle, and Tato, a rust-colored Irish Setter. She did the cleaning for Harry to pay for her room and board and spent most of her time gardening, sometimes into the middle of the night.

"After the divorce, I stayed on at Harry's house in Hialeah for another seven years doing the cleaning and taking care of the yard," Bettie told the author in 1992. "I had become very interested in tropical plants. In the backyard I had a mango tree, an avocado, a Valencia orange, a pineapple orange, a grapefruit tree, and a calamondin tree."

She bought dozens of books about tropical trees, learning all she could, and she planted them until the spacious backyard she shared with Harry resembled an orchard. She meticulously watered and cared for the plants as if they were the children she never had. Her favorite project, however, was a pear-shaped pond that she built from a design in one of her books. Bettie dug the hole and poured the concrete herself, forming a quiet, tasteful oasis in the backyard. Unfortunately, tree frogs found it a restful place, too, and made it their home—a very noisy one. Harry and Bettie couldn't sleep with all the croaking at night. Then, when the frog eggs hatched, the little pool filled with wriggling black tadpoles. Bettie drained the pond, but she wouldn't admit defeat. She would still spend time reading by the empty concrete crater, in spite of the frogs who had taken away her creation.

"She was always a very, very intense person," Harry said of Bettie. "When she was going to do something, she would do it. Like when she was planting a lot of those things out in the back, all kinds of exotic plants, she would start work in the afternoon and she would work almost all night long. She would work until three or four in the morning. She was a very strong woman, because she was in such good condition all her life. She could outwork me easy."

Bettie also doted on Po the poodle. He could often be seen riding on her lap as she drove her old, wood-paneled station wagon back and forth to the grocery store and bingo games. "Bettie didn't care too much about animals, but she just loved Po to death," Harry recalled.

Harry and Bettie remained friendly, if distant, and Bettie now seemed almost comfortable with Harry's diminished role in her life as friend and landlord. In fact, in 1992 Bettie said, "Harry and I are still good friends. We have been writing to each other throughout the past fourteen years; also, he sends me some money every few months."

By 1978, at the age of fifty-five, Bettie's alimony from Harry had run out, though he was still helping her out in little ways. He wanted to retire, to move away from Florida. He never had liked the climate. No changes. No winter. He ended up moving to South Carolina. With Bettie having no place to go, Bettie's brother Jimmie once again came to her rescue. He had recently divorced and was lonely, so he invited her to move into his suburban California home near Santa Monica. After eleven years, and with some sadness, Bettie packed Po and her belongings and left behind the only constant home she had ever known during her entire life. She also left behind Tato, the Irish Setter, who stayed with Harry's mother.

According to Bettie's authorized biography, she lived with Jimmie for the next nine years, looking after him and cleaning his house. But this is clearly a fabrication by Bettie and her family designed to mask the truth of her tragic descent into madness. While she may have lived with Jimmie off and on, it's doubtful how long she really stayed with him. Some, including her former agent, J. B. Rund, say that Bettie acknowledges that she lived at various addresses during the time, though they say she isn't clear about the location. Rund says that Jimmie, who was reportedly a biology and science teacher in the California public school system, has retired and now lives in Las Vegas.

In 1979, a little over a year after she moved to California, Bettie wasn't staying with Jimmie. Instead, she was living in Lawndale, California, in a trailer owned by an elderly married couple who lived at 14723 South Firmona Avenue. Bettie's address was 14723 1/2 South Firmona. She had no car, phone, or job. She was probably still living off money from Harry Lear.

At 1:45 on the afternoon of April 19, 1979, Bettie's insanity reasserted its dominion over her. She stabbed her elderly landlords for no apparent reason. The victim's names are partially obliterated on the police report, but it appears the wife was named Esther Trevin. Her husband's middle name was Hunter. Again, their personal information is not legible, but it appears she was sixty-seven and he was seventy-seven. Bettie was three days short of her fifty-sixth birthday.

Ten minutes later, at 1:55 P.M., a Los Angeles County Sheriff's deputy responded to an emergency call about a woman with a knife at 14723 South Firmona Avenue. "Upon arriving, I was immediately contacted by the victims, who are man and wife," Deputy Ast wrote in his report. "The victims told me that the suspect had attacked and assaulted them with a knife. The victims said that they had recovered the knife, Evidence Item No. 1. The victims added that the suspect was inside her trailer, which is in the rear of the victims' house. I observed that both victims had sustained knife wounds. I asked the victims why the suspect attacked them. The victims told me that the suspect was crazy and that the attack was completely unprovoked. The victims added that the suspect may have been a mental patient at one time."

According to Mrs. Trevin, just prior to the stabbings, she had been taking clothes off her clothesline in the backyard next to Bettie's trailer. When Mrs. Trevin had gathered all the clothes into her basket, she started walking back to her house, which took her in front of Bettie's trailer. As Mrs. Trevin passed by, Bettie came out of the trailer wielding an eight-inch-long serrated bread knife with a brown wooden handle. Bettie ran toward Mrs. Trevin without a word, and stabbed the older woman, falling to the ground with her and rolling on the driveway beside the Trevin's backdoor. Mrs. Trevin screamed shrilly.

Hearing the commotion, Mr. Trevin came outside and found his wife struggling in the driveway with Bettie. Mr. Trevin tried to wrest the knife away from Bettie, but she stabbed him in the right hand, so he retreated to the garage where he picked up a crescent wrench. He ran back and threatened to hit Bettie if she didn't drop the knife. When he got no response from Bettie, Mr. Trevin brought the wrench crashing down upon Bettie's head, knocking her unconscious. He quickly and carefully took the knife from Bettie and helped his wife back into their house, afraid that their tenant would come to her senses before they reached the door. Once safe inside, he called the police.

After talking to the Trevins, Deputy Ast decided that Bettie was a danger to herself and the community. He called for backup and, with the aid of a Deputy Lintz, knocked on Bettie's trailer door, and after gaining her permission, entered, and arrested her on two counts of assault with a deadly weapon, both felony charges. The Trevins told the deputies that they definitely wanted to press charges. Local fire paramedics responded not long after, treating Esther Trevin for a painful three-inch-long laceration to her left underarm and several small defensive slash wounds to her arms. Mr. Trevin suffered a one-inch-deep cut to his right hand. Both went from the attack to their family physician. Bettie was taken by police to Hawthorne Community Hospital, where doctors sewed six stitches in her head, closing the wound she had received when Mr. Trevin hit her with his crescent wrench. The deputies then took Bettie to Lennox Station in Lawndale, and processed and booked her.

An investigator at the station had no luck getting Bettie to state a motive for the stabbings or even acknowledge that she'd committed them. "Suspect is mentally unstable," the investigator wrote in his report on April 19. "[Did] not interview as investigator could not get suspect to understand or make intelligent [recognition] of [her] rights." He described Bettie in the report as unemployed, divorced, and cooperative at the time of arrest. Her preliminary hearing was held on May 11, 1979, and she was arraigned fourteen days later, on May 25. Bail was set at $1,000. Upon reviewing court-ordered psychiatric reports, however, a Los Angeles County Superior judge found Bettie mentally incompetent and ordered her involuntarily committed to the care of the California Department of Mental Health, which placed her in Patton State Hospital in Highland, California, one of the state's largest mental health treatment centers.

Bettie's motions for bail were granted almost a year later, on May 1, 1980. On May 22, 1980, the court ruled that Bettie had committed the stabbing, but the judge found her not guilty by reason of insanity. Deciding that she had not recovered from her mental illness, the court committed her to Patton State again and, on July 24, sentenced her to five years incarceration and treatment. But by February, 1981, on the recommendations of her doctor, Bettie was released from Patton State and began to receive outpatient treatment, after serving a total of less than two years. Her outpatient status was renewed in February 1982, four months before she committed the vicious stabbing that would lead to her trial for attempted murder.

13

Insanity

THE LONG knife glistened, lit by moonlight, as Bettie straddled Leonie Haddad in the darkness, pinning her to the bed. Still groggy, Haddad struggled to come to her senses. Her eyes could make out the knife pointed just inches from her face, and her mind was racing to comprehend what was happening.

Suddenly, Bettie slashed at her, slicing her from the corner of her mouth to her ear. In a blur, Bettie raised the knife again and lunged for Haddad's face. But Haddad jerked her head away and the blade only grazed her cheek. Then, in rapid succession, Bettie stabbed Haddad four times in the chest, narrowly missing her heart. Haddad freed her left hand and raised it in front of her, desperately trying to fend off the attack. Thrashing back and forth in a violent frenzy, Bettie stabbed the hand eight times, severing the top of Haddad's third finger.

With her other hand, Haddad grabbed the telephone from her night table and smacked Bettie in the face with it. The knife dropped from Bettie's hand and clanged to the floor. Haddad screamed. Startled, Bettie looked around as if waking from a trance. Her chest heaved, her breath was deep and ragged. She stumbled backward out Haddad's bedroom door, never turning away from Haddad. "Don't go anywhere," she said, and went off to her room.

Haddad stood up shakily. By the time she had broken free of Bettie's berserk attack, she had been stabbed over twelve times. "I had a blue-green nightgown," she said. "When I stood up, it was red. It was a nightmare." From her severed finger, veins hung loose like shoe-strings. Blood covered the bed, drapes, and carpet. Haddad made her way to the front door, struggling with the knob, and ran across the street to her neighbor's house, blood trailing behind her. When the neighbor finally awakened and made it to the door, still pulling on a robe, she saw Haddad slumped on her front porch and bleeding profusely.

"Oh, God! What happened to you?" the neighbor asked. Haddad could barely answer. The neighbor loaded Haddad into her car and took off to the hospital. As the car started, Haddad slipped into a deep unconsciousness. . . .

An hour later, on the morning of June 12, 1982, the Santa Monica police arrived at the little house on Linda Lane. Getting no answer, they broke in the door. Searching the house, they found Bettie standing in the shower with her clothes on, trying to wash out the bloodstains. She kept the police waiting for an hour before she dried herself off.

When Leonie Haddad awoke at Cedars-Sinai Hospital in Los Angeles, she was surrounded by police detectives and a team of doctors. Nurses had to feed her through tubes because of the severe slash wounds to her face and mouth. One of her lungs was punctured. The police didn't know if they'd have another chance to interview their elderly victim, or if the case would become a homicide.

"When I wake up and see the police, I started to cry," Haddad remembered in a June 1994 interview. "My son, God bless him, was there [at Cedars-Sinai] in ten minutes. He was so worried."

Haddad continued: "It's so scary. It cost me so much money for psychoanalysis. I left my home. I sold my home and never went back. My blood was all over the bed, the drapes. I don't know how I am still alive. I am very lucky."

Healing took a long time. "My hand, it was cut so deep. I was cut from my mouth to my ear. The nurse had to feed me. I couldn't do nothing," she said, adding she considers herself fortunate that Bettie's weapon wasn't a butcher knife. "It was a bread knife, otherwise I could be dead," Haddad said. "She gave me a scar near my heart. I had a heart attack last year."

Bettie was charged with one felony count each of attempted murder and assault with a deadly weapon, and was committed again to Patton State under ninety-day observation to determine her competency to stand trial. Her bail was set at $50,000 but was nullified by the commitment.

She was ruled competent, and more than a year later, on September 26, 1983, Bettie Page stood trial for attempted murder. Those who saw the sixty-year-old in court described her as quiet, almost scared, and seemingly incapable of the violent stabbing of Leonie Haddad—at first. Haddad's lawyer, James Hirsen recalled years later that with her deep tan and her long, straight, black-dyed hair cut in bangs, Bettie looked like a Native American.

Her pinup girl days were long gone. Nobody there would have guessed she was *that* Bettie Page, even if they *had* seen her pictures. "She looked a little haggard the way I remember it," says Charles Wilson, a retired police investigator who worked the case.

Earlier, Bettie pleaded not guilty but later changed her plea to not guilty by reason of insanity after two California Department of Mental Health doctors testified that she was insane and had confessed to the attack. They also testified that she presented a danger to herself and others. California Superior Court Judge David Fitts decided to accept her plea.

Judge Fitts, who is now deceased, was an unremarkable-looking man save for his ruddy skin, according to those who knew him. "He had a reputation of being a very firm judge even though he was pretty relaxed in the courts," Wilson recalls. "When he would recess the court, he'd say, 'Court adjourned for a fifteen-minute break,' and then he'd say, 'Who won that game between the Dodgers and St. Louis last night?' talking to the attorneys and police. He was well liked by the other attorneys, his peers, and so forth."

Because Bettie was ruled insane and presented a danger to others, Fitts ordered her committed to Patton State for ten years, minus fifty-five days for good behavior and minus the 471 days she had already been in the hospital's custody. As soon as the verdict was reached, Bettie's calm demeanor disappeared. She was dragged kicking and screaming from the courtroom, insulting Haddad, the judge, the prosecutor, and the public defender; calling them all liars in her deep, booming Southern drawl. A shaken Leonie Haddad held her son's hand and watched from the courtroom gallery as the bailiffs carried Bettie away.

Haddad filed a $1.75 million lawsuit against the state of California and Westside Independent Services for the Elderly because, she said, Bettie's state caseworker had lied to her about Bettie's status as a mental patient. Haddad accused the elderly housing placement service of having been negligent in not following through on a background check that would have revealed Bettie's history of violence.

"I told the social worker Bettie's not normal. She goes into the bathroom and talks to herself," Haddad said. "I'll never forget the social worker. She didn't tell me [Bettie] was crazy. I ask the social worker what she is coming here for and she said it was because Bettie had problems. She never mentioned Bettie was in jail. She said it was because Bettie left her husband."

Martha Fitzgerald of Westside Independent Services for the Elderly, the service that had placed Bettie in Haddad's home, denied responsibility for Haddad's stabbing in an interview with a local newspaper, saying, "We assume that the people are adults and can check each other out."

It was just one more scandal for Patton State, which had released Bettie less than a year after her previous stabbings of the Trevins. The hospital's executive director was fired in 1983 by the State Mental Health Department, citing Patton State's growing criminal population and the hospital's need to have more "sensitivity to the community." Before Bettie stabbed Leonie Haddad, more than a dozen patients incarcerated at the hospital had escaped in 1981 and 1982 while on "therapeutic field trips" to nearby shopping malls and parks. In another incident, a patient already convicted of two rapes and the sexual molestation of a thirteen-year-old girl walked out of the facility with an employee with whom he had a romantic relationship. The State Department of Corrections later took a large role in administration at Patton State, because of its numerous patients who, like Bettie, had committed violent crimes or were serving criminal sentences concurrent with their treatment at Patton State.

The state of California settled Leonie Haddad's lawsuit out of court in 1987 for $70,000. Her lawyers took 40 percent, and the rest barely covered her medical expenses, which included plastic surgery to her face and hands, nerve reconstruction, and psychological treatment. "It wasn't a good settlement," Haddad said. "It's not worth it to give me $70,000 for what I've been through."

It had taken Haddad two years to heal from the accident. She moved in with her son, selling the house she had lived in for thirty years. Almost all her bedroom furniture had to be discarded because of the blood stains. She also got a phone call from Esther Trevin, Bettie's previous stabbing victim, who had seen Haddad on the TV news and wanted to console her. The two had a brief conversation, talking about their shared victimization at the hands of Bettie Page. Haddad had become afraid to walk the streets. She decided to get away from the crime-ridden United States and later traveled to London, where she lived briefly with relatives.

A little more than twelve years later, in 1994, Haddad, then in her early eighties, still had no feeling or movement in two fingers on her left hand. Doctors told her that the heart attack she suffered in 1993 was also possibly due to injuries from the stabbing. She said, "I've suffered a lot. I got two fingers I can't bend. They stay like this. I feel my fingers like they are numb. It cut the tendons and nerves. It was quite a story."

After returning from London, Haddad lived with her sister in a small house in Irvine, California, for several years, and spent summers in Lebanon with her family. Since she was interviewed for this book in June 1994, she and her sister have moved and left no forwarding address.

Bettie wrote Leonie Haddad a letter sometime in the 1980s, apologizing for the attack and saying that she hoped that she could visit Haddad in person one day to express her regrets. "When she was in jail, she [sent] me a letter from the crazy house. She told me, 'I was sorry for what I did to you. Regret it. Want to visit you one day,'" Haddad recalled.

Haddad still fears that possibility. She instructed her second lawyer, Jack Diamond, to tell Bettie not to contact her: "I told him, don't let her write me again."

Looking back on her ordeal, Haddad offered some cautionary advice to others: "Don't let anybody stay with you that you don't know."

At Patton State, doctors diagnosed Bettie as having "schizophrenia, paranoid type chronic," according to a progress report filed by Patton State on January 10, 1989, for Bettie's mental health review hearing in Los Angeles County Superior Court on February 2, 1989. The report describes her clinically and matter-of-factly: "Ms. Bettie Page is a 65-year-old female admitted to Patton on . . . commitment . . . [she] is 65 1/2 inches in height, weighs 183 pounds, has . . . blue eyes." The report also describes her as "fair complexioned," which suggests that Bettie lost her tanned look after years inside the hospital. The court reports also refer to her previous stabbing in Lawndale and her commitments to Jackson Memorial Hospital in Florida during the 1970s.

Doctors at Patton State prescribed drug therapy to combat Bettie's schizophrenia. Intensely unhappy much of the time, her weight fluctuated between 161 pounds and 183 pounds, depending on her mood. She received yearly court reviews of her treatment and progress, all of which came to the same conclusion: She was still ill and needed treatment.

Knowing that Bettie was schizophrenic explains a lot of the erratic behavior later in her life, but the nature of her madness is particularly intriguing. Why did she exclusively choose a knife as the instrument of her violent biddings? Was she inspired by the religious imagery of Christ pinned by nails to the Crucifix at Calvary? Was it a deeper, Freudian, even sexual impulse, driven by the phallic nature of the knife as a tool to penetrate the flesh? Most interesting is that the knife she selected was usually about the same length—eight to twelve inches, and serrated. When she stabbed the Trevins, Bettie was living at the rear of their property in a separate trailer, much like she was when she lived with Harry Lear after their divorce. Bettie's state social worker told Leonie Haddad that Bettie was still upset over the divorce from Harry. Was the stabbing of the Trevins a reenactment of the day she held Harry and her stepchildren at knifepoint a decade earlier? Was it an attempt at consummating that act, directing her anger at Harry through others?

Or did the anger go much, much deeper—and to a place much, much earlier in her memory? Bettie's victims were smaller or older than she, and not in as good a position to defend themselves against her attacks. Could her lashing out at them have been a manifestation of her suppressed inner rage over her sexual abuse at the uncaring hands of her father, Roy Page? Was she consciously or unconsciously trying for once in her life to become the powerful instrument of aggression and domination rather than the victim? It certainly seems in her modeling years that she used her sexuality as a weapon of defense, a means of overcoming her childhood trauma and confusion. Perhaps as her stunning beauty faded, she became violent and angry at the world that left her bereft of her greatest asset.

"My hunch is it's posttraumatic stress disorder," says Dr. Mary Clement, a professor of criminal justice at Virginia Commonwealth University who has worked as a counselor for victims of sexual assault. It's not unusual to see someone as late in life as Bettie react to a childhood trauma like her father's sexual abuse, she says.

The fact that Bettie chose women as the focus of her attacks is interesting. Speaking as not just an expert, but a fellow victim of a childhood sexual assault herself, Clement says she believes Bettie was "projecting her self-hatred of the feminine part of herself" when she stabbed Haddad and Mrs. Trevin. When sexual abuse victims attack or even kill someone, they tend to be extremely emotional. They don't stab someone once or twice, they stab them several times, Clement says, like Bettie did with Leonie Haddad.

"They lose sight of who they've got and they pour out all the anger," Clement says. "That person isn't a person, it's an object, and they're doing to that object what was done to them."

Peter Smerick, a retired profiler for the FBI, thinks the stabbings could be a reaction at Bettie's anger over her sexual abuse, too, but he thinks Bettie could have been symbolically punishing her mother. "Let's say if the father was assaultive to her in her formative years, and her mother stood by and did nothing about it or refused to believe her, then if she encounters another woman who has the same personality traits as her mother, that could be the triggering episode."

As for Bettie's choice of a knife, Smerick says he thinks there may be a more mundane reason than Freudian or religious symbolism: "If you were looking for a Freudian connotation as the knife being a substitute penis, then you'd almost be expecting her to be attacking men, if a male's penis caused her hurt and trauma in her early years."

Instead, Smerick says, women are more familiar and comfortable with knives than handguns as a weapon, because the knife is a common kitchen implement.

Smerick now works in Manassas, Virginia, for the Academy Group, a consultant group made up of former FBI and Secret Service agents who perform threat assessments for corporations and give lectures to law enforcement agencies. They're also one of the groups that *X-Files* creator Chris Carter seeks advice from for his *Millennium* television series on Fox. Smerick himself is best known as the profiler who assessed cult leader David Koresh at Waco.

Knowing that Bettie was diagnosed as a paranoid schizophrenic at Patton State, Smerick says, "If you're looking for a logical answer for her behavior, there may not be one." To Smerick, Bettie sounds like a woman who was gradually mentally deteriorating throughout her life.

"It might be all psychiatric," he says. "If you've got somebody who is certifiably paranoid schizophrenic, you don't know what's going on in their mind. They're delusional. Their relationship with reality is different from yours and mine. It may not be attributable to anything in her environment. It might just be the mental condition she was going through.

"She could have had all the loving and caring in the world in her formative years and turned out exactly the same way. If there was a gene in her system for paranoid schizophrenia, at some point it was going to begin manifesting itself."

By the sketchy accounts available from court records, Bettie's struggle against her illness was a long one. Harry Lear, who stood by her during her years in and out of Jackson Memorial, was still supportive. Hearing about her incarceration from her brother Jimmie, Harry wrote to Bettie constantly during her stay at Patton State and occasionally sent her money to help her out. It wasn't out of character for Lear, who, after all, had supported Bettie and given her shelter for years after their divorce.

Though Bettie battled hard over the next several years to overcome her mental illness and receive early release, the California courts continued to deny it, deeming her a threat to herself and others. By 1992, when she had completed her sentence, Bettie began to be treated on an outpatient basis and, presumably, had gained control over the restless and violent voices echoing in her head. At the age of sixty-nine, with the better part of ten years of her life having been lost in mental institutions, Bettie Page sought help from her family and church placement groups, who helped her get herself back on her feet. According to Harry Lear and her brother Jack, she initially moved into a Baptist home with some other women and lived off the modest sum she earned from Social Security.

Today Bettie says she's tackled her illness. "I wish I could erase the years from 1979 to 1992 . . . [but now] I am in very good health, for which I am very thankful." Now in her seventies, and living in Los Angeles County, Bettie Page is still only beginning to rediscover the world outside Patton State's walls. At her lowest point, released from nearly a decade of incarceration as a mental patient, she reemerged to find herself a hero.

Ironically, Bettie, who spent much of her life struggling with the problems that her sexual attractiveness seemed to bring, is now an inspiration to some women, who say she helped make them feel more comfortable about their own sexuality. As a living icon, Bettie now has a new lease on life from her growing cult status as a pinup legend, a phenomenon of which she was only marginally aware during her lost years.

14

Have You Seen This
Pinup Queen?

IN THE LATE 1960s, Bunny Yeager, the outstanding photographer from
Florida who shot Bettie's January 1955 *Playboy* centerfold, bumped
into Bettie and her third husband, Harry Lear, at a downtown Miami
department store. Bunny and Bettie talked briefly, and Bettie promised to keep in touch, but she never did. That chance meeting would
stick in Bunny's mind, though, as the years went on and a new generation of fans began to discover Bettie Page.

It all started almost a decade earlier, in the early sixties, just a few
years after Bettie moved away from New York. The quietness of her
departure started a slew of rumors that persisted until her
reemergence in 1992. Some said she killed herself in embarrassment
after the Kefauver hearings. Others said she was rubbed out by the
Mob for witnessing something she shouldn't have seen, or that she
moved abroad to get away from her past. Some of the rumors were
closer to the truth: Bettie became a born-again Christian; she settled
down and married. However it happened, the mystery and the allure
of New York's one-time hottest pinup model was passed down from
father to son and from big brother to little brother as her fans began to
search for ways to preserve their memories of Miss Page. It seemed
that every year, she set hearts blazing and pulses pounding with her

friendly Christmas centerfold. Servicemen posted the image in bases all over the world. Post–Korean War airmen reportedly had it (altered to include a bikini) stenciled on their planes. There are even quite a few forty-year-old "Miss Bettie" tattoos floating around on the arms of regular guys across America in remembrance of the greatest American pinup queen.

By 1960 or so, a series of pocket-sized retrospective digest-style magazines of topless, commercially posed photos of Bettie began to emerge with titles like *Betty Page at Home* and *Betty Page Outdoors.* And the Klaws' Nutrix mail-order company rereleased many of Bettie's photos in books like *Betty Page in Bondage, Volume One*—illustrated with twenty-five photos.

Bettie's pictures continued to be top sellers throughout the sixties, as her former bosses milked her old photos for everything they could get. However, with the advent in the early 1970s of more explicit magazines like *Hustler* and *Penthouse* and the availability of X-rated movies like *The Devil in Miss Jones,* demand for Bettie's innocent cheesecake photos fell off.

A large contributing factor to Bettie Page's climb to widespread fame during her absent years was journalist Gay Talese's bestselling book, *Thy Neighbor's Wife,* a compelling and painstaking documentation of America's changing sexual mores. Published in 1980 by Doubleday, the book tells the story of *Playboy* founder Hugh Hefner, from his days of raising funds for a new magazine that he laid out on a card table in his apartment, to his reign as America's sexual superman. It also provides fond, glowing recollections and praise for the hottest Playmate of all time—Bettie Page. Just four years earlier, in 1976, the late publisher Leonard Burtman's Eros Goldstripe Publications issued a special $5 magazine devoted to Bettie called *A Nostalgic Look at Bettie Page.* Slowly, during the late 1970s and early 1980s, an underground demand began to build again for Bettie's pictures, and Bunny Yeager started getting inquiries for reprints.

In 1975, she heard from Talese, who was trying to track down Bettie for an interview for *Thy Neighbor's Wife.* Bunny knew the time was growing near for a Bettie Page revival, and she hoped to hop ahead of the trend by writing Bettie's biography. Unable to remember Bettie's married name, though, Bunny took out an ad in the *Miami Herald,* looking for information about Bettie's whereabouts. Harry

Lear answered the ad. He called Bunny and told her that he and Bettie were now divorced, but that Bettie was living in the addition on the back of his house. He brought Bettie to the phone.

Bettie wanted nothing to do with the revival. "I don't think the Lord would approve," she told Bunny. Bunny tried to get Bettie to tell the story of her salvation, but Bettie still wasn't interested, and Bettie thought the matter had died there. However, as Bettie's mental health deteriorated and her incarcerations kept her separated from society, her fan following was growing exponentially, unbeknownst to her.

From 1978 to 1980, publishing entrepreneur J. B. Rund (who later briefly became Bettie's agent in 1996) revitalized the marketing of Bettie Page to a new generation with his four *Betty Page—Private Peeks* magazine-format books. The now hard-to-find low-budget publication featured paintings and many never-before-seen photos of Bettie, including some taken from private collections that were more explicit than anything previously published.

Rund discovered Bettie in the 1950s. He's a self-admitted bondage enthusiast. "I've been interested in bondage and fetish stuff since I was a teenager," he says. How did he get interested in it? "The same way I was interested in chocolate ice cream. It's genetic," he says.

Born in 1943, Rund's first memory of sexual arousal is from when he was about twelve years of age, he says. He got an erection while playing cowboys and Indians and tying up neighborhood kids. At that age, bondage material is hard to come by, let alone understand, and so Rund says he found early inspiration for his fantasies in television shows such as *Sheena, Queen of the Jungle* and torture sequences in comic strips like *Prince Valiant* and *Dick Tracy*.

By the time he was fourteen, a friend in his Boy Scout troop showed him a men's magazine called *21*. Inside was a bondage serial comic strip called *Madame Adista*. It was a seminal moment in Rund's life, to discover that there was sexual material that catered to his desires.

Rund grew up in a repressed Irish Catholic neighborhood in New York. "In my neighborhood, a lot of Irish kids would carry a condom around in their wallets, so you could see the round outline in their back pockets. It was a sign you were ready for action. Of course, I don't think any of those condoms left those wallets."

The boys in the neighborhood furtively traded small digest girlie magazines like *Pick* and *Laff,* where Rund first recalls seeing swimsuit pinups of Bettie Page.

"Here was this girl-next-door type. She wasn't a movie star, she was just this model," Rund says. "She seemed to be sexual but she was wholesome looking, which was odd to me because I thought only Marilyn Monroe or Jayne Mansfield or all those other women with big tits were sexual. To me, they were whores. You could sense they weren't virgins. But to me, Bettie Page was a virgin. She was on a level above these movie stars."

It wasn't until Rund discovered an ad for Irving Klaw's Nutrix mail-order company that he was able to obtain a source for bondage photos and found to his amazement that Bettie Page was a bondage model as well. "Most of the bondage models were not beautiful women, but here was this beautiful woman doing it," Rund recalls. He bought the Klaw pictures out of the seven-dollar-a-week salary he made working in a drugstore as a teen, and, when he got them, he kept them hidden under his mattress.

When Rund entered college, he started working in the mailroom of a publishing company where he learned the business and cultivated his interest in erotic literature by collecting out-of-print books of Victorian erotica. After he was burned on a purchase that he thought was a pornographic novel but turned out to be a nineteenth century racist potboiler, Rund vowed to learn everything he could, eventually becoming an expert on the history of pornography and erotica.

When Sothebys offered its first sale of antique erotic books in 1971, Rund was consulted on the collection's value. Over time he became his own publisher, starting with reprints of nineteenth-century erotica, and moving on to interests closer to his own heart, such as a collection of the bondage comic strip, *The Adventures of Sweet Gwendoline.* Rund's company, Belier Press, eventually published a compilation of the works of noted underground cartoonist Robert Crumb as well as the first anthology by Art Spiegelman, who would later script *Maus,* the acclaimed graphic novel about Spiegelman's father's experiences in the Holocaust.

Soon Rund was printing compilations of 1940s and 1950s bondage photos and comics, many from Irving Klaw's studios, in books like *Bizarre Comix, Bizarre Fotos,* and *Bizarre Classix.* He had also been collecting photos of Bettie Page, but kept them out of his early books, thinking he might do a separate book on Bettie. Around this time, two pivotal things happened: The first was a phone call from Gay Talese who was trying to locate some nude photos of particular actresses, and called Rund for help. Rund turned him on to Bettie Page. Amazingly, Talese had never heard of her before.

The second thing that happened was that a friend of Rund's, Richard Merkin, called to tell Rund he had some full-frontal nudes of Bettie Page, and he claimed to also have a pornographic loop film starring Bettie. The film turned out to be of another actress, but the photos were Bettie Page—like almost no one had ever seen her before. In a series of from fourteen to twenty black-and-white photos taken at the same location, Bettie poses with her legs open, exposing her vagina.

"When I saw these photographs, it was like the missing link," Rund says. "You never saw Bettie [fully] nude in the 1950s. You never saw pubic hair. I went home and thought about what I had seen, and looked at what I had with all the bondage and cheesecake photos. Now I had an idea to do a Bettie Page book."

Merkin published some of the photos in an article about Bettie in *High Society* magazine in April 1977. Most of the rest were published by Rund in his *Private Peeks* magazine, which was totally devoted to Bettie.

Years later, Rund would pay Bettie royalties for the photos and find out to his dismay that she had never intended to have the graphic photos published and was deeply upset by them. "I was wrong to do it," Rund says. "I can never do anything to make it up to her fully. It was the wrong thing to do. I knew it at the time. I thought I could get away with it."

Nevertheless, Rund's magazines were an enormous hit, earning some $50,000 through mail orders. The price on the pastel-colored covers of Rund's *Private Peeks* mags ranged from $6 to $7—expensive for a premium magazine of a forgotten pinup queen—but soon the magazines were being traded at comic book conventions, introducing Bettie to a cultishly nostalgic and obsessive new group of collectors.

Rund says he's never sold one himself for more than $7, but he's seen them sold at conventions for as much as $50 to $100.

"I was at a comic book show around 1979 or 1980, and a fellow had *Private Peeks Number Three*," recalls Steve Brewster, president of the

Bettie Scouts of America, the official Bettie Page fan club. "This was the first time I ever had something in my hands with Bettie on the cover, and it was just like magic. My jaw dropped and I just could not believe the beauty [and] the exotic appeal this lady had.

"From that point on, I just kind of started scouting, to use the term, for more Bettie material. It kind of went from me going to a comic book show to me looking for men's magazines with anything Bettie on it."

"I am not responsible for the interest in Bettie Page. Bettie Page is the reason for the interest in Bettie Page," Rund says. "I provided a document that was the catalyst for it.

"But if these other people didn't respond to it, it wouldn't have caught on like it did. They're an important part of what happened because they disseminated Bettie Page. These people are putting Bettie Page in their culture. I only provided a cue, a beginning, a wellspring."

Bettie Page was slowly becoming the private darling of many fans, from collectors and publishers like Brewster and Rund to gallery artists and comic book writers, who would help popularize interest in her through their work over the next decades.

"A common bond with Bettie Page collectors is that they usually start out thinking they're the only men who ever noticed her," Brewster says. "They start out thinking she's their dream girl and no else knows about her, but eventually they find out how popular she really is."

Erotic pinup artist Olivia De Berardinis began a twenty-year career of painting and drawing Bettie Page in 1978, when Rund, her former agent, introduced her to his *Private Peeks* books and she was entranced by Bettie's party-girl smile and sultry looks. Known in the art world by her first name only, Olivia's work has appeared in *Playboy* and in other books and magazines, and her annual Bettie Page calendars, prints, and trading and greeting cards are coveted and valued among collectors. As interpreted by Olivia, Bettie Page is cotton candy; a vision of airbrush-smooth black bangs and flowing tresses over creamy skin hues. Olivia has called Bettie a black-haired Marilyn Monroe, and she likes no model better. Her images of Bettie are many-faceted, ranging from the humorous and light to the sizzling and serious.

She places Bettie in situations both enticing and absurd. In one painting, Bettie gives you her best bedroom eyes as she sits nude, save for her black opera gloves, high heels, and stockings, atop a cushion. On closer inspection, however, one sees that she's not alone. A tiny hand, curled boots, and a belled hat can be seen protruding from under her bottom on the cushion. The painting's title? *Betty and the Very Happy Elf.*

Olivia's paintings have a fantastic and fetishistic edge. She favors drawing Bettie in stiletto heels, corsets, garter belts, and leather. In one work, Bettie even sits atop a giant high-heeled shoe. In another, she's a mermaid with a shiny black vinyl tail. In yet another, she's a devil in red leather, ready to make a deal. She's naked and bound, teasing you with her tongue pressed against her bottom teeth, and she's joyful and exuberant in white lace. Sometimes she's tattooed, and other times she's the whip-wielding dominant Bettie. In totality, Olivia has captured in her work all the moods of the many faces of Bettie; both the Queen of Curves and the Dark Angel. Still, Olivia only goes into the twilight world of bondage.

The dark is the realm of Robert Blue.

Blue, fifty, is famous for his life-sized photo-realistic fetishistic pop-art paintings of Bettie as bondage queen, blown up from magazines. His images of Bettie are beautifully rendered with unbelievably attentive care to detail: individual strands of hair, fabric texture, and super-realistic shadowing. The overwhelmingly blue tints in his painting give them an air of fantasy and memory, providing the atmosphere of a world in darkness.

As portrayed by Robert Blue, Bettie is often dominant, sometimes submissive. She's donning high-heeled black leather boots with spurs as she ties up a pretty young model on a fifties-style sofa. Or, clad in lingerie, she's tied up and being spanked by a pretty blonde, or she's spanking another model herself, with a look that says both that she'll give no quarter and that she's really into this. Other paintings have her hog-tied with a ball-gag in her mouth or simply by herself, wearing only black stockings and a look suggesting danger ahead.

"Power," Blue says, is what his paintings are about. But, it's a power that largely affects only fetishists. "Most people who look at my paintings don't see the power in them," he says.

"The idea that she was a pinup is ridiculous. Many other models were doing good, clean beach poses in the 1950s. If Bettie Page didn't do this other stuff, no one would remember her," says Blue.

"I don't care how sweet people say she is, she's not the pinup queen," he says. "She's the bizarro queen. Everybody who thinks she was this innocent country girl who just got sucked into this, well, guess what? She hand-sewed the costumes herself. She invented the scenarios." Blue is the son of the Hollywood comedian Ben Blue, who starred in films with Jimmy Durante during the 1940s and was friends with W. C. Fields. As a boy growing up near Los Angeles in the 1950s, the younger Blue found Bettie in the pages of the late Leonard Burtman's *Exotique,* the bondage magazine from which Blue later took the inspiration for many of his paintings.

Exotique was a small-format digest-sized magazine that sold for $3.75, about seven times more than the big girlie magazines—a fortune for something that didn't even feature nudity. It was one of a number of "taboo" magazines, wrapped in cellophane and kept under newsstand counters.

"I discovered this stuff when I was seventeen or so, because I used to dig around in old bookstores," Blue recalls. "I used to get a bus and go to Los Angeles looking for what I call a 'virgin' bookstore, where the magazine stacks hadn't been raided, and I would find this stuff, and the stuff just radiated power.

"It was like the Ark of the Covenant in Steven Spielberg's *Raiders of the Lost Ark* for me. . . . If the Ark of the Covenant shoots out rays of energy, if that is what the Ark of the Covenant does, then on the dark side, *Exotique* magazine was shooting out rays of dark-side energy, and that is a fact."

Soon Blue became an *Exotique* devotee, a move that opened him up to the other side; to a world of bondage and erotica. "You would go to the newsrack that sold men's magazines, and in the fifties, you weren't supposed to be at this newsrack anyway, that's seedy enough, but then to ask for one of these publications that weren't displayed, that took guts.

"There was something in this magazine that was so erotic and so taboo and so bad and so unbelievably on the other side, that you'd have to go through those lengths to get it. You'd have to know about it, you'd have to request it. You couldn't even flip through it and preview it like other magazines," Blue recalls.

In the 1970s, Blue began painting Bettie and other *Exotique* models in his photo-realistic way, blowing up the magazine's small photos to life size. As he began exhibiting his work in New York galleries, Blue at first didn't know that Bettie had any special significance to anyone but him, but he says he soon found otherwise. "What I discovered is there was a following, a cult of Bettie, like the followers of Do," referring to the Heaven's Gate cult and its leader, Marshall Herff Applewhite.

He remembers the time when he had a visitor to the one-room studio he had in a cold-water flat in a Jewish neighborhood: "This guy comes to visit me to ask about my involvement in Bettie Page, and I figure he's a client wanting a painting. He's a strange European little man and I start picking up a strange vibe from him. He's got a ring with a silver skull on it. And I remember I've seen the ring somewhere before. It's an SS ring. I realize that the guy is like an old Nazi, and he finds me and he wants to talk about what Bettie's done to his life, and all of a sudden I start meeting all these characters."

Eventually, a show of Blue's work was held at the *Playboy* mansion by one of Bettie's biggest fans, Hugh Hefner. Through that show, Blue met one of his most famous clients, Jack Nicholson, who purchased a painting from Blue after he won his Best Actor Oscar for *One Flew Over the Cuckoo's Nest* in 1975.

Blue's paintings have attracted severe, harsh, and personal criticism from mainstream newspaper art critics, but they are widely reprinted and loved, breaking all convention for a normal gallery painter, who would be dead in the water after a bad review. His fame as a fetishistic painter was even immortalized in an acclaimed 1984 film based loosely on his life, *Heartbreakers,* in which actor Peter Coyote plays an erotic painter named Arthur Blue. Speaking about the staying power of the images of Bettie Page and *Exotique,* Blue says, "The stuff still has this power. The idea that these things are kind of an art joke, that they're funny in a contemporary art sense, they're not." As evidence, he recounts the story of when an acquaintance who was a heroin addict came to visit his studio in the 1970s and was so shocked by Blue's paintings of Bettie that he never spoke to Blue again.

"A lot of contemporary art is based on being ironic," Blue says, and his art certainly qualifies for that. The images he paints were taboo and forbidden in the 1950s, but by the time of the sexual revolution in the 1960s and 1970s and the pornography that came with it, Bettie's bondage photos were no longer as risqué. Yet they still retained their power.

"It's 1975 and it's going to be ironic to blow up pornography that isn't really pornography anymore," Blue explains. "In 1975, you have full-on nudity, you have *Penthouse* magazine putting it in your face," Blue says. But while his bondage paintings of Bettie weren't explicit or pornographic, "It was a thousand times more powerful than anything Bob Guccione ever had a wet dream about."

For all the impressive quality of Blue's work, his paintings only reached a narrow segment of society, those who were either art gallery patrons or bondage enthusiasts, and their word of mouth about Bettie spread slowly.

To truly popularize Bettie, it took the work of cartoonist Dave Stevens, the most famous of the Bettie artists and the closest to her personally. He was among those who discovered Bettie in her second wave of fandom, during the late 1970s, and his comic book, *The Rocketeer*, almost single-handedly started the third wave of Bettiemania in the 1980s.

While an animator at Hanna-Barbera studios, Stevens was intrigued by a magazine ad for some of the Movie Star News 8mm loop films of Bettie, and ordered them out of curiosity. He played the silent dancing movies for his colleagues during his lunch hour on a secondhand Keystone projector, with music from Cab Calloway playing in the background. Bettie was a major hit with his friends, who requested to see the films over and over, whistling and causing a commotion over the black-and-white Bettie. His friends' reaction stuck in his mind for a long time, until Stevens was asked to write and draw a short comic-book story for an upcoming anthology.

After mulling it over for a bit, Stevens produced *The Rocketeer*—the immortal and fanciful retro tale of a 1950s flyboy named Cliff Secord who becomes a flying superhero thanks to a jet-powered backpack. And who played Lois Lane to Cliff's Superman? No one less than "Bettie Page" herself! Stevens was a master at depicting Bettie's glamour, grace, and humor, and his comic was such a success that it spawned the 1991 Walt Disney motion picture of the same name, which made more than $100 million internationally. As depicted by Dave Stevens, Bettie is closer to her image in the Bunny Yeager photos: a sunny, smiling pinup girl with the knockout looks of a dark Marilyn Monroe.

"She didn't become an icon until Dave Stevens started using her in *The Rocketeer*. Dave was able to capture her aesthetic quality in his cartoons. People began to see he was not just cobbling it out of his artist's inspiration. If it hadn't been for Dave, she would not have had that comeback," says noted author Harlan Ellison, who wrote an introduction to one of Stevens's *Rocketeer* books. "That's why she and Dave are friends now. They see each other all the time."

Taken collectively, Stevens, Olivia, and Robert Blue form a triumvirate; a holy trinity of Bettie artists. "Dave Stevens, Olivia, and me, it's through our hard work that people begin to understand who Bettie is and start delving deeper into the history," Blue says. "We're the conduit."

Fueled largely by *The Rocketeer*, Bettie publications and Bettie memorabilia became a hot commodity by the late 1980s and early 1990s. Through statuettes, prints, trading cards, T-shirts, and comics with titles such as *Betty in Bondage* and *Tor Love Betty*, the Tease From Tennessee became a multimillion-dollar business. Soon other talented artists who had been painting Bettie for years began receiving more acclaim than just gallery shows and newspaper reviews as the ever-widening ranks of Bettie fans discovered their works.

One of the most popular publications of the wave that followed Stevens's *Rocketeer* was Greg Theakston's *Betty Pages*, a small independently published magazine that celebrated the nostalgia of all things Bettie. Theakston remembered sneaking peeks at Bettie as a kid in copies of *Time Out*, a sixties men's magazine he often found in his father's underwear drawer.

"Whereas other models made you feel creepy, Bettie made you feel good," Theakston said, explaining his fascination with the Queen of Curves. "Sheer determination and hard work put her where she was. It's inevitable that good work will be recognized, even if not in the time it was created, because of the sexual stigmas attached to it then."

Stocked with rare photos, collector's information, and Theakston's own wonderful drawings and paintings of Bettie, *The Betty Pages* was a smash success with fans, eventually spawning nine issues, two book-sized soft-cover annuals, and a sequel magazine by Theakston called *Tease* that celebrates cheesecake photos and pinup art in general.

Theakston is probably the person most responsible for launching the image of Bettie Page as an enigma, a mysterious woman like Greta Garbo, separated from her past and wanting to be left alone. Through an in-depth series of investigative articles in his magazine, Theakston pieced together the first partial biography of Bettie Page, as he searched across the country for the clues that could lead him to the truth about her mysterious disappearance from the public eye so many years ago.

"Everybody loves that Judge Crater kind of mystery, the 'Where is She?' angle. She was at the top of what she did and she walked away. It was the hardest research project I've ever done," said Theakston, who got his start writing articles about comic book artists and movie monsters for fanzines, and later became a top commercial artist whose work has been seen in *Playboy* magazine and DC Comics.

Though his research was largely focused on Bettie's modeling days as he looked for her films and photos, Theakston uncovered a valuable trail of information, and was among the first to discover Bettie's Tennessee roots. Ending every one of his magazine columns with a "Goodnight, Ms. Page, wherever you are," the New York City–based artist enticed amateur and professional journalists across the world to seek out Bettie's trail. As for Theakston, he came to the conclusion (correctly) that Bettie Page was still alive and for some reason didn't want to speak about her past. That was enough for him at the time. He was satisfied with the memory of her as a pinup and didn't want that sullied. The same couldn't be said for a lot of other fly-by-night publications and cheaply made video productions that proliferated rumors and cheap innuendo ranging from the believable (she was a retired grandmother living in Florida) to the bizarre (she had been assassinated by the FBI).

In November 1992 the speculation ended. Earlier that year, Tommy Goldsmith, a columnist for the *Nashville Tennessean,* found and interviewed Jack Page, Bettie's younger brother, a sixty-five-year-old retired machinist who was still living in Nashville. With that piece of information, the author of this book and the producers of the syndicated television program *Lifestyles of the Rich and Famous* separately contacted Bettie Page. As if by destiny, Bettie had just been released from Patton State and was beginning to learn about her fan following (the only previous indication she'd had of it was a short piece about herself she had seen on *Entertainment Tonight* at the hospital one evening).

For all Bettie's current fame, though, she hasn't had much of a chance to savor the fruits from it. Today Bettie leads a reclusive life, refusing to be photographed and preferring to communicate only by letter or phone. She wrote the author of this book a six-page letter in the summer of 1992 on unlined stationery in the precise and pretty handwriting of a former English teacher. It was her first acknowledgment of the world that clamored to know both her and the solution to the mystery of her disappearance. In the letter she answered some questions and provided more clues and information about her whereabouts for the last forty years. Pieces of that interview, her first since her comeback, were published in an article written by the author for the second *Betty Pages* annual and the last issue of *The Betty Pages*. Soon after she wrote the author, Bettie also wrote a few select fans, including Steve Brewster, who would become the president of her licensed fan club, the Bettie Scouts of America. She also provided Robin Leach and *Lifestyles of the Rich and Famous* with a thirty-minute audiotape of her slow, deep Southern voice answering interview questions. Portions of that were aired in a November 1992 segment. She has since done short interviews for a variety of publications including *Playboy* and *Interview* magazines and E! Entertainment Television, which aired a two-hour documentary about her in April 1997.

Ironically, though her image has made many hundreds of thousands of dollars for others, Bettie hasn't seen much money herself. She was living on Social Security and Medicaid when she reentered the public eye in 1992. Some artists and publishers such as Dave Stevens and J. B. Rund, who had made profits from her image, immediately sent checks to Bettie, wishing to make reparations with their dreamgirl, now seemingly returned after four decades from the shadow world of the dead and missing. These men's love of the young black-banged woman in their cherished photos has led to a loyalty not to be trifled with. In the 1950s, men would have fought to have her. Today, denied that possibility, those who admire her treat her very protectively as a treasure or a cherished loved one or even a favorite grandmother. Dave Stevens is one of the handful of people outside Bettie's family who have met with her in person since her reemergence. Stevens and

Playboy magazine founder Hugh Hefner reportedly screened a private showing of the film version of *The Rocketeer* for her at the Playboy Mansion on the West Coast. Stevens refused to be interviewed for this book, because he didn't want to participate in an unauthorized biography. Equally loyal, actor Robert Culp, Bettie's former drama teacher, wouldn't consent to an interview without Bettie's permission, even though he hadn't seen her in forty-five years.

Not everyone believes she's back, though.

In 1954, when Richard Merkin was sixteen, a buddy slipped him a "special" photo of Bettie Page that he'd bought at a joint on New York's 42nd Street. It may not have been the first time Merkin had seen a picture of Bettie, but it was the first time he saw her in an uncensored bottomless pose. "A lot of people don't realize today, because we live in such different times, but in those days, nudist magazines were doctored so that people had these strange blank areas," Merkin recalled. "To see this dreadfully beautiful woman with her legs spread apart and obviously fully aware of it. . . . I don't know how Moses felt when he got the tablets, but it had a certain kind of staying power. I still have the picture today, and the fact that a fifty-eight-year-old man would keep this photo all his life is indicative of something about her charisma."

Merkin, now a writer and illustrator, is best known as a contributing editor to *Vanity Fair* magazine and for his column, "Merkin on Style," which appeared in *GQ* magazine during the late 1980s. His paintings have appeared in both *GQ* and the *New Yorker*.

In recent years, however, Merkin has gained some measure of notoriety—if not infamy—among Bettie fans for his intimation in an article in the August 1993 issue of *GQ* that Bettie Page's partial reentry into public life may be nothing more than a money-making hoax.

"Bettie Page's disappearance was a very gradual thing for someone of my generation. I think there was always a question of whether or not she was alive. The rumors that she became a religious zealot, the rumors that she killed herself. Certainly no one knew anyone who was in contact with her," Merkin said.

"I'm not a dumb man. I'm fifty-eight years old and I remember the whole Clifford Irving thing," he continued, referring to the author of the bogus biography of Howard Hughes who duped the American public and press for a considerable time in the 1970s. "All I know is, if you hear some woman with boll weevils in her voice calling from three thousand miles away, and you say, 'That's gotta be Bettie Page,' my only question is Why? If you can fake Howard Hughes, why can't you fake Bettie Page?"

Hugh Hefner and Bettie's one-time attorney, James Swanson, were both angry with his article, Merkin said, and Swanson even threatened *GQ* with legal action. "Swanson didn't want anybody raining on his parade. He had a real money-maker here, whether she was alive or not," Merkin said. "He wanted to scare the magazine. I merely questioned whether or not she was alive. *GQ* knew that we were on very solid ground. *GQ* felt like if push was ever going to come to shove on this thing, Bettie Page would have to come out of her cocoon and go to court. And it was unlikely that was going to happen."

Some have accused Merkin of trying to make a name for himself with the controversy, but as he points out, the question of Bettie's life or death was not even the focus of the article. It was a minor point made at the end of a piece about pinup art. New York columnists and reporters in *USA Today* picked it up and made a story out of it. Apart from his column and artwork, Merkin is also known for his small contribution to rock and roll history—as a young art student in London, he was photographed among the cardboard cutouts on the cover of the Beatles' *Sgt. Pepper's Lonely Hearts Club Band*. ("I'm right in the back row," Merkin will tell you. "Look over Fred Astaire's right shoulder and you'll see a man in kind of a blurry picture, wearing a fedora with glasses and a dark mustache—that's me.")

"I don't understand why a seventy-two-year-old woman who, long after the fact, is being feted as the reigning goddess of her time absolutely refuses to stick her head out her window when there are people writing checks," Merkin said. "Here's a lady who lives in Hollywood with all these cameras around her and all this hubbub in recent years developing about her and there ain't a single picture. I don't understand how all of these people like J. D. Salinger who are doggedly reclusive, somehow they get photographed by some enterprising paparazzi, but no one has snapped her and no one has seen her except for these anointed people like Swanson who go out to dinner with her.

"How long can one perpetuate this thing? I realize at this point if she is alive, from what everybody says, she is totally reclusive. She wants nothing to do with anybody seeing what she looks like now. But let's face it, I've been told that enormous kinds of deals have been thrust in front of her, and all she's got to do is show up at Barnes & Noble for three hours and then take a wheelbarrow to the bank. I don't get it. I'm not great-looking, but I'd do it."

When Merkin was offered a phone interview with Bettie for an article in *Vanity Fair,* he held out for an in-person interview. Bettie's handlers flatly refused it. To Merkin, Bettie's reclusiveness may be nothing more than a smokescreen hiding a conspiracy to keep people from discovering that she really died. He even postulates that reporters might have been unknowingly fed false "interviews" with an actress portraying Bettie. It's only fair to point out here that when Merkin was interviewed, he didn't know about Bettie's battles with mental illness or her incarceration in Patton State, and the court papers that document the fact that she is still alive. That's also not to mention the letter she sent me, the author, which included many personal details that had not been previously revealed about Bettie, and some of which only she could have known.

While it's safe to say Merkin was wrong about Bettie's return to semipublic life being a hoax, he was asking a smart question. Any journalist worth his or her salt should have been wondering the same thing. And with the recent advent of tabloid TV, it's amazing that a show like *Hard Copy* hasn't tracked her down. Only now, with the new revelations of Bettie's violent past does it start to make sense why she should want to avoid public scrutiny outside the comforting controlled environment of screened phone calls and letters.

And Merkin adds that, "I got a letter saying that [J. B. Rund] had gone out to Los Angeles and had dinner with Bettie Page. Like me, [Rund] was also an agnostic about the whole business, but this letter was like getting a letter from a born-again Christian. It was filled with exhortations like, 'It was the most wonderful moment in my life.' "

If anything, Merkin feels a little left out. He wants dinner with Bettie, too. Who wouldn't?

This is the kind of fidelity Bettie breeds, even in her disbelievers— admirable, dogged, good-hearted, and, unfortunately, sometimes misplaced. Many of Bettie's fans, famous and otherwise, were so incensed by reports that she was living in virtual poverty after her reemergence that they were willing to participate in anything that carried her agent's so-called authorized label, either by buying, selling, or creating it, believing Bettie would be enriched by it and finally realize some earnings from her photos. A good example is Stevens, who contributed a lot of work to the layout and design of Bettie's authorized biography, apparently without understanding just how little of it reportedly actually benefited Bettie. A more mundane instance is the receptionist at an art gallery featuring paintings of Bettie, who at first refused to transfer a call for the author to the gallery owners, because this book is an unauthorized biography and doesn't benefit Bettie. Even Billy Neal, Bettie's erstwhile husband, who doesn't harbor much love for Bettie, refused to talk, because he said there's nobody who is really helping Bettie financially. Strangely, he's probably closer to the truth than anyone else.

15

The Battle of Bettie

TAKING her place as a modern celebrity has rocketed Bettie Page into
a new era, far removed from the innocent fifties. The 1990s are a
world of lawyers and deal-makers to whom Bettie is a commodity, and
everyone is either buying or selling. Bettie's bashful first dance with
the world that adores her has turned from a graceful minuet into a
scramble for cover on a battlefield of legal troubles and greed.

What should be a cause for joy has splintered lifelong friendships
and left many wondering whom they can really trust. At the heart of it:
the yet-elusive millions that everyone thinks Bettie Page Inc. can be
worth.

Jack Page was largely behind brokering Bettie's first "public" appearance, providing *Lifestyles of the Rich and Famous* with tapes of
her voice in 1992. When Jack appeared on *Lifestyles* himself, he told
the show's producers that he was handling his older sister's business
affairs. In truth, the retired machine worker was looking for someone
to do it for him. Offers were coming in fast. *Life* magazine reportedly
called Jack offering to put Bettie on its cover if she would agree to be
interviewed and photographed. Jack hadn't seen Bettie in nearly fifteen years, but she was family, and as a small businessman of many
years, he knew there was considerable money that could be made or
lost depending on the decisions that were made in the coming
months. He also knew that Bettie wouldn't be interested in being

photographed or revealed to the world the way she is today. Anyone looking in from the outside would think Jack took all the right steps and did all the things one would logically do to protect Bettie's fame and fortune. So what went wrong? Here's the behind-the-scenes story, taken from court records and interviews with those close to the Pages:

Sometime in 1992, Jack Page heard about Everett Fields, a Los Angeles lawyer and showbiz agent who is the grandson of W. C. Fields. Everett Fields began seeking profits for his grandfather's estate after a W. C. Fields beer mug found its way onto store shelves in California. Upset by what he considered the misappropriation of Fields's image, the grandson of the famous Vaudeville comedian became instrumental in drafting state laws that entitle the families of famous performers to retain the rights to their images and a cut of the profits from spin-off products, even after the death of the famous family member. Fields signed Bettie Page in January 1993. Jack Page wanted Everett Fields to personally represent Bettie, but Fields recommended one of the partners in his firm as the agent to represent Bettie—the now-controversial entertainment agent and attorney James L. Swanson. Fans and publishers alike say they feared Swanson, and found him iron-fisted and threatening to deal with, though none is willing to say much on the record, fearing litigation.

"At the time, at the very beginning, Jack felt a little uncomfortable because he really wanted Everett Fields himself. He wanted the real person, but he felt that Swanson was in the family," one friend of the Pages said. So it ended up that Bettie would be represented by Fields's firm, but Swanson would be the Pages' sole liaison to Fields.

In January 1993, Jack and Bettie Page signed a three-year contract making Everett Fields and James Swanson "their exclusive, worldwide agents for the purpose of exploiting merchandising rights in association with products, services, premiums, advertising, and promotion . . . from February 1, 1993 through February 1, 1996."

Fields's firm promised to begin an aggressive marketing and licensing campaign, including seeking fees and royalties from unauthorized Bettie products; signing deals for new merchandise such as T-shirts, posters, cards, photos, and clothing; licensing Bettie's likeness for movies, TV shows, books, and look-alike contests; managing all licensed products; "maintaining quality control" over those products; and safeguarding Bettie Page's copyrights and trademarks.

The Page family agreed to turn over to Swanson all requests and leads for business deals concerning Bettie. In exchange, Swanson said he would take no action regarding licensing or merchandising of Bettie Page products without prior approval from Bettie and her family.

According to the terms of their contract, "The Pages will receive 65 percent of the income, including royalties, advances, and other payments, collected from licensing or merchandising the image of Betty Page." Swanson—and Fields—would take 35 percent, and would "not deduct from the Pages' 65 percent share any routine office expenses or overhead." However, the contract continued, "From time to time, the duties of the agents will require that they attend trade and gift shows to monitor or promote Bettie Page merchandise." Those expenses would come out of the profits of licensed Bettie Page products, the contract stated, but not without an earlier agreement from the Pages.

In a letter from Swanson to Jack Page dated January 11, 1993, he cited his firm's expertise in cases involving protecting entertainers from the unauthorized uses of their image and assured Jack Page that he would strive to make sure that didn't happen with Bettie. He also advised the Pages to create a corporation owned by Bettie and her family members to handle the corporate side of Bettie's business dealings and distribute her royalty earnings. However, it was never formed while Swanson was her agent. In his letter, Swanson had written:

> No agent should own any part of your family business. We should be working for you and not be partners and part owners of your corporation. It is a conflict of interest for the person who organizes your merchandising program to own any part of the business. If there is a falling-out, or you are not satisfied and want to make a change, you will be joined at the hip to an outsider who owns part of your family business. That kind of long-term relationship does not make sense. Being in partnership with an agent will also be expensive and will cut into the income you should be receiving. For example, I suspect that anyone who wants to be part of your corporation will want to deduct various "expenses" from funds that should otherwise go to your family. Every dollar applied to office rent or the various other costs of doing business is one less dollar for you. Furthermore, in time, the corporation

will have value as an asset in itself, separate and distinct from the annual income it produces. You must retain complete ownership of this valuable family asset.

In theory, that's what was supposed to happen when Swanson took over the Pages' business dealings. In practice it has been another matter, at least according to the Pages' agents today, Curtis Management Group (CMG) Worldwide Inc., who allege that Swanson engaged not only in practices that placed him in a conflict of interest as Bettie's agent and attorney, but that he also fraudulently misrepresented himself for his own gain.

On November 12, 1995, about two and a half years after the Pages signed with him, Swanson submitted an amendment to his contract with Bettie. According to some close to Bettie, Jack Page had begun asking questions about some of Swanson's deals and was concerned because Swanson had left Fields's firm and taken Bettie's contract with him. Jack was also reportedly having trouble getting in touch with Swanson. The matter ended with Swanson recommending Glamourcon Inc., a Washington State entertainment corporation, as a substitute agent for himself in the contract.

Glamourcon put on large conventions that promoted the Bettie Page merchandise and was run by Bob Schultz, a trusted fan and collector who had published a low-budget Bettie Page fanzine called *Fond Memories*, mainly full of photocopied pictures of Bettie from old magazines. Jack Page was initially hesitant to have Schultz as their agent, but Schultz assured Jack that he would straighten everything out with Swanson, friends say. Believing Schultz would become their new agent and Swanson would no longer be negotiating deals for them, the Pages signed. What Swanson didn't tell them, according to a lawsuit filed on the Pages' behalf by CMG Worldwide Inc. on February 11, 1997, in the Superior Court of Marion County, Indiana, is that Swanson is a principal in Glamourcon—possibly a co-owner or officer.

Another source of contention in the suit is a top-selling authorized biography of Bettie written in part by Swanson. The book, *Bettie Page: The Life of a Pin-Up Legend* was published in 1996, but apparently had been in discussion since before Glamourcon took over Bettie's representation, as she wrote the foreword to the book in early October 1995. Bettie Page fans both famous and obscure contributed to the book, eager to help her out by participating in an authorized biography that they believed would benefit her financially more than anyone else. Several, such as photographers Art Amsie and Don Whitney, contributed their work for free. As previously mentioned, Dave Stevens took care of the design chores. Other famous artists who have made Bettie the subject of their art, such as erotic painters Olivia De Berardinis and Robert Blue, also participated in the book and were interviewed. Famous actresses such as Demi Moore and Debi Mazar were photographed in Bettie-inspired poses by top fashion photographers for the $40 coffee-table book. New York, and Los Angeles fashion designers quickly jumped on the Bettie train, too.

Helping Swanson write the book was Karen Essex, a Los Angeles writer who had written an early biographical piece about Bettie in *L.A. Weekly* that Bettie said had showed real understanding of her. Swanson also took a joint authorship credit with Essex for an article of excerpts from the book published in the December 1995 issue of *Playboy* magazine. Swanson also apparently was going to author a sequel to the book. CMG's lawsuit against Glamourcon charges that Glamourcon committed not only a conflict of interest but a violation "of its fiduciary duties by assigning to or otherwise permitting Swanson to author the proposed biography and to participate in the proceeds from the sales thereof." Swanson's participation in the books while Bettie was his client is "a transaction specifically prohibited" by the Illinois State Bar's Rules of Professional Conduct, the lawsuit states. However, as of March 1997, no complaints had been filed against Swanson, according to the bar's disciplinary arm, the Illinois Attorney Registration and Discipline Commission, and no punitive actions had been taken against him.

It's unclear how much money Bettie earned from the Swanson-Essex book, if any, but sources close to her say that she received little compared to the book's total profit, and they also allege that she never signed a contract authorizing the book.

Until shortly before Bettie's contracts with Schultz, Swanson, and Glamourcon were terminated in May 1996, she had received only about $15,500 out of an account that totaled probably between $80,000 to $90,000 in royalties from licensed Bettie Page products, sources say. CMG's lawsuit alleges that Swanson never advised Bettie or Jack Page to seek independent legal counsel for advice about his dealings with them. Swanson, who was in control of the above-mentioned bank accounts, "disbursed and diverted funds to himself from the accounts he maintained for the Pages' purported benefit for unauthorized purposes, for purposes beyond the scope of his agency, and for his own personal benefit," the suit charges.

It continues: "Despite repeated requests and demands, Swanson failed to properly account to the Pages and to B.M.P. with respect to use, disposition, and diversion of the Pages' and B.M.P.'s monies and other property. Similarly, Swanson failed to remit and pay sums due to the Pages and B.M.P. and to otherwise timely deliver their property to them."

A source close to the Pages and the legal negotiations claims to have seen checkbook stubs from an account at Chicago's La Salle Bank that Swanson managed for Bettie. The source, who we'll identify here by the pseudonym Terry, says that out of the approximately one hundred checks that Swanson wrote, virtually all of them were made out to himself. "Very few checks were written to vendors," Terry says. "Let's say he paid for an airplane ticket. It's not written to the airline or a travel agency. It's a reimbursement to himself."

Terry alleges that many of the expenses Swanson incurred were not only questionable, but most were never approved by the Pages, as the lawsuit affirms. "Take my word for it," Terry says. "The Pages are telling the truth. Swanson may have asked them about one or two specific items, but not a hundred. There's no way."

There is at least $25,000 in expenses that Bettie's lawyers are questioning, the source says. For instance, Swanson allegedly claimed more than $16,000 in travel expenses for promotions related to Bettie, but that includes instances such as when he traveled to the Playboy Mansion to be present when Bettie and Hugh Hefner were signing limited edition prints of her Christmas centerfold. Terry says the Page family contends there was no reason for Swanson to be there, except to make a name for himself with Hefner and *Playboy*, with whom Glamourcon wanted to make business deals. "Bettie would never have consented to that," Terry says.

Other expenses include $5,000 for books, periodicals, and reference materials, and $783 for framing and photographs. Covered in the latter, Terry alleges, is at least one framed picture of Bettie that Swanson gave as a present to a model. "Why should Bettie pay for that?" Terry asks angrily. Another allegation from the Pages' lawyers, Terry says, is that Swanson may have wrongly spent nearly $2,000 of Bettie's money on research for his book.

Terry says the Pages are extremely concerned because they don't have statements from the first three months after the account was opened, a time period that includes deposits such as a cash present that Dave Stevens gave Bettie for her birthday. To the Pages' knowledge, Bettie has never received the money from Stevens's gift, Terry claims.

"Out of between $80,000 to $90,000, Bettie got $15,500. In almost three years, that's all she got from him, and the rest of it he kept," Terry says. "Thirty-five percent of it is legally his, but the rest of it is not."

When Glamourcon (Swanson and Schultz) took over as her official representatives, there were still long delays in getting money to her, and still questions about the way the money was being accounted for, Bettie's new agents, CMG, say in their suit.

Terry says that when Schultz sent royalty checks to Bettie, he did not send statements outlining what the money was for or the amount of the gross receipts from which Bettie was receiving a percentage. Terry also alleges that the Pages cannot produce contracts for some deals because they were never given copies by Swanson or Schultz.

Bettie's lawyers and CMG have asked for a jury trial to settle the matter and have asked the court to force Glamourcon to cease producing any new Bettie products and destroy already existing products that were ostensibly made without Bettie's approval.

Their suit also charges that Swanson, who published an open letter in the *Comics Buyer's Guide* in 1993 asking for makers of Bettie Page–related products to tithe 10 percent to her, did not aggressively pursue manufacturers of bootleg Bettie products. And when he did take legal action against one alleged copyright infringer, the suit claims he did so without seeking Bettie's permission to sue and without advising her of what legal and financial risks it could open up against her.

That suit was filed against Something Weird Video, a mail-order company that was marketing home videotape versions of the films *Teaserama, Strip-O-Rama,* and *Varietease.* All the films were in the public domain by this time, and though model-release forms could not be located for all the films, it was widely assumed that Bettie had in fact signed the forms, which would have allowed commercial use of her image in the film without her consent. However, Swanson retained a California law firm to sue Something Weird Video, claiming misappropriation of Bettie's likeness, not in the films, but in Something Weird's catalog ads for the movies. The lawyers contended the ads were a commercial use of her image separate from the films and thus would have required her permission.

A judge disagreed and in a summary judgment ruled against the plaintiff Bettie Page and ordered that she pay Something Weird Video's legal costs. That decision left Bettie personally holding the bag for some $84,000 in legal fees, Terry says.

Friends and lawyers tried to negotiate a settlement for Bettie with Something Weird Video instead of filing an appeal, but since Something Weird was legally entitled to the fees according to the judge's ruling, initially it was not inclined to accept other proposals, which included offers for services equal in value to the fees they claimed. As of April 1997, Bettie's options were looking increasingly limited. "There's a way Bettie can get out of it," Terry said then, glumly. "She can declare bankruptcy." Fortunately, it didn't come to that.

On June 12, with the help of Bettie's longtime admirer, *Playboy* founder Hugh Hefner, the suit was settled. Something Weird reportedly agreed with Hefner's lawyer to drop Bettie's financial obligation in exchange for free advertising and publicity in *Playboy* for Something Weird's Bettie Page video. It's just one example of Hefner's kindness toward Bettie, Terry says.

There's some question as to whether Bettie signed an attorney-client retainer agreement authorizing the law firm to pursue the lawsuit against Something Weird Video on her behalf, Terry says, claiming that a law enforcement officer in Tennessee who specializes in handwriting examined a photocopy of the retainer agreement supposedly signed by Bettie and declared the signature a fraud.

Glamourcon, Swanson, and Schultz filed a countersuit against Bettie and Jack Page in U.S. District Court of Central California on March 10, 1997, subpoenaing the Pages and charging them with defamation, breach of contract, and interference with past contracts. Swanson and Schultz are seeking almost $3 million in damages. Through the documents filed with the court, a clash of wills and personalities begins to emerge, with Jack and Bettie Page on one side and Swanson and Schultz united on the other.

According to the Swanson and Schultz lawsuit, Jack Page terminated Glamourcon's representation of Bettie on May 17, 1996, telling Swanson and Schultz that he would notify all the licensed Bettie Page vendors that they were not to make future payments to either Swanson or Schultz. Jack later made good on the threat, sending out a letter to all makers of approved Bettie Page products, telling them to send royalties to him personally, not Glamourcon. When Kitchen Sink Press, a noted publisher of underground comics and "longtime and valued licensee" of Bettie Page products, responded to Jack Page's letter by telling him that they would hold all funds in an escrow account until it could be determined who was legally supposed to receive them, Jack Page voided all deals and contracts with Kitchen Sink.

The suit continues to allege that Bettie did not live up to an exclusive oral contract to sign books and photographs for Glamourcon in 1996, and instead signed autographs for competitors. Friends of the Pages say that Bettie did so because they considered Glamourcon's contract legally terminated, since they believed Glamourcon had breached its management contract.

As for the biography Swanson wrote with Karen Essex, Swanson claims that Jack Page interfered with it and caused General Publishing Group to break its contract with him. Jack Page "falsely stated that Bettie M. Page had been cheated on the book project and would not receive any profits from the book," the suit says. It also states that after the biography was published, Jack's "conduct was wholly inconsistent with his cooperation and authorization" of the book. The suit says that Jack complained that certain photographs were used without his or Bettie's approval and he "attempted to harass the publisher into dropping one hundred photographs from the book before the second printing."

Friends of the Pages agree with the basic facts, but they say it was Swanson who was duplicitous. Bettie was reportedly upset that photographs showing her pubic hair were published in the book, and she and Jack have told friends that they didn't want those pictures included and wouldn't have approved them.

A sequel to the Swanson and Essex book is a sticking point in both

The Kitten With a Whip: Bettie hated this bad-girl photo because it portrayed her as a smoker. In real life, she was a teetotaler and claimed that explicit photos that had shamed her in the fifties came from the one time she was drunk. (*Movie Star News*)

One of the more bizarre and surreal of the Klaw studio film loops: "Bettie's Clown Dance." (*Movie Star News*)

Bettie at her sexiest.
(*Movie Star News*)

Displaying her attributes.
(*Movie Star News*)

An example of Bettie's early
burlesque modeling for Robert
Harrison's cheesecake magazines,
like *Wink* and *Titter*. Harrison
taped his models' breasts together
to achieve the desired effect.
(*Author's collection*)

Age thirty-nine, in her 1962 yearbook from Multnomah School of the Bible in Portland, Oregon. Religion became both a quest and a violent obsession in Bettie's later life. (*Multnomah School of the Bible*)

Showing her rapid disintegration, these 1972 mug shots were taken after one of Bettie's many brushes with the law. She was voluntarily committed for the second time to Jackson Memorial, a mental hospital in Florida, after these photos were taken. (*Hialeah Police Dept.*)

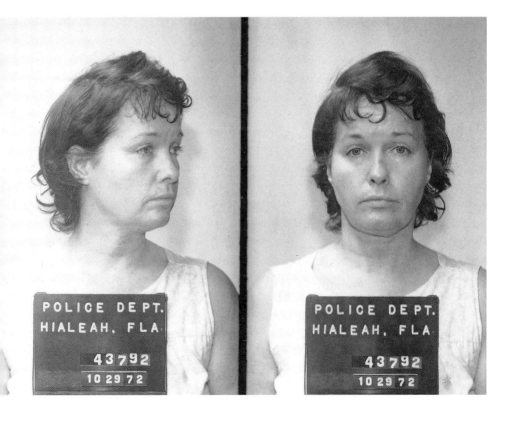

POLICE DEPT.
HIALEAH, FLA
43792
10 29 72

POLICE DEPT.
HIALEAH, FLA
43792
10 29 72

lawsuits. According to the suit CMG Worldwide filed, Glamourcon persuaded Bettie and her brother to sign a contract authorizing Glamourcon to "create, publish, and market" a sequel to her authorized biography. The deal created a "conflict of interest" for Glamourcon since it would be both Bettie's agent and a licensee producing a product, the suit charges.

The contract, dated April 19, 1996, forbade Bettie from doing any interviews or other projects until a year after the publication of the book and would give Glamourcon temporary exclusive use of family photos, which included a cache of one hundred family snapshots of Bettie recently unearthed by her brother Jimmie.

As for Bettie, her book contract with Glamourcon would have given her a nonrefundable $1,000 advance on future royalties—$500 paid up front and $500 after its publication. She would receive $1.50 for each book sold at retail, and 75¢ for each sold below retail. She would also receive $10 in royalties for each book she signed at Glamourcon's request. Glamourcon agreed to be responsible for its own publishing and research costs. If the book sold just fifty thousand copies at a retail price of $40, the book would gross $2 million and Bettie would receive only $75,000. If she signed, say, an additional 1,000 books, that would make it only $85,000.

According to the Swanson and Schultz suit, Bettie wrote a two-page handwritten letter to be used as a foreword for the new book, but then reneged on the agreement by not providing interviews, photos, and other materials. Swanson and Schultz further allege that the Pages denied the existence of a deal to create the book.

Either way, it may play out in court if it's not settled. And that's a major problem for everyone on Bettie's side because of Swanson's subpoena. Serving a subpoena against Bettie, her friends say, is a sour-grapes tactic designed to force a resolution, because unless Bettie settled out of court, she would be forced to appear in public, something she has steadfastly refused to do thus far.

"She's really upset," says Steve Brewster, president of Bettie's fan club. "This really bothers her. She just wants this to be behind her. Unfortunately, that's working in [Swanson and Schultz's] favor. Their tactics are working. She has resigned herself to a life of seclusion, but she has said she is to the point, she is so mad, and so upset with these guys, that she is ready to face the world."

Terry says, "Swanson thinks that Bettie will never show her face in public, but Bettie has told Jack she can go to court for that. You can only corner a cat so many times and a cat's going to fight back. Swanson's fooling himself. He's deluding himself," if he thinks she won't show up. "That's what he's counting on. I think it's a dirty trick."

"Bettie does not like James Swanson," Terry says. "Bettie said to me, 'Butter wouldn't melt in his mouth.'"

So, it appears that unless a settlement is reached, the world may soon get its first look at Bettie Page since 1957. One wonders if some fans will choose, like Lady Godiva's villagers, to look away from her shame. It will probably be impossible, given the media onslaught that can be expected to result if the reclusive Bettie Page enters a courtroom in broad daylight. Would she conceal herself like Michael Jackson or walk unmindful through the anticipated gauntlet of TV news cameras and microphones? It would certainly provide an unwelcome reminder of the Kefauver hearings for her, and though she says she's in better mental health now, it could be an enormous strain on her.

Bettie has been on an "extensive diet and exercise routine," according to Brewster, and has lost thirty-four pounds in case she must testify. Her weight has long been cited as one of the reasons she wishes to stay hidden from the public eye. Though Brewster says Bettie plans to appear in court "only if she's forced to," he also resolutely says that "I think she realizes there's no way to fight this court thing without being in the public."

As of the time this book was being written, Bettie and her agents and lawyers were still trying to broker a deal with Swanson and Schultz that might bring the whole matter to a quiet close, away from newspapers and television. Some close to the matter have hinted that *Playboy* founder Hugh Hefner is involved and providing lawyers and money to Bettie.

In early 1996, after the expiration of the contract that made Swanson and Glamourcon her agents, Bettie took on J. B. Rund briefly as her agent. Rund reportedly did a great job in taking on manufacturers of unlicensed products. He also helped the Pages establish their own family-owned corporation—the Nashville-based Bettie Mae Page (B.M.P.), Inc.—to handle Bettie's earnings and disburse them to family members. It's something that was never accomplished under Swanson's tenure, Rund points out proudly. In 1997 Curtis Management

Group became Rund's successor, though he still claims to be an employee of the Pages in certain deals. According to several sources, within months of representing Bettie, Rund and CMG Worldwide had made more money for Bettie and put more of it in her pocket than Swanson and Glamourcon did in three years. However, without all the financial records, which are largely absent from court documents filed so far, that's impossible to confirm, and Rund and CMG aren't telling.

It's certain that the extra money has been a comfort to Bettie in all the turmoil created since she resurfaced and she and her family have sought to protect the use of her image. However, the quest for royalty money and the fallout from the rift between the Pages and Swanson and Schultz have had far-reaching and sad ramifications for those fans and friends close to the center.

Some of the bad feelings started early on. Olivia, for example, was reportedly angered in 1992 when *Lifestyles of the Rich and Famous* allegedly broadcast some of her paintings without her permission, and during a segment that mentioned makers of bootleg Bettie products. Olivia is not cooperating with Bettie Page projects now, people who know her say, and she was not interviewed for a recent cable TV documentary. Greg Theakston apparently met with Bettie's wrath because he printed an interview with her that she now claims was a private telephone conversation between them, a source says.

Bunny Yeager had a falling-out with Bettie over her photos, which Bunny sells in various formats, including trading cards and comic books. She reportedly has told Bettie that if Bettie wants her pictures, the price is $200 a print. According to the book published by Swanson and Essex, Yeager asked in a letter, "What has Bettie Page done for me lately?" Bettie might be the first to say "plenty." Bunny's still making money off her photos of Bettie, photos for which Bettie often posed for free.

The rift between the Pages and Swanson and Schultz has divided almost everyone else into two camps, into those who either do or do not defend Bettie against Swanson and Schultz. Several longtime collectors who corresponded and talked frequently in the old days, comparing their lists and sharing Bettie Page news and pictures, now don't talk to each other anymore because of it. Most are afraid to get into the middle. Some, like Dave Stevens, are reportedly responding by not responding, defensively refusing to talk publicly about anything to do with Bettie, even at the cost of valuable publicity.

Luckily, the volleys from the Battle of Bettie have largely not reached the ground-level fans, who are still fervently buying her pinups and posters and magazines. Oblivious to the struggle for their dollars, the fans keep buying her products and perpetuating the Bettie Page legend, making her the most famous pinup girl alive, more than forty years after her career ended.

16

....

Bettiemania

WHY, after more than forty years, does Bettie Page endure as one of the most passionately loved pinup queens of all time? How is her appeal able to span age groups from teens to seniors, males and females, gays and straights, and extend to all races, ethnic groups, and nationalities across the world? And more than that, why does her popularity increase exponentially, year after year, spawning books, T-shirts, figurines, comic books, magazines, fanzines, Internet web sites, and Hollywood documentaries?

"Why is Bettie still popular? There's the mystery of all mysteries," says fan-club president Steve Brewster. "I've asked myself that a lot, and I think I have an answer: Because she simply is the most attractive woman who ever lived. Whether she's the reincarnated Cleopatra or Helen of Troy, or Eve herself, there's something so magnetic about her.

"I've had hundreds of letters from men who say once you lay eyes on her, you're magnetized by her radiance. You can't say that about Marilyn Monroe or Jayne Mansfield, as much as I love those ladies. They don't have that kind of spark. For years we didn't even know what Bettie's voice sounded like or what her personality was like. For something like that to come out of a still photo, that's pretty amazing."

It's a testament to Bettie's enduring mystique that in a readers' poll in *Glamour Girls: Then & Now*, a magazine devoted to pinup girls both past and present, Bettie was recently ranked as the third-most-popular glamour girl of all time, after Marilyn Monroe and Jayne Mansfield, and ahead of contemporary beauties like Cindy Crawford and Tyra Banks. In a subsequent survey, Bettie fell two places to fifth —after Brigitte Bardot and Raquel Welch, but ahead of Sophia Loren. That's still pretty good for a woman who never made a mainstream movie, and with whom America at large is only now becoming fully acquainted.

"Nobody thought of her as anything but this extraordinarily pretty woman. Who was to know she would become an icon?" asks noted author and pop-culture critic Harlan Ellison.

During the 1950s and 1960s, Ellison worked on various magazines that featured Bettie's photos. He frequently found himself writing filler copy to go along with the layouts of Bettie.

"I must have written twenty [articles] on Bettie," Ellison says with a laugh. "With the exception of Greg Theakston, I think I've seen more photos of every inch of Bettie's young epidermis than anybody in the universe."

In a field where it was an everyday task to look at pictures of naked female models, Bettie was unusual, Ellison says. After a while, the impact of all that flesh is numbing—the editor begins to look at his photos as an artist might look at his canvas, assessing the aesthetic value of the elements but not receiving the same visceral reaction from it as his audience. Does the model have the right smile? Is her leg at the correct angle? It's often not an arousing experience, but Bettie had the ability to wake up even the most jaded editors.

"There was a thing about Bettie where the elements were all in harmony," Ellison says. "With Bettie, there was always that quality of sexuality that stirred the primal yahoo, but beyond it, there was something about it that said if I couldn't actually be her lover, I'd like to know her. She's so nice to look at."

Bettie produces a twin reaction in her fans and admirers, Ellison says. On the one hand, they desire her because of the sexual charisma she exudes through her photographs, and on the other, they revere her. He quickly adds, however, that there can be no Italianate Madonna–whore parallel to the way Bettie is adored because she is above that. No matter what Bettie was doing in her photos, bondage or otherwise, she was never a slut. She was, Ellison says, "absolutely untouched by human depravity."

"Bettie's appeal is deserving of nothing but respect and admiration; the kind of admiration you extend to a work of art. You can't just say the things you would say in a barroom about her," he says. "You have to say the things you would say in a museum about her."

Unlike the Bettie fans of the fifties and seventies who were generally the average mens' magazine readers, Bettie's fans today are hard to pin down into just one category. In the 1990s, Bettie has followers in high fashion, comic books, fine art, punk rock—almost every subgenre of 1990s American culture that considers itself slightly alternative or exclusive has taken a shine to Bettie in one way or another.

Brewster's Bettie Scouts fan club has two hundred to three hundred members on its regular "true-blue hardcore fan" mailing list and another four hundred or more Bettie fans have contacted him at his address in Kansas City at one time or another for information or newsletters. His two club vice presidents hail from Europe and Canada.

"The original guys, like this Korean War guy I know with a tattoo of Bettie, about 10 percent of my letters are from those guys," Brewster says. "Some of them, they're so old, the handwriting is shaky and you can hardly read it. Some of them write to tell you they remember Bettie and others want me to forward letters to her.

"Then you have the revivalist ones. I feel like I'm part of that second wave with *A Nostalgic Look at Bettie Page* or *Private Peeks,* the first ones that were looking back," Brewster says.

"Wave Three is the new group that I kind of lump together: *The Rocketeer, The Betty Pages,* or the kind of punk movement, the people who like to dress in the black leather and all that. Bettie's like their goddess. They don't really mix well with the *Rocketeer* crowd, but they're the modern fans. I cannot tell you how many people have Bettie Page tattoos all over the place now, both male and female," he says in amazement.

"There are very many female Bettie fans. I've talked to a lot of these girls on the phone about Bettie. One hit it right on the head," Brewster says. "To her, Bettie represented guilt-free sexuality. To me, that's it. She was not ashamed. She did not do these kinky fetish things and feel embarrassed or naughty. She did it, she was smiling, she looked like she was having a ball, enjoying every minute. 'What an easy way to make a living!' To me, that's the expression on her face.

"I think that's why you have so many girls participate in the Bettie look-alike contests at the comic stores and conventions. They feel very bold and comfortable. They're not doing something they're ashamed of. They're proud to stand up there in their leather gear."

Not surprisingly, Bettie Page has found one of her strongest fan followings among today's sadomasochistic and bondage enthusiasts, who have taken her into their leather-clad embrace and made the Dark Angel their matriarch. In New York City, not far from where S&M fans forty years ago would buy photos of the whip-wielding or rope-bound Bettie under the counter from Irving Klaw, sits Pandora's Box, an "S&M establishment" (featured in an HBO documentary) where dominant mistresses exert power over willing slaves for a fee.

"We like Bettie Page," says Lady Kayla, a twenty-five-year-old who has been a domina since she was eighteen. "She was a switchable. She was just as submissive as she was fierce and dominant. She was also very beautiful, one of the most beautiful sadomasochistic types in a time when what they had then were people who weren't that attractive getting into this."

Lady Kayla prefers to be called a domina, or dominant, because she says the words *mistress* and *dominatrix* have become too tired and overused. Explaining her lifestyle, she says, "There's no sex involved. It's erotic overtures and foreplay. It uses pain to make it more pleasurable. It's like erotic, erotic pain, and it's also not bad. It's an aggressive woman dominating, or an aggressive man. It's a power play. It's an interchange."

Pandora's Box is about fantasy, and its world is one in which the 1950s Bettie Page probably wouldn't have felt uncomfortable. In the role-playing room at Pandora's Box, there are pictures of Bettie posted on the wall in an environment that looks not unlike the old warehouse where she shot a lot of her bondage pictures for the Klaws. Many of the dominas are Bettie fans, and a few even emulate her raven-colored bangs and fifties-era bondage costumes.

"Most of the people who are involved in this are very, very intelligent," Lady Kayla says. "A lot are powerful people in their own lives and they want to give that power over to someone else for a little while. It's an exchange."

Talking about the role that Bettie Page plays as an unofficial ambassador for the bondage world, Lady Kayla says, "She made it a little more mainstream. I think it influenced a lot of sadomasochistic types, more for it to come out in public, because generally this stuff is underground."

Interestingly, Bettie imagery abounds in the modern fetish world. A fetish magazine in England, for example, has dubbed its annual awards—the S&M equivalent of the Oscars—as the Bettys.

"I can say without a doubt that the hardcore collectors and the hardcore fans of Bettie Page are involved with Bettie Page not because she's a pinup model, but because there's something else there," says the painter Robert Blue, known for his fetishistic paintings of Bettie in bondage.

"The thing is," Blue says, "if you went into a fetish club in Japan or in California or New York or Denmark or Germany or France, if you went into any fetish club in the world and you just wore a little button with Bettie's face on it smiling, or the word Bettie, or just any reference to Bettie Page on this little button, it means something. And it certainly doesn't mean that I like pinups.

"It's a buzzword," Blue says. "It's a secret word for people who play-act their sexual fantasies. It's the password to get in to the other side: The password is *Bettie*."

Bonnie J. Burton, a former member of the Denver fetish performance group UZI, now runs a fanzine on the World Wide Web called Grrlzine, where she offers some fetish-oriented pictures and photos of herself in a black rubber nun's habit. "The S&M crowd almost crown Bettie as their queen," Burton says. "I'm not into the S&M scene as an active participant as far as sex games are concerned, but I do love the fashion.

"I think, deep down, there's a curiosity for every woman to try on a corset just once. Personally, I have a massive corset collection from vintage styles of the 1930s to rubber ones from the 1990s. I love the fetish fashion scene because I think they will always be on the cutting-edge of fashion."

Bettie clearly appeals to all sorts of counter-culture types, from rock-and-rollers to bondage queens. But Lady Kayla says that Bettie is something more to the S&M crowd—she was a trendsetter and a trailblazer.

"She's just made it more acceptable, more pleasing to the eye, I guess," Lady Kayla says. "Most people think that dominants, masters, mistresses, tops, bottoms, are monsters. But we're not. We like alternative lifestyles. We're nonconformists. We refuse to have society mold us into these type of citizens where you work, you come home to your family, you watch TV, you go on your vacation, you work some more, and then you die. Especially now, with Generation X, I guess we need something else to do."

Bonnie Burton has some similar thoughts to Lady Kayla's when it comes to Bettie's appeal.

"I think younger fans are so bored with sex right now," she says. "It seems like everything has been done already. Nothing shocks us anymore. So many of the Gen-X crowd, myself included, like the playfulness of sex depicted in men's magazines in the 1950s. Marilyn Monroe, Rita Hayworth, Jayne Mansfield, and Bettie Page all had that fun aspect of sex surrounding them. I think that's why women like that are held in such high regard as sex symbols. They knew how to make sex seem less dangerous.

"Now with AIDS and everything else attached, it's hard to look at sex as something that could be fun and worry-free. Aside from the sex element, Bettie was a natural beauty and a striking image. Many of the images most copied, aside from her trademark bangs, are all those hand-in-whip photos she did with Irving Klaw. Just the other day I saw a rave flyer with that printed on it. I see those pics everywhere."

Burton, twenty-four, is a web editor for the @Home Network, and a freelance writer for computer magazines. A curvy, raven-haired brunette with black bangs like Bettie's, Burton has competed in Bettie Page look-alike contests, and collects Bettie photos and memorabilia. Her twenty-first birthday cake even read, "Happy Birthday Betty."

She's a prime example of the new Bettie Page fan—smart, savvy, witty—and female. Gone are the days when Bettie was the sole possession of men who discovered her for the first time as adolescents rummaging through their father's pinup magazines.

"I'm not sure what first drew me to this Southern Belle of Bondage, but I ended up on a quest to find out about her life and pay tribute to her in any way I could," Burton recalls in "I Was a Teenage Betty," her online essay. "I collected all comic books that borrowed her image —such as *Pentacle, Phantom Lady, The Rocketeer,* and *Vampirella.* I went into a mad frenzy to dig up her January [1955] holiday pinup picture in *Playboy* magazine from the archives, where they keep the porn and nudie mags, in my college library."

Burton was introduced to Bettie Page while still a freshman in college. "I went with my roommate to the local comic-book store in Boulder, Colorado, and some guy working behind the counter said I looked just like Bettie Page. I didn't know who that was, so he shoved a copy of the *Betty Pages* magazine in front of me and I've been a loyal fan ever since."

Like a lot of fans, "I own a ton of Bettie Page comics, trading cards, magazines, calendars, T-shirts, rings, pins, flyers, movies, and so on," she said. "My favorite has to be my collection of 3-D Bettie Page comic books, because they are so damn campy. I love the Irving Klaw bondage 3-D comics better than the Jungle Bettie series."

She says: "I'm a Bettie fan for the mere fact that she's gorgeous. No other model has been photographed more than her, and for good reason: She's the best there is.

"I love Bettie because she sort of brought innocence back to sex. When you mention pinup models and men's magazines to most people, they think you're talking about porn or smut. With Bettie, you aren't embarrassed to appreciate looking at her, whether she's being spanked, trying on stockings, or playing in the buff on the beach. She makes sex seem okay instead of a sin. I think a lot of older fans left over from the 1950s appreciated that quality in her when she was in magazines like *Playboy*. She made you feel at ease with your sexuality, and most of all, she had fun with it."

17

....

Memory and Desire

THESE DAYS, Bettie Page is not Bettie Page. At least, she's obviously not the pinup girl everyone knows from the photos. Age, her battles with mental illness, her failed marriages, and living with the memory of her remarkable past glories have changed Bettie into a quiet, devout old woman who is paradoxically as interested in preserving her pinup image for history as she is in personally leaving her past behind her.

Only a few people outside her family have met her in person, knowing she was once *that* Bettie Page. Among their ranks are those already familiar to Bettie fans: Hugh Hefner, Dave Stevens, Karen Essex, James Swanson, and J. B. Rund. And only a precious few more, like Greg Theakston and Steve Brewster, can count themselves among those who have spoken to the reclusive Ms. Page by telephone.

Rund visited Bettie in April 1996, when her brother Jack flew to California for a weekend visit. He was privileged to spend fifteen hours with Bettie over three days, and he walked away with a rare and unique glimpse into her world today; one that certainly fits like a puzzle piece into the rest of her life.

"On Saturday afternoon, after I spent a couple hours at Glamourcon, I went out to where Bettie lives and I met her for the first time," recalls Rund. "Of course, I didn't know what to expect, but she's still a very pretty woman.

"She's put on a little extra weight, but her face is Bettie Page's face, except it's puffy—a puffy version of it. And she's still got bangs, though her hair is shorter, and, of course, her bangs are grey now. She's also got these incredibly clear blue eyes and she's got the same smile. You look at her, and it's Bettie Page."

Rund remembers Bettie wearing trousers and a long-sleeved blouse, and that her weight showed mostly on her arms and legs, which sounds similar to Leonie Haddad's recollections of Bettie's appearance. He estimates that she probably weighed about 180 pounds at that time.

For obvious reasons, Rund won't disclose exactly where Bettie lives. According to Swanson and Schultz's lawsuit against her, however, she lives in Los Angeles County. Sources close to Bettie says she now lives as an outpatient in a type of group care home. Friends describe it as a house in a nice, secluded area with a private double courtyard that cannot be seen from the street. Bettie shares the house with one other man, though there have been more people staying there in the past.

A counselor visits or stays at the house, and Bettie sees a psychiatrist or psychologist once a week, a source says, though Bettie can apparently come and go as she pleases, walking and shopping nearby.

"She's got a little garden there. It's gorgeous. She spends a lot of time with it," Rund says. The interior of the house is sparsely decorated. The only reminder of her pinup past was a current Bettie Page calendar hanging on the wall of her small bedroom. He could recall no religious icons or pictures of Jesus displayed.

"The only income she has is social security," Rund says. "She lives very frugally." According to some friends, phone calls for Bettie go through the group home's switchboard. It's unclear whether Bettie has a phone of her own. In fact, the only luxury items in her house are probably in the living room: The television and VCR on which she faithfully watches local and national news and old movies.

Bettie's fan club president, Steve Brewster, has some insights into Bettie's current life, too, though he's never met her in person. He says, "I speak with her by phone about once every month just to see how she's doing. At first I was in total shock and total awe. She is so sweet, she comforts you. Now it's like talking to my best friend."

Brewster says, "We talk about movies, current events. She doesn't go out to the movies much, but she watches a movie at home on videotape almost every night if there's nothing on cable. She likes the old movies more than new movies. Her favorite movie is *Dark Victory* with Bette Davis. She loves Sharon Stone and watches all her movies. On television, her favorite television show is *Xena, Warrior Princess.* Bettie watches every one of those. I'm not sure why she likes it. She loves those fantasy-type pictures, and she's always had a thing for muscular-type guys. She's attracted to them, so that may be part of it. She thought Steve Reeves—Hercules—was pretty good looking, I know that."

Rund recalls that Bettie wanted to talk about musicals and old movies, and the only common ground they could find at first was the 1952 Burt Lancaster film, *The Crimson Pirate,* which both of them had watched recently. However, when Rund told Bettie that he mostly enjoyed action-adventure flicks, she said, "You know that Jean-Claude Van Damme? He's sure got a hot body."

"She's seventy-three years old and she makes a remark like that," Rund says. "I was really taken aback by that. When I get to be seventy-three, I hope I'm still interested in that."

When he visited her, Rund also brought some of Bettie's legendary modeling photos to show her and discuss. "Bettie loves to look at these old pictures of herself. It seems like it's compulsive, you know," he says. "She's sitting down in her house and she's looking at every single picture and she's got stories about all these old photo sessions, and I'm fascinated."

However, Rund says that he found Bettie's take on the pictures, particularly the Klaw bondage photos, to be innocent and "naive."

"She said, 'Irving used to get suggestions from his customers as to what kind of photos they wanted to see. A lot of Irving's customers liked me with a ball gag in my mouth.' Very matter of fact," Rund recalls.

"I realized right then and there that she doesn't understand any of this. She doesn't understand foot fetishism or bondage. I said, 'Bettie, does it ever occur to you that guys are masturbating over these photos?' and she says, 'Yeah, I guess so,' you know, like it doesn't matter. She had no understanding of any of this.

"She said to me she thought it was funny. She does not understand that people get erections from it. Her sexual interests are very normal. Bettie still drinks milk."

He says, "The thing is, she really doesn't have anything revealing to say about her work. She went there and posed and that's it."

Rund describes Bettie's current attitudes as consistent with those of a girl raised in a religious atmosphere of sexual guilt, not the sexual revolutionary she later became. "Bettie does not use four-letter words," he says. "She discusses sex in euphemistic terms. She doesn't know the word *fellatio*."

Despite her adamant refusal to be photographed or filmed as she is today, Bettie is not the Howard Hughes or even J. D. Salinger brand of recluse, Rund and others say. Though she lives in seclusion from the public eye, she is hardly solitary. She goes for walks along the Pacific Ocean, shops at local stores, rents videotapes, and goes out to dinner and the movies. She and Rund ate in the middle of a big family-owned restaurant near her home when he visited.

"She had a hearty appetite," he says. "That lady is as middle-American as she can be. She eats country cooking, home cooking, and she likes ice cream, but she's kind of frugal. I don't think she'd buy something like Ben and Jerry's."

Bettie doesn't drive, and anytime she wants to go out for some distance, she needs someone to take her. Frequently, that responsibility has been shouldered by *Rocketeer* cartoonist Dave Stevens, who has become like a son or grandson to Bettie, Rund says.

"Dave Stevens is her chauffeur. He's her best friend without question," Rund says. "He spends a lot of time with her. I think in part Dave feels a kind of responsibility for what happens. He feels he exposed her to unwanted publicity because of the Bettie character in *The Rocketeer*."

A devoted friend, Stevens usually sees Bettie at least twice a month. "If it's something nearby, he'll take her," Rund says. "He takes her to doctors' appointments and he takes her out to dinner and a movie every other week. He's the only person she really trusts."

Occasionally, in her excursions close to home in Los Angeles, someone on the street will recognize Bettie, and in a Tennessee accent "so strong you can cut it with a knife," she'll completely deny that she's ever heard of anyone named Bettie Page, Rund says.

"I can't believe that nobody's found her," Rund says in amazement. "What if somebody does, and then *Hard Copy* shows up on her doorstep? Then what? They'll make her life a nightmare."

But if Bettie doesn't want to be found, why has she taken such a semipublic role in making her presence known? Why not stay completely hidden? And why doesn't she want anyone to see her today?

"She's a devout Christian lady," Brewster says. "She takes her religion very seriously. We've had some discussions about it. She's not ashamed of her past. She said she does not feel guilty then or now. She has a very positive attitude about her career. She thinks those seven or eight years she modeled were kind of a time in her life when she was kind of lazy. The time period we think of as the Golden Age of Bettie Page, to her, she kind of kicked back in New York and made a few dollars modeling. She left New York and went to Bible college and started her real career.

"She's very flattered that people still think of her and collect her magazines and photographs. She's kind of mystified that she left this thing thirty-five years ago and people are still interested in her. She's very comfortable with a very simple life. The only reason she's even sought out an agent and royalties is really for her family, her brothers, sisters, and her nephew.

"If people are cashing in, it's only fair that the family should benefit in some way. Bettie has no desire to live wealthy. She's contented with a very simple life."

Rund says he believes Bettie's reliance on religion is a "crutch," but he respects the fact that it's an important part of her personal life. He says he believes the reason she hasn't accepted requests for filmed interviews and personal appearances is both simple and at the same time, deeply complex: "She doesn't want anybody to see what she looks like because she thinks nobody's going to like her," Rund says.

"My impression of Bettie is that she actually has no self-confidence. I think she's got low self-esteem. Maybe it's got something to do with what her father did to her," Rund speculates, referring to Roy Page's sexual abuse of Bettie. "There's something deep there. She has no ego at all. When she looks at those old pictures, she says, 'I wish I looked like that.' "

Even without her help, however, Bettie's celebrity has grown of its own accord into a thing alive, independent of her simple life. And she must stare in wonderment as she watches it unfold on her television and through talks with her few trusted friends. She's finally achieving her dream of becoming a film and TV star, ironically without stepping on any stages in person.

Her cult status as pop-culture icon has been firmly cemented in recent years in a number of hip reverential nods from fans in the entertainment industry. In 1997 Fox's science fiction megahit *The X-Files* featured a segment about a man haunted by a pinup girl tattoo on his arm that drove him to murder through its whispery accusations. With a syrupy sweet Southern accented voice supplied by Jodie Foster, the malevolent tattoo was Bettie, plain and simple, no question about it, even in name. An episode of *Batman: The Animated Series* in 1993 also featured an appearance by a femme fatale Bettie doppelganger. And many Bettie fans have been quick to point out sultry actress Patricia Arquette's homage to Bettie with her black bangs and Klaw model-inspired posing in director David (*Twin Peaks, Blue Velvet*) Lynch's 1997 film *Lost Highway*.

Just weeks after Bettie's reemergence in 1992, rumors abounded of high-dollar offers from Hollywood for the rights to her story. Actress Kim Cattrall, among others, reportedly had expressed interest in playing her on the big screen. Now it finally seems some of those deals are coming to pass, though not yet in the blockbuster cinematic ways many had originally envisioned.

In April 1997, the E! Entertainment cable channel broadcast the first of the Bettie movies: An original two-hour documentary on Bettie's life in the *E! True Hollywood Story* series titled, "From Pinup to Sex Queen: Bettie Page." At roughly the same time, HBO Pictures was working on a docudrama based on Bettie's life written by Henry Cabot Beck, directed by Mary Harron, and starring actress Guinevere Turner as Bettie. Finally, Single Spark Pictures, headed by the Academy Award–nominated documentary filmmaking brothers Mark and Thorp Mori, is reportedly working on a documentary brokered by Glamourcon and James Swanson.

Bettie is attracting attention all over the place. She could soon take her place at Howard Stern's side as the Queen of All Media. Early on, there were rumblings of Japanese investors who were offering Bettie $100,000 for a one-time personal appearance and autograph signing. Whether or not that's true, Bettie clearly hasn't accepted any public invitations. But fans will be able to get closer to the Queen of Curves through a CD-ROM documentary, *Betty Page—The World of a Pin-Up Queen.*

The popular country group BR5-49, from Bettie's hometown of Nashville, have even written a song about her called "Bettie Bettie." She wrote a fan letter to the group's leader, singer Chuck Mead, thanking him for the song. "Your hillbilly twang takes me back to my early years in Nashville when I was such a big Grand Ole Opry fan," Bettie said.

"That blew me away," Mead says in disbelief during a May 1997 phone interview from Nashville. "It got sent to [BR5-49's record label] Arista through her lawyers. I got the letter in December and it just blew me away."

Mead, thirty-six, has steadfastly collected Page memorabilia for more than ten years, starting with bargain items found in thrift stores. Now he has a modest collection of postcards, books, and cardboard standups of Bettie.

"I love Bettie. It's the whole naughty-and-nice thing," he says, explaining her appeal. "Of course, there's a certain amount of sex in there, too, but there were tons of tittie magazines [in the fifties]. She stands above those because her performance is of such quality."

Mead wrote his tribute to Bettie before he moved to Nashville in 1993, but since becoming acquainted with Bettie's hometown, he says he feels even closer to her. "The more I find out about her, the more amazing it is to me," he says. For instance, "I'm living right down on Shelby Avenue near Shelby Park where she met her first husband. And every time I pass Hume-Fogg High School, I think of her." In fact, when BR5-49 started its first gigs, it played clubs in the old lower Broadway section of Nashville, Bettie's childhood stomping grounds.

Playing country music with what he calls a "hillbilly blues sensibility," Mead's band takes its name from the phone number of comedian Junior Samples's used-car lot on the television variety show *Hee-Haw.* BR5-49's music harkens back to a time in the 1950s when America was stronger and purer and country music was beginning to spin off into the rockabilly sounds of Jerry Lee Lewis and Buddy Holly.

That fifties nostalgia is also a large reason behind the love that Mead and millions of other fans across the world now have for Bettie Page. As he says, "You can see quality in her performance and modeling, and anytime that shines through, it's going to be timeless, it's going to be appreciated."

For the pretty girl who was practically born in a Nashville movie theater and spent her life seeking the fame and unconditional acceptance of the silver screen, Bettie's finally found it. In her lifetime, Bettie Page has taken her place among American icons such as Marilyn Monroe and James Dean who have been rendered immortal in our memories.

"She always lives undimmed in beauty in those photos," Harlan Ellison says. "She's forever. She's for eternity."

Some stars like Monroe and Dean probably owe their immortal celebrity in part to the brevity of their careers. Look at Dean, Ellison says. He made only three popular movies and he's on a United States postage stamp. Bettie's disappearance came at the exactly appropriate moment to protect her image in our minds for the long haul.

"She will always be undimmed by time, unmarked by life," Ellison says. "She is eternal in her beauty. She's like Venus rising from the sea in the great painting, and that's the way I want to remember her."

Bettie's fans will preserve her memory in many different ways because there are so many different sides to Bettie: pinup girl, bondage model, centerfold, mystery woman. But why does Bettie persist? Everyone has their own answer, but Robert Blue may come close to the ultimate one.

"The fact of the matter," Blue says, "is the people who were Bettie Page collectors, they were interested in something else. What was that? Here is my theory: My theory is that it's the other side, the dark side.

"The idea that Bettie doesn't know about that, that Bettie's ignorant of this, that's too much to take, that's too much to swallow, because Bettie Page self-imposed her own exile and she became a Christian in repentance for what she's done." And what has Bettie done? Nothing less than transform the world's culture, Blue asserts. With her swimsuits and smiles and black leather and bondage, she unleashed a Pandora's box of sexual frankness for generations to come, a world of *Penthouses* and *Hustlers* and adult videos and fetish clubs and fetishistic play-acting.

"She's the prime mover," Blue says, "and if I had this responsibility as someone in the 1950s who changed the second half of the twentieth century, I would not show my face either, and I would be a born-again Christian, too, in repentance for what I've done to the world. But she's got to take responsibility for it. It's her fault."

With just a touch of irony, however, Blue also says, "Thank God for perverts and thank God for Bettie Page. Without all of this mix, it would be a pretty boring world. We might be sentenced to be living a Norman Rockwell existence out there."

Blue pleads to readers not to think of Bettie as just an innocent, cheesecake model. "One thing, please don't do: When you read something in the Bible, don't demystify it. You're making a mistake. And when you read and hear about Bettie Page, don't homogenize her. Don't mix it in with milk, because it doesn't mix. It's like oil and vinegar. Bettie's the other side of milk."

To some, like Dave Stevens or Ellison, Bettie Page was fantasy, the ideal woman. To others, like Blue, she was a dark queen ensconced in leather and lashes. Still others might describe her as a naive country girl who was seduced and exploited by her own ambition.

Her fame is independent of her physical self. Her image continues to grow more and more famous without any contribution from her.

At the same time her photos were making her famous, her demons were driving her literally insane. From the spectre of her father sexually abusing her as a girl, to her failed marriages, struggles with religion, and guilt over the violent acts she wreaked, stabbing the Trevins and Leonie Haddad in misplaced vengeance, the human Bettie is a very fragile creature, limited and fallible, and nothing like our fantasies.

"I think that Bettie is psychologically fragile," Rund says. "I think there's a lot of damage from what happened from her father. I think she's kind of distant from things now. She certainly didn't show any emotion at all, not in my presence."

When the Bettie who's seventy-four now is long dead, however, we will still have the Queen of Curves with us, alive and well, shaking her stuff and living it up in Irving Klaw's loop films and bondage photos, because we, as her fans, have rewritten history and made her greater than she herself could ever have hoped or imagined to become.

There's a line in T. S. Eliot's poem "The Waste Land" that goes like this: "April is the cruellest month . . . mixing memory and desire." Perhaps it's no mistake that April is also the month that brought us

Bettie Page. She was the brightest star who never was. And she remains that way, trapped somewhere in the twin heaven and hell of perpetual April where memory is stronger than the present.

Famous or infamous, Bettie Page, with her black bangs, trademark curves, and girl-next-door looks, now belongs to time . . . and the hearts of those who remember her smile.

Epilogue

ON DECEMBER 11, 2008, Bettie Page passed away of natural causes in a Los Angeles hospital. She was 85.

The pin-up queen and sex symbol, whose racier photos and magazine spreads were once sold furtively under countertops and secreted away under mattresses, was eulogized by mainstream media outlets ranging from *The New York Times* to CNN to *Time* magazine.

Pulitzer Prize–winning *New York Times* writer Robert D. McFadden remembered her as "the most famous pinup girl of the post–World War II era, a centerfold on a million locker doors and garage walls." Back in 1956 when Page left behind her dreams of show business stardom, the notion of one day receiving this kind of recognition and approval would have been a surreal fantasy.

Penning a paean to her ever-growing mystique, the late *Time* magazine film critic Richard Corliss wrote that Bettie "was rich Corinthian leather to connoisseurs of specialized, subterranean erotica." He dubbed her "the Garbo of bondage movies," a pop culture icon with "a radiance, a mystery of personality, that transcends technique and passeth understanding."

In the 20 years since this book was first published, many of the other key figures I interviewed or mentioned within its pages have also passed on, including, notably:

- Model turned pinup photographer Bunny Yeager, who shot Bettie's iconic 1955 *Playboy* centerfold. In her 2014 obituary

Time magazine remembered Yeager, 85, as "the photographer who immortalized a '50s sex goddess."

- Steve Allen, the first host of NBC's *Tonight Show*, died in 2000 from injuries sustained in a minor car crash. He was 78.
- Robert Culp, who taught some of Bettie's acting classes and later found fame via the classic TV series *I Spy* and *The Greatest American Hero*, died in 2010 at age 79.
- Amateur photographer Art Amsie, who took some of the best camera-club photos of Bettie and carried a torch for his unrequited love his entire life, passed away in 2006 at age 78. Amsie was an outsized man, both in demeanor and build. He and I met in person for the first and only time at a book signing I did at a Fredericksburg, Virginia, bookstore in 1998. What I mainly recall of him are his booming voice, good humor, and generosity. He was a man who relished being the center of attention, and as the first Bettie Page fan, he clearly appreciated both Bettie's new celebrity status and the recognition he received for being part of her story.
- Bettie's third husband, Harry Lear, died in Florida in 2011 at 87. Lear was one of the first people I'd tracked down when I was initially writing Bettie's story, and in his first interview with me, he revealed Bettie's history of mental illness and violence. The details he gave me led me to uncover press clippings and court and police records, which in turn helped me locate and interview stabbing victim Leonie Haddad. Initially Lear and I had discussed collaborating on a biography focusing on his tumultuous marriage to Bettie Page, as he insisted he had much more to divulge than he had stated in his previous on-the-record interviews with me. We had agreed to split any proceeds of such a book, but our negotiations broke down after Lear wanted me to sign a contract granting him 50 percent of proceeds from any future writing I did, whether or not it was related to Bettie Page. As a professional writer whose entire income would have been up for grabs under those terms, that was a nonstarter for me. I respectfully declined and went on to write this book without any further cooperation from him. In an interview in *Playboy*'s January 1998 issue, Lear confirmed that the accounts

of Bettie's troubles in this book are factual but then went on to say, "I don't like that guy Foster," adding the highly dubious claim that I had said to him I would do "anything for money." (In case it needs to be stated more clearly, I did not say that.)

- Cartoonist Dave Stevens, who immortalized Bettie as the love interest in his comic book series *The Rocketeer*, tragically died from hairy cell leukemia in 2008 at age 52. As one of Bettie's closest friends and confidants in her later years, he heard about this book as it was going to press and unexpectedly called me at home to express his concerns about its discussion of Bettie's mental health problems and run-ins with the law. What was probably intended to be an angry call wound up being a brief, pleasant conversation, in which Stevens talked to me about his friendship with Bettie Page, and I affirmed my admiration for his work. Steadfastly loyal, Stevens wouldn't go on the record for the book but did answer some of my questions, confirming things I'd heard, and in turn I answered a few queries he had, hopefully allaying some of his fears about my book.
- Just a little over a year after Bettie's death, the Rev. Morris "M.O." Wright, who had brought Bettie to Jesus, died at 79 in Key West, Florida, where he had been preaching since the late 1950s. In subsequent retellings, the Baptist minister would paint Bettie as suicidal when she had her religious epiphany, an allegation she firmly denied. (This flourish was notably absent from his story when I spoke with him in 1993, the first time he had ever been interviewed about Bettie Page.)
- Entire books could be written about legendary *Playboy* magazine founder and publisher Hugh Hefner, who died in September 2017 at age 91 at his equally legendary (and scandalous) Playboy Mansion home. Hef stayed true to his pajama-clad, swinging '60s persona for decades and decades after it had passed from fashionably provocative social statement to trainwreck reality-TV fare but he remained a permanent celebrity.

Hefner's legacy will long be a topic for debate: Was he an exploitative soft-core pornographer who objectified women and reinforced negative gender stereotypes, or was he a social warrior, ahead of his time, who advocated for civil rights and championed freedom of sexual expression? Future viewpoints of the man will likely evolve as society does.

One thing that *is* certain, though, is that Hefner was faithful to his friends and he remained loyal to Bettie Page after she reemerged from obscurity.

For my part, as a Gen-Xer growing up in the 1970s and '80s, Hefner's centerfold girls loomed large in my sexual awakening as I sneaked peeks at not-so-well-hidden *Playboy*s belonging to my male relatives. In my 20s, as an aspiring young journalist, I developed an admiration for the editorial pluck and entrepreneurial verve the young Hefner had exhibited in launching a media empire from a magazine first laid out on a card table in a modest Chicago apartment.

After I landed the first interview with Bettie Page in 1992, the first call I made was to *Playboy* magazine. I was an ambitious young journalism student, still a sophomore in college. My first professional freelance article, an interview with Marvel Comics patriarch Stan Lee, had just been published a couple months previously in the *Richmond News Leader*, my local afternoon newspaper.

I don't recall which *Playboy* editor spoke with me, but I do remember that he was (1) very interested in the fact that I had tracked down Bettie Page, and (2) not at all interested in giving me any credit for the accomplishment. He was willing to pay me some money, he cajoled, if I would just tell him how I found her. I was naïve, but not that naïve.

My next call was to Greg Theakston, publisher of *The Betty Pages*, the fanzine that had first turned me on to the mystery of Bettie Page's disappearance at the height of her fame. Theakston immediately sent me a check and hired me to write what was the first (albeit partial) biography of the reclusive pinup queen.

A few months before this book was published, I received a phone call from Steve Brewster, then president of the Bettie Page fan club, who told me that Hefner had somehow acquired and read an uncorrected proof of my book.

Coinciding with the release of *The Real Bettie Page*, Hefner commissioned an interview with Bettie in the January 1998 issue of

Playboy that was obviously intended as a rebuttal of this book's revelations of Bettie's difficulties. (Hefner's success on that front could
charitably be described as limited, however.) Hefner and Stevens
were present for the interview. Asked about this book and its author,
Bettie told the interviewer, "Richard Foster is the devil posing as a
human. A monster. He wants to make money, and he doesn't care
what he does to my reputation."

In the article, written by former *Golf* magazine editor-in-chief
Kevin Cook, Bettie both disputed and confirmed accounts of her
mental illness and incarcerations. She was unable to recall holding
Lear and his children at knifepoint, she said, probably because "I was
out of my head. . . . I heard voices. I heard God and the angels talking to me, talking about fighting the demons in me. They talked out
loud with my voice. That scared poor Harry. Of course, in the state I
was in, I thought it was perfectly normal to talk to angels." She described being forced to take the antipsychotic medication Thorazine
after she was committed to a Florida mental hospital following that
episode.

Regarding the incident at Bible Town, in Florida, she denied waving her .22 handgun as outlined in a police report, insisting instead
that the gun "never left my dresser drawer." In the case of the stabbings of her elderly landlords in 1978, despite police reports and
court records to the contrary, Bettie claimed that she was the victim
and that her landlords committed an unprovoked attack on her.
Bettie acknowledged that she had brandished a knife but demurred
as to whether she had stabbed the couple. She also confirmed that as
a result of the subsequent trial, she was diagnosed with paranoid
schizophrenia and involuntarily committed to a state mental hospital.

As for her brutal 1982 attack on the widow Leonie Haddad, Bettie
admitted going into Haddad's room at night as she slept, straddling
the older woman while wielding a knife and demanding receipts for
rent she'd paid Haddad. The two "fought," Bettie said, and Haddad
hit her in the head with a telephone. Bettie flatly denied, however,
that she had stabbed Haddad at all, let alone more than twelve times,
as documented in court and police records, as well as by Haddad's
interview for this book.

"I wasn't insane. I had no intention of cutting that woman," Bettie protested in her *Playboy* interview, insisting that the judges in both her stabbing trials had not let her speak or give her side of events.

At the interview's close, Bettie said that after spending eight years committed in Patton State, she was living in a small house next to a mental health center that provided her with outpatient treatment.

Hefner was hardly the only Bettie Page supporter to take issue with my decision to write about Bettie Page's entire life, warts and all. Many fans preferred to live with the image of the celluloid fantasy woman, forever vibrant, young, and sexy. They wanted the glamour of the Queen of Curves, unburdened with the dismaying knowledge of the decades she had spent in and out of institutions, not to mention the very real harm she had inflicted on others.

Bettie herself must have realized this to some extent as well, stating in the interview that her reason for choosing to remain out of the public spotlight was that "I want people to remember me as I was," a sentiment that echoed nearly verbatim her 1992 missive to me.

Nevertheless, Bettie briefly emerged from her self-imposed Garboesque exile in 2003 to attend Playboy's 50th anniversary gala at the Playboy Mansion, taking a photo with her fellow famous centerfold alumnae Pamela Sue Anderson and Anna Nicole Smith. Bettie was unmistakably recognizable, still sporting her signature brunette fringe, slightly heavier but looking happy and remarkably younger than her 80 years. During the same time frame, Bettie took another photo at the mansion with Hefner and pinup painter Olivia De Berardinis. That image gives a glimpse of the private Bettie, with undyed gray bangs and clad in a comfortable plaid shirt, proudly posing alongside an idealized De Berardinis painting of her younger incarnation garbed as a sexy nurse.

In the intervening decades since this book was published, Bettie Page's allure and mystique have continued to grow, her look emulated by a new generation of celebrities from singers Katy Perry and Christina Aguilera to supermodel Eva Herzigová to the transgender porn star Bailey Jay. A host of fashion designers, including Todd Oldham, Betsey Johnson, and Dolce & Gabbana, have been influenced by Bettie's timeless appeal. Famous and noteworthy Bettie Page fans that I have encountered as a result of writing this book range from

Go-Go's bassist Jane Wiedlin to Darth Vader himself, actor Dave Prowse.

And as for her ever-expanding new millennial fan base, Bettie Page is as familiar a sex symbol and retro style icon as Marilyn Monroe. She is the unquestioned patron saint of their burlesque counterculture, and as far as they're concerned, there has never been a period when Bettie's name wasn't recognizable. In the social media age, dozens upon dozens of Facebook pages are devoted to Bettie Page fan groups, Bettie-influenced models and burlesque performers, and an array of products. There are roughly 140,000 images with Bettie Page–related hashtags on Instagram. In Santa Monica, California, there is an officially licensed Bettie Page store devoted to Bettie-inspired women's fashion and accessories, including shoes, clothing, lingerie, and swimwear, all inspired by Bettie's actual outfits. Fans seeking the complete Bettie lifestyle can even pick up Bettie Page brand wine and faux Bettie bangs.

Adding to Bettie's legacy, HBO Films in 2006 released the big-screen biopic *The Notorious Bettie Page*, based in part on this book and written and directed by Mary Harron (who also helmed *American Psycho*, featuring future Batman star Christian Bale). The film stars Gretchen Mol (*Boardwalk Empire*, *Mozart in the Jungle*) in a stunning performance channeling both Bettie's fresh, girl-next-door appeal and her lingerie-clad bondage-babe persona.

"With her blue-black hair, Mol looks so much like Page that this could be a documentary," observed *New York Magazine* film reviewer David Edelstein, "and her swings between modesty and exhibitionism are amazingly fluid."

Other cast members of note include Sarah Paulson (who would later win an Emmy and Golden Globe for her portrayal of prosecutor Marcia Clark in *The People v. O.J. Simpson: American Crime Story*) as photographer Bunny Yeager and Norman Reedus of *The Walking Dead* fame as Bettie's first husband, Billy Neal.

Received with mixed critical reviews, the film captures Bettie's early life and heyday, along with the unwanted spotlight of the Kefauver hearings, leading up to Bettie leaving her modeling career behind and finding Jesus. Closing with her handing out Bible pamphlets on the street, the movie makes no mention of her troubled later life. The film review website Rotten Tomatoes summed up the critical response thus: "This biopic only skims the surface of Bettie Page's life, leaving her as a cipher, and additionally fails to place her iconic status in historical context."

Bettie had humbly protested in the 1998 Playboy interview that her life wasn't "interesting enough for a big-time movie," but there is plenty to like about Harron's look backward at a more innocent time when nudity was shocking and naughty lingerie photo shoots were perceived by some as nothing less than a threat to the nation's very moral fiber.

More than sixty years after Bettie Page smiled into the camera for her last modeling session, many fans are still trying to find a way to time-travel back to that mythical 1950s embodied by our curvy, raven-banged siren. As Bettie Page takes her place in the pop-culture firmament, it doesn't appear we will stop anytime soon.

March 2019

Appendixes

Cyber Bettie
Bettie Page on the World Wide Web

Now woefully outdated, this material is retained from the original 1999
edition for historical interest. It offers a snapshot of what 1990s
Bettie Page fandom was like on the fledgling Internet at a time when
Yahoo! and AOL were the biggest names in cyberspace and dial-up
phone modems chirped and warbled in households across America.
Needless to say, the links mentioned below are no longer working,
but remnants of some may be found via the Internet Archive's
Wayback Machine.

It's fitting that Bettie Page, a trendsetter in American sexuality, should be conquering another new frontier in her old age: cyberspace. So many counterculture types have embraced Bettie already—punk rockers, artists, bondage and S & M aficionados, comic book fans, supermodel devotees, erotica collectors—and now you can add to their ranks the self-described cyber-geeks who are giving Bettie electronic immortality. Though it's not clear if she has a computer herself, Bettie has done a few on-line interviews by now, and Bettie-philes from all walks of life—men and women, young and old—have crafted dozens of creative and sexy websites in tribute to the Tease From Tennessee. Some are fetish-driven, others are information providers and references for shopping for Bettie-related pinups and souvenirs, but many are just simple paeans to the eternal warmth of her country-girl smile. Taken collectively, they form a jigsaw puzzle picture of the vast and diverse network of Bettie fans who want to share with the world their love for their black-banged Queen of Curves.

"I did [my] Bettie Page web site initially because there wasn't a lot out on the Net about her. I felt that she deserved a place in cyberspace where fans could network and share gossip. When I first put up the page, she hadn't been found yet," said Bonnie J. Burton, whose Grrlzine site includes a sizable homage to Bettie.

"I've received e-mail from fans all over the world, especially Japan and Germany. More and more people are rediscovering Bettie and the image she's made popular. I get a lot of e-mail from women who find Bettie appealing because she really did call her own shots when it came to modeling and even acting. After all, not many women can say they turned down both Hugh Hefner and Howard Hughes for dates. She's led a very interesting life, and people admire her for that."

Bettie's prominent presence on the Internet is just one more sign of her staying power. Who knows? Maybe one day, decades from now, you'll be sitting in your friendly neighborhood cyber-cafe, wired into a virtual reality where you'll share a cup of joe with a holographic Bettie. Just don't get fresh!

So, what are you waiting for? If you haven't done it already, get on-line and plug into Bettiemania! Here's a list with summaries and descriptions of some of the many sites where you'll be able to find Bettie on the Web.

Surf's up, Ms. Page!

Dave's Bettie Page Page

http://www.fantasies.com/bettie/bettie/.shtml
http://www.xnet.com/~dav /bp/bettie.shmtl

"Betty? Bettie? Bette? The way she signs her name is . . . Bettie Page." So says Dave Holle, who claims his site is licensed by Bettie Page. His site is more of a resource page than a pictures page, though it does offer some nice Bettie pinups by Olivia as well as some of Bunny Yeager's photos of Bettie on the beaches of Miami. Here you'll find recent RealAudio interviews with Bettie as well as transcripts of Internet interviews; links to shopping for Bettie videos and photos; links to other Bettie fans; and an offer for fans to buy pictures jointly autographed by Bettie and Bunny Yeager. Holle says proceeds from the limited-edition photos directly benefit Bettie and her family. Though they'll probably be gone by the time this book reaches print, prices ranged from $150 to $350 for a single photo or $595 for a set of five. Portfolios offered included Yeager's Bettie-as-Cleopatra poses, "Bettie Nude on a Boat," "Bikini Bettie at Funland," and "Jungle Girl Bettie."

Bettie Page—A Goddess

http://www.bitnik.com/bettie.htm

Fetish is the theme for this page, particularly the black leather high heels that adorn its background. You're greeted by a Klaw studio photo of a whip-wielding Bettie in black bra and panties sitting atop a display case of high-heeled shoes. The site's creator says, "Other people's pages tell more about Bettie. These pages just let her beauty speak. Enjoy." The photos on this page are mostly Klaw studio shots, with an emphasis on pictures of Bettie wearing high heels and carrying riding crops. Links to other pages are reached through a box with a picture of—guess what?—a pair of high heels!

The Bettie Page
http://www.grrl.com/betty.html

This is a spin-off of beautiful Bettie fan and writer Bonnie J. Burton's GRRL Guide and Grrl Enterprises, which she describes as "a playground for weird, wired women." Her Bettie site is aesthetically pleasing, with an animated Olivia drawing of Bettie as a devil girl (or is that grrl?) to welcome you inside. There's also an amusing appropriation of Netscape's "Netscape Now!" icon into "Bettie Now!"

Most of Burton's selection of Bettie photos are the cute, saucy type from the Klaw studios. She includes links to buy Bettie books, comics and videotapes, as well as links to other fan pages and interviews and articles. Her news and gossip section is lacking, but she makes up for it with a colorful guide to her other interests that incorporates everything from fetish photos to Lucy from the *Peanuts* comic strip.

Burton says her cyberzine is "for ALL girls from the truly girlie (though I won't admit it) to the bitchy punker lost in a different decade. It's for skate chicks to fashion Betties to Goth girls. Basically, if you don't have a Y-chromosome, this site is meant for YOU." But men will find something to enjoy here, too.

Also look for:

I Was a Teenage Betty
http://pobox.com/slt/revenge/betty.html

Bettie fans will find Bonnie Burton's account of her Bettie fandom well-written and highly entertaining, if a little repetitive of past biographical information about Bettie. It's a little too heavy on Bettie's background and doesn't include enough first-person information about aspiring author Burton, who has competed in Bettie Page look-alike contests and collects Bettie photos and memorabilia. Still, it's a small gripe. Read her essay.

Esa's Betty Page Page
http://www.clinet.fi/~esa/betty.html

Esa Aaltonen's simple page gives a few links to other Bettie Page pages, and has several black-and-white Klaw pictures. The orange background isn't very pretty, but he does include an interesting timeline of Bettie's

early life and modeling days that makes a good primer for a starting Bettie
fan.

Lou Nigro's Bettie Page Pages
http://www.hiheels.com/

Another fetishist—this time, devoted to "REAL nylons" and high heels.
The page's background features stiletto-heeled boots. A somewhat explicit
non-Bettie photo greets visitors. Nigro, who says he's been a Bettie fan
since the fifties, also has a strange sense of humor (check out his link to
cheesecake). His animated devils tell you that "panty hose are the work of
the devil" and he invites you to join the movement to eradicate the
dreaded hose. He has some hand-colored Klaw pictures, as well as photos
of nineties cheesecake-bondage model Darla Crane impersonating Bettie.
Nigro's "Betty Page Tour" is an attractively packaged trip through the
various looks Bettie sported in her short career, with a little history added
for good measure.

Also see:

Bettie Page Bondage
http://www.hiheels.com/bbond/htm

A spin-off site from Nigro, this one features a small bit of text and
comments, but mostly serves up what its name implies: Klaw bondage pix
of Bettie.

A Bettie Page; Hyperlist of Sites
http://www.weber.ucsd.edu/~dmckiern/bettie_page.html

Not much in the way of pictures here, but you can jump from here to
just about any Bettie picture or site imaginable. It's an incredibly thorough
and comprehensive list of Bettie and Bettie-related pages, from "Louie's
Limbo Lounge" to a Spanish page, "Blasfemias y masoquismo." Topics
include: Home Pages; Paintings, Drawings, Sculpture, Tattoos; Foreign
Language Sites; Marketing Sites; Neo-Bettie Pages; Bettie and Music;
Usenet; and Missing or Terminated Sites.

My Bettie Page

http://www.canuck.com/~garyp/myfav.html

"Damsel in Distress" pix of Bettie and a short list of links.

Bettie Page Link Collection

http://www.it.kth.se/~tomi/bettie.html

A few pictures, including a shot of supermodel Eva Herzigova as Bettie, and about a dozen links.

My Bettie Page Page

http://www.angelfire.com/ma/LIZZIEMONSTER/BettiePage.html

This website's author says: "I get nothing but infuriated when I show a guy a picture of Bettie and the only comment he has is 'She's okay, but she would never make it today.'!!! Now I'm not preaching that my way is the way, but isn't it ironic that the women with lasting beauty were women like Marilyn Monroe, Tempest [Storm] and especially Bettie—all voluptuous and curvy?"

Bettie's Page

http://www.public.navisoft.com/b/e/bettiepage.index.htm

An official page? Still under construction when this book was written, this page describes itself as a nonprofit venture to promote all things Bettie. It promises pictorials, a biography, an art exhibit, and updated information on Bettie and her fan clubs.

My Bettie Page Page

http://www.geocities.com/Hollywood/2667/warning.html

Lots of links, some nice graphics, and a series of animated Klaw photos.

Joe's Betty Page

http://www.joebates.com/betty.htm

Joe Bates's tribute to "the amazing" Bettie Page comes with this strange (and hopefully, tongue-in-cheek) endorsement: "Recommended by Bob Hope."

Bates writes to his visitors: "There was no one like her in the fifties—

we're talkin' Beaver Cleaver, Ike, Boy Scouts, and Mom and apple pie. Was she a visionary or the pawn of those who photographed her? Now, leather, S&M, bondage, and other such fetishes are talked about openly on daytime talk shows, but Bettie was definitely ahead of her time." The star feature of this page is a fun, animated gif of a dancing Bettie. Bates has dozens of Bettie pictures posted and includes a plethora of info about fifties-themed stuff like stripper Tempest Storm, pulp fiction magazines, fifties men's digests, comic books, and links to colorful sites with names like "Teenage Dope Fiends" and "Sleazy B-Girl Movie Posters."

Neon Knight's Bettie Page
http://www.execpc.com/~jnorton/bettie.html

This site contains about two dozen Bettie photographs as well as art by Dave Stevens and Olivia. It advertises an interactive moving Bettie puzzle, but it wasn't available when I visited.

Page . . . Betty Page
http://raita.oulu.fi/~apeiron/betty.html

This site has fun and obscure Bettie links posted by a *Rocketeer* fan who admits that he knows *Bettie* is the preferred spelling.

The Page Page
http://www.picpal.com/bphome.html

At this site you'll find a campy, kitschy presentation with an easy-to-read text on a white background decorated with textured images of Bettie dressed as a harem girl. You can order hard-to-find movies of Bettie here, from the Klaw 8mm dance loops to her three feature films, *Teaserama*, *Strip-O-Rama*, and *Varietease*.

Don't miss the neat interactive "on-line centerfold" here. It's ginchy!

Craig's Bettie Page Page
http://www.users.interport.net/~fpod/

Under construction when I last visited this site, Craig says he's going to rechristen it "The Beauty and the Beast Page" in an ever-lasting tribute to that long-standing Hollywood couple, Bettie Page and Godzilla. Yup, Bettie and Godzilla. "A match made in heaven," is what Craig calls it. Craig must be a disturbed individual. I can't wait to see the finished page.

Bettie Page—Sex Without Shame

http://bostonphoenix.com/archive/styles/96/10/BETTIE_PAGE.html

This site consists primarily of a well-crafted article about the cult of Bettie written by Charles Taylor for *The Boston Phoenix,* a weekly arts and entertainment news magazine in Beantown. It also includes an extensive list of Bettie links.

The Bettie Page Picture Gallery/Land of Make Believe

http://www.geocities.com/Hollywood/5339

This attractive, simple site has high-quality reproductions of some fifties magazine covers and Bunny Yeager's Jungle Girl Bettie photos. Hosted by Hampshire College photography student David Uzzardi (also known as David Alan Interior), the page also features a portfolio titled "Naughty Girls in Black Leather."

Melissa's Bettie Page

http://www.bridge.net/~negumi/bettie.htm

Extra points for originality! This site features a Bettie photo gallery on a leopard-print background, as well as a Dewars Scotch–style profile of Bettie. The introduction contains what may or may not be a bit of hyperbole, claiming that Bettie is the "most photographed woman in American history, surpassing Marilyn Monroe and Cindy Crawford combined."

The most interesting thing about this site is its disclaimer. Voicing the mortal fear most Bettie fans and journalists have felt of her various lawyers, Melissa writes: "To All Those Lawyers (including Ms. Page's): I am NOT making any money off this site and it is strictly for fans. So don't bother suing me because I have no money to begin with."

Superfuzz's Bettie Page

http://www.redestb.es/personal/superfuzz/bettie.htm

A foreign language page. You know, I took three years of Spanish in college, and to my professor's eternal chagrin, all I could make out here was "Bettie Page, Queen of the Pinups." Or maybe it said, "Bettie Page, '57 Buick of the 1996 Olympics." I can't be sure.

Betty Page 3-D Photos

http://www.giramondo.com/n9604/mattatore/captrash/3dshow.htm

Italian. Even better. I took Latin in high school. I'll be damned if I could understand anything on this page. It's a neat idea, though, featuring a keen photo of Bettie outlined in red and blue, intended to be viewed with 3-D glasses.

Bettie Page

http://www.ipr.nl/cultuur/cult/bettie-p/page.htm

A *Swedish* Bettie page. At least they didn't make her a blonde. It has lots of Klaw pix. Other than that, again, I'm at a loss as to what it's saying.

3-D Betty Page

http://www.ligobal.com/ent_fun/3d/betty3d/

Keep those glasses out. (But take them off if you're going out driving, or on a date, for that matter). This page features a way-cool three-dimensional comic-art drawing of Bettie. Unfortunately, it also appears that this page was last updated in 1991. According to the biographical information of Bettie at this site, "To this day, no one knows what happened to Betty Page." Boy, is my face red—and blue.

Let's stay on top of current events, people.

The Hungarian Betty Page Page

http://www.idg.hu/internetto/kepscar/index.html

Hoo boy. Maybe your grandad who came over from the Old Country can translate for you. You should know by now that I can't. If he can translate, I'd like him to explain to me, too. This site is damnably odd. It looks cool and has a nice layout and a table of contents, so I'll venture it's an on-line magazine called *Internetto*. Now as for its contents: Bettie shares space with links to pictures of socialist propaganda, cigarette ads, a guy in a raincoat that pipes in rain, and anatomically correct polar bears. Is it art? I'm not sure, but I like it.

The Japanese Betty Page Page
http://www.digitalogue.co.jp/Betty_Page.html

Oh, this is much better. This site has five—count 'em, five!—words in English: "20's Avat [sic] Garde Expand Book." It also has one picture of Bettie. This is the work of a dadaist or an art student, or maybe both, I know it.

The Betty Page Social Club
http://www.infobahnos.com/fetishad/betpage.htm (Montreal)
http://www.halcyon.com/elf/seattle (Seattle and Vancouver)

The name makes it sound like the kind of atmosphere in which you might have tea and cookies, and you might at that, but you'd probably also find yourself asking, "Could you please remove your whip from my tea and cookies?" This is a bondage and S&M society that pays homage to Bettie with weekly and monthly "fetish nites." There are also club chapters in Tokyo.

Bettie Page–Related Sites

Movie Star News
http://www.moviestarnews.com

The on-line home for the late Irving Klaw's great pinup empire. This is the source for Bettie photos taken from the original negatives, still sold the way they were in the fifties. You can also find nice glossy photos of almost any movie entertainer imaginable here.

The Pin-Up Mall
http://www.pinupmall.com

You can buy pinup girl books, CD-ROMS, posters, and lithographs at this site, which features the art of Olivia, among other notable artists. Besides Bettie Stuff, it's also a resource for fans of modern pinup models and B-movie scream queens like Linnea Quigley and Monique Gabrielle.

Atomic Books
http://www.atomicbooks.com/catalog/pinup.html

Your one-stop source for Bettie books, cards, 3-D picture books, trading cards, and magazines. Among the merchandise offered here you'll find *Bettie Fetish Comix.*

A final word: Bear in mind that the World Wide Web is a fluid, ever-changing medium. Not all of these sites may still be in operation, or at the same addresses. If you have trouble locating a web page listed above, or you want to see if any new Bettie Page pages have cropped up, I recommend using an Internet search engine such as WebCrawler, Lycos, AltaVista, Yahoo!, or MetaCrawler.

The Catalogue of Curves

An Inventory of Everything Bettie

Compiled from fan club lists, the author's collection, and other sources, here is a partial, select inventory of Bettie and Bettie-inspired books, magazines, merchandise, and memorabilia. Since many are pretty obscure or one-shot toss-offs, publishers are often not available, and because of that, are not listed. In most cases, these are long-out-of-print magazines, the type you'd see in the back of an antique store, at a garage sale, or in your father's or grandfather's attic. Happy hunting!

Albums and Compact Discs (Songs and Photo Covers)

Ain't Misbehavin': Music of Fats Waller (publisher unknown, 1950s).

"Bettie Bettie" song on *Live From Robert's* by BR5-49, Arista/Nashville.

The Betty Page Collection, Vogue 74321135722 (French), boxed set and 20-page book, 1993.

Betty Page: Danger Girl, burlesque music, Q.D.K. Media.

Betty Page Is Back, Gretschen Hofner, Blueeyedog Records, CDOG02 (UK).

Bizet's Carmen (publisher unknown, 1950s edition).

Do What You Wanna Do, Lords of Acid, (publisher unknown) 1995.

Forbidden See, The Loafin Hyenas, Sympathy Records (UK).

Halo's Best Musical Comedy Songs, (publisher unknown, Bunny Yeager cover photo of Bettie with twin leopards).

Sexplosion!, My Life With the Thrill-Kill Kult, Wax Trax Records, Waxcd 7163, 1991.

A Tribute to Bettie Page, Cleopatra Records, Los Angeles, 1997.

Books

Bettie Page, by Isabel Andrade, (Spanish). Midons Editorial S. L. Avd. Baron de Carcer, Valencia, Spain, 1996.

Bettie Page, The Life of a Pin-Up Legend, by Karen Essex and James L. Swanson, General Publishing Group, Santa Monica, California, 1996.

Bettie Page, Queen of Hearts, by Jim Silke, Dark Horse Books, Milwaukie, Oregon, 1995.

Betty Page Confidential, by Bunny Yeager and Buck Henry, St. Martins Press, New York, New York, 1994.

Bunny's Honeys, by Bunny Yeager, Taschen Books, 1994.

Bunny Yeager's Photo Studies, by Bunny Yeager, publisher unknown, 1960.

Fetish, by Valerie Steel, Oxford Press, 1996.

Glamour Girls of the Century, by Steve Sullivan, Glamour Girls; Then and Now, P.O. Box 34501, Washington, D.C. 20043, 1997.

I Was a 1950s Pin-up Model! by Mark Rotenberg, Shake Books, 449 12th Street, Brooklyn, NY 11215, 1995.

The Playmate Book, by Gretchen Edgren, General Publishing Group, 1996.

Va Va Voom! Bombshells, Pin-ups, Sexpots and Glamour Girls, by Steve Sullivan, Rhino, 1-800-432-0020.

Book Covers

Sex Merry-Go-Round, Tuxedo Paperback no. 120, by Jack Moore, Tuxedo Press, 1950s.

Shad Run, by Howard Breslin, publisher unknown, 1950s.

CD ROMs

Betty Page Special Edition Highly Interactive CD ROM, digi-glam, 3015 Main Street, Suite 390, Santa Monica, California, 90405, 1994. (310-450-9556).

Betty Page, The World of a Pin-Up Queen, Q.D.K. Media, Grobe Elbstr. 146, 22767 Hamburg Germany 040.389.37.37, April 1997.

Comic Books

Bettie Page Comics, 1996–present, Dark Horse Comics, 10956 SE Main Street, Milwaukie, Oregon 97222.

Betty Page: Captured Jungle Girl 3-D, The 3-D Zone, Box 741159, Los Angeles, California 90004.

Betty Page Fetish Comix no. 1, by Dirk Vermin, 1992, Fetish Press, P.O. Box 27801, Las Vegas, Nevada 89102.

Betty Page in Jungleland, 1992, Bunny Yeager, 9301 NE 6 Ave., Miami, Florida 33138.

Betty Page in 3-D Picture Book, The 3-D Zone, Box 741159, Los Angeles, California 90004.

Betty Page Punk Comix no. 2, 1994, Fetish Press, P.O. Box 27801, Las Vegas, Nevada 89102.

Betty Page: The '50s Rage, November, 1991, Illustration Studio.

Betty Page 3-D Comics, The 3-D Zone, Box 741159, Los Angeles, California 90004.

Betty vs. Nosferatu, David Lasky, 2705 20th St., San Francisco, California 94110.

Eroticom vol. 1, no. 1; publisher unknown, 1990.

Kiss Comix no. 6 (Spanish), 1992, Ediciones La Cupula S.A. Plaza Beatas no. 3, entlo. 08003 Barcelona, Spain.

Personality Comics Presents, 1992, Personality Comics, 5500 Sunrise Hwy., Massapequa, New York 11758

The Rocketeer no. 1, by Dave Stevens, Oct. 1982, April 1983, Pacific Comics.

The Rocketeer Adventure Magazine no. 1, July 1988, Comico. Later issues published by Dark Horse Comics, 1995–present, 10956 SE Main St., Milwaukie, Oregon 97222.

The Rocketeer Graphic Novel, Eclipse Comics.

The Rocketeer Special Edition, Eclipse Comics.

Tor Love Betty, 1990, Monster Comics, Box 25070, Seattle, Washington 98125.

Young Lust Comics, publisher unknown, 1990.

Film, Video, and Laserdisc

The Betty Page Collection (includes three theatrical releases: *Striporama, Teaserama,* and *Varietease,* plus trailers and dance films.) Available from Cult Epics, P.O. Box 55670, 1007 ND Amsterdam, Netherlands; Sight & Sound, 27 Jones Road, Waltham, Massachusetts 02154. (617) 894-8633. Laserdisc.

Betty Page Uncensored—The Irving Klaw Bondage Classics—Volumes 1 and 2, Klaw films, 70 minutes each. VHS. (Cult Epics).

The Bound Beauties of Irving Klaw, Back to Back Betty, Movie Star News

Klaw studio loop films on VHS, Movie Star News, 134 W. 18th St., New York, New York 10011-5403. (212) 620-8160.

The E! True Hollywood Story: Bettie Page, From Pin-Up to Sex Queen, documentary, E! Entertainment Television, April 1997.

The Exotic Dances of Bettie Page, Klaw loop films, 90 min. VHS (from Cult Epics).

One Hundred Girls by Bunny Yeager (Available from Cult Epics and Sight & Sound) Laserdisc.

Striporama (1952 color) Venus Films, producer Martin Lewis. Starring Joe E. Ross, Lili St. Cyr, and Bettie Page (available from Something Weird Video, P.O. Box 33664, Seattle, Washington 98133), (206) 361-3759; also available from Cult Epics) VHS.

Teaserama (1955 color) Movie Star News, producer Irving Klaw, 65 minutes (available from Something Weird Video and Cult Epics), featuring Tempest Storm and Bettie Page. VHS.

Varietease (1954 color) Movie Star News, producer Irving Klaw, 51 minutes (available from Something Weird Video and Cult Epics), featuring Lili St. Cyr and Bettie Page. VHS.

Magazines

A1 True Life Bikini Confidential no. 1, 1990.

Adam, mostly Bettie in ads—vol. 2, no. 1, 1957; vol. 2, nos. 3 and 5, 1958; vol. 5, no. 12, 1961; vol. 7, no. 4, 1963; vol. 8, nos. 1–12, 1964; vol. 33, no. 1, January 1989.

Adam Annual, 1957.

Adventure, October 1955, February, October 1956.

After Hours, 1957, vol. 1, nos. 1 and 4.

All New Betty Page, 1962.

Amateur Art and Camera, March 1954; March 1956; vol. 8, no. 2, 1957.

Amateur Screen and Figure Photography, April 1955.

Amazing Heroes no. 138, April 1, 1988.

Amazing Heroes Preview Special no. 145, July 15, 1988.

American Beauty, 1960s.

American Photographer, "Innocent Fascination" by Barney Cohen; July 1987.

Art Alternatives no. 8, October 1996.

Art and Camera, July 1955; March 1956.

Art Photography, October 1950; May, August 1951; June 1952; August
    1954; April, May, July, August 1955; February, June 1956; July 1957.
AS&P, April 1955; October 1956.
Bachelor, April 1966.
Backstage Follies, June 1957.
Bare, October 1954, vol. 2, no. 4.
Beauty Parade, September 1951; April 1952; January, May, July 1953;
    January, July, September, November 1954; January, March, June, Au-
    gust, October, November 1955; December 1955; February 1956.
Bella Donna, no. 1, date unknown.
The Best of Glamour Girls: Then & Now vols. 1 and 2, 1995.
Best of London Video vol. 1, no. 1, 1989.
Best of Screw, Summer 1976.
Bettie Page, New York, Diamond Publishing, date unknown.
Bettie Page no. 1, 1963.
Bettie Page, America's Foremost Figure Model no. 26, 1959.
Betty Being Bad, 1990.
Betty Page, 1958.
Betty Page, 1963.
Betty Page no. 4, 1980.
Betty Page: A Nostalgic Look, 1976.
Betty Page And, 1960s.
Betty Page in Bondage nos. 1–7, 1960–61; no. 1, 1970s.
Betty Page Outdoors, 1962.
Betty Page—Pin-Up and Figure Model, 1958.
Betty Page—Private Peeks vols. 1–4, 1978–80.
Betty Page, Queen of Bondage, 1962.
Betty Page 3-D Picture Book, 1989–90.
Betty Pages, The, issues 1–9; 1987–93.
Betty Pages Annual 1, 1991.
Betty Pages Annual 2, 1993.
Bizarre no. 14, 1954.
Bizarre Life no. 9, 1969; and new reprints nos. 1 and 2.
Bizarre of the Unusual no. 21, 1958; vol. 1, nos. 5 and 6, 1962.
Black Nylons vol. 1, nos. 5, 6, 8, 1962–63; vol. 2, no. 2, 1963.
Black Nylons Semi-Annual no. 2, 1963.
Black Nylons and High Heels vol. 2, no. 2, 1963.
Black Satin vol. 1, no. 6, 1963.
Black Stocking Parade no. 2, 1963.

Bold, February, March, June, December 1955; April, August 1956; May 1957.

Bold Girls! vol. 2, no. 1, 1960.

Bondage Photo Treasures no. 7, September 1984.

Bondage World, mid-1980s.

Boudoir Noir vol. 2, no. 2, 1989, no. 14, Summer/Fall 1996, "Who Owns the Real Bettie Page?" by Diane Wilputte, Toronto, ON Canada.

Boston Phoenix, 1996, "Bettie Page—Sex Without Shame," by Charles Taylor; and October 18, 1996, "Sane and Sexy," by Charles Taylor.

The Bound Beauties of Irving Klaw vols. 1–5, 1977–78.

Brave, November 1956.

Breezy, December 1954; February, June, August, December 1955; February, April, December, 1956; April, October, December 1957; August, December 1958; June, October 1959.

Brief, October, November 1954.

Bunny Yeager's ABC's of Figure Photography, no. 54, 1964.

Bunny Yeager Photographs Famous Models, 1965.

Buttock Fetishism, 1965.

Cabaret, March, May, November 1955.

Camera Art no. 4, 1950s.

Candid no. 5, 1959; vol. 9, no. 1, mid-1960s.

Candid Photography, 1955, 1956.

Candid Special Edition no. 1, 1960.

Candid Whirl, June 1953.

Candida vol. 2, no. 2, 1960.

Caper, January, September 1957; January, November 1958.

Caper's Treasure Chest, 1959; January 1960.

Carnival, June 1956; December 1958.

Cartoon and Model Parade nos. 53, 59, 65, 72, 78, 85, 91, 97, 104; 1952–1956.

Cartoon and Model Parade Annual Catalog nos. 1–3, 1952–1956.

Cartoon Comedy, November 1954; May, July, November 1955; January 1957; March 1958; March, May 1960; May, July 1962.

Casanova vol. 1, no. 1, May 1957.

Catfights Galore no. 1, 1983.

Celebrity, November 1954; October 1955.

Celebrity Sleuth vol. 5, no. 2, 1992.

Charmand's Catalogue of Fashion, Summer 1955.

Cheeks, June 1990.

Chic, August 1989, November 1990, May 1992, Beverly Hills, California, L.F.P. Inc.

Chicks and Chuckles, August, October 1955; August 1956; April, November 1957.

Cinefantastique vol. 22, no. 1, August 1991.

Classic Photography no. 1, Autumn 1956.

Collector: The Photos of Irving Klaw and John Willie, 1976.

Comedy, January, November 1954; May, July 1955; July 1956; March, July, September 1957; March, July 1958; January 1959; May, September 1960; March 1961; January, July, September 1962.

Creative Figure Photography, Modern Camera Guide no. 459, 1960.

Damsels in Distress, date unknown.

Dare vol. 1, no. 8, August 1953.

Demoiselle vol. 1, no. 1, 1960s.

Dedicated to Betty Page, Cult Model 1950s no. 2, 1990, Italian publication.

Details, May 1989; June/July 1989.

Devils in Skirts, 1964.

Diva-Bizarre, November 1985; December 1987.

Diva-Mania, 1988.

Diva—Uncertain Regard, January 1987.

Domina no. 10, 1989.

Dominant Damsels no. 1, 1958.

Dominant Whip Girls/High Heels no. 2, 1961.

Draw at Home, 1952.

Drawing the Human Figure Using Photographs, 1965.

Elegantly Bound III, Fond Memories/Glamourcon Inc., P.O. Box 2594, Woodinville, WA 98072.

Ellery Queen's Mystery Magazine, January, September 1953.

Entertainment Weekly, April 15, 1996.

Escapade, February, March, August, September, December 1956.

Esquire, January 1955, appears in advertisement, page 132; August 1994, "The Wild One—Betty Page, the first naked woman in America," by Willie Morris.

Exotique nos. 1, 3–5, 8, 13, 17, 18, 21; 1956–1957.

Exotique Illustrated, 1960.

Exotique Photo Album no. 5, 1960s.

Eye, October, November 1954; April 1955; October, December 1960.

Eyeful, August, December 1951; April, June August, October, December

1952; August, October, December 1953; February, June, August, October, December 1954; February, April 1955.

Fabulous Fotos, date unknown.

The Face vol. 2, no. 3, December 1988.

Fantastique nos. 1 and 6, 1953.

Fem Fantastique no. 1, 1988.

Femme, 1960, U.K. publication.

Femme de Joie vol. 1, no. 2, September 1979.

Femme Fatales vol. 5, no. 8, February 1997, "Kim Cattrall on Bettie Page."

Fetishism no. 6, 1962.

Figure nos. 5 and 6, 1955.

Figure Photography Annual no. 8, date unknown, 1950s.

Figure Photography Quarterly no. 12, 1955; nos. 13 and 14, 1956; Spring, Fall 1958; Fall, Winter 1959; no. 26, 1960; no. 32, 1961.

Figure Studies Annual nos. 7, 10, 12, 1955.

Filmfax no. 56, May/June 1996, "Lights, Camera . . . Bettie! The Making of Striporama," by John S. Carroll.

Flirt, August 1951; February, June October 1952; February 1953; February, June, October, December 1954; February, April 1955.

Focus on Bettie Page no. 1, 1963.

Follies, November 1955; July 1957; July 1958; January 1960; November 1962.

Follies de Paris et de Hollywood nos. 69, 70, 96, 102, 126, 150, 151, 190, mid–late 1950s.

Follies de Paris et de Hollywood—Special Nuits de Broadway, 1957.

Follies de Paris et de Hollywood—Special Striptease Follies, mid-1950s.

Fond Memories, assorted issues variously numbered and titled, American fanzine, 1990s.

For Men Only, May 1955.

Forty Private Peeks, 1990.

Forum, February 1989.

Foto-Rama, April 1955; March, May, December 1956; March 1957.

Frauds vol. 1, no. 8, February 1957.

French Frolics vol. 1, no. 1, 1960s.

French Pastry vol. 1, no. 1, 1950s.

Frolic, August 1953; April 1954; October 1954; February, April, August, October 1955; June, December 1956; February, August 1958; April 1959; July 1961; April 1962.

GQ, August 1993, "Hothouse Roses," by Richard Merkin.

Gaieté, 1960s one-shot.

Gala, September 1952; March, July 1953; May, July, November 1954; March 1956; March 1957; January, July 1958; January, March 1959; June, December 1963; March 1966.

Gaze, February, April, October, December 1956; February, June 1957; February, August, October 1958; February, April, August, October 1959; February, June 1960; February, June 1962.

Gee-Whiz, January, July, November, December 1956; January, July 1957; January 1959; May 1960; December 1961.

Genesis, October 1979; September 1989.

Gent vol. 1, no. 1, September 1956.

Girly no. 44, 1960, U.K. publication.

Glamour Girls: Then and Now no. 9, 1995, Steve Sullivan, P.O. Box 34501, Washington, D.C. 20043.

Glamour International, May, October 1986; May, September 1987.

Glamour Parade, August 1956; December 1957; February 1959.

Glamourous Betty Page, the Cult Model 1950s, Books 1 and 2, 1989 and 1990.

Glamour 7, October 1986.

Glance, March, June 1958; February, October 1959.

Glo, 1960s one-shot.

Good Photography no. 297, 1956.

Grandeur no. 4, 1960s.

He, May, October 1955; January, March, April, August, October 1956; November 1957; September 1965.

Heavy Metal, July 1991.

High Heeled Women vol. 2, no. 2, 1989.

High Heels vol. 2, nos. 2, 5, 6, 1963.

High Society, April 1977; October 1980; February 1992.

History of the Pin-Up no. 1, 1990s.

Hit Show, September 1961.

Hot Talk, September 1988; February 1989.

How to Take Figure Photos no. 38, 1962.

Hum, April 1957.

Humorama, April 1957; January 1958; July 1962.

Hustler, April 1978; August 1978.

I Gialli di Ellery Queen, Italian, no. 42, June 1953.

In Praise of Bettie Page, July 1983.

Inside, March 1955.

Interview, "The Real Betty Page," by Bunny Yeager, July 1993.

The Irving Klaw Years 1948–1963 vols. 1–10, 1976.

It's Only a Movie no. 3, "Why Women Love Betty Page," 1990.

Jest, November 1954; January, April, May, July, November, December 1956; January, July, November 1957; January 1959; January 1962.

Jet Set Sex no. 103, 1950s.

Joker, April 1954; April, June, December 1956; December 1957; February, June, August, December 1958.

Joy, August 1959.

Just Teasing, 1992, Ursus Imprints, Kansas City, Missouri.

King vol. 1, no. 3, 1959.

Kitbuilders Magazine no. 17, Winter 1995, color cover of Bettie model.

Kontinental Kuties vol. 1, no. 5, 1958.

L.A. Weekly, October 11, 1991, "In Search of Bettie Page," by Karen Essex.

Laff, April 1952; April 1961.

Lark vol. 1, no. 1, date unknown.

Late Show, U.K., no. 3, 1991, "Betty Page Queen of Curves."

Laugh Digest, February 1964.

Laugh Riot, December 1961; February, June 1962.

Leather and Lace Annual, 1962.

Leg Show vol. 1, nos. 1, 4, 1993.

Lucky, July 1961.

Male Life, June 1955; January, April 1956; January 1957.

Male Point of View, March 1955; May, August 1956; August 1959.

Man's Cavalcade, April 1957.

Man's Conquest, August 1955.

Man's Delight, one-shot, 1972.

Man's Epic, April 1965.

Man's Illustrated, September 1955; April, June 1957.

Man's Magazine, December 1954.

Man's True Danger vol. 2, no. 1, 1950s.

Man's Way, October, December 1956.

Master Photography no. 3, Winter 1958.

Master Sex, 1966.

Mediascene, February 1974.

Meet the Girls nos. 1–3; 1957–59.

Meet the Girls Special vol. 1, no. 3; 1955.

Memory vol. 47, nos. 7, 9, 1982.

Mermaid vol. 1, no. 5; date unknown.

Midweek Reveille, November 12, 1956.

Mirages, one-shot, date unknown.

Mr. Annual, Winter 1956.

Model, The no. 2, 1955.

A Model Catfight, 1960.

Model Studies Annual, 1956, 1958, 1960.

Modern Continental vol. 20, no. 1, 1955; vol. 20, nos. 1 and 2, 1957 and 1958.

Modern Man, November, December 1954; February, May, June, July, October 1955; November 1957; September 1958; July, August, October 1959; December 1961; August 1966.

Modern Man's Hunting Annual vols. 2 and 3, 1955.

Modern Man's Yearbook of Queens vol. 6, 1957.

Modern Sunbathing and Hygiene, October 1954; February, June, September 1955; April, October 1956.

The Movie Star News Story, New York, Black Cat Books, 1990.

New Modern Continental vol. 20, no. 1, 1950s.

The Nose, no. 11, March 1992.

A Nostalgic Look at Bettie Page, 1976.

Nugget, June 1977.

Nugget Yearbook, 1977, "Irving Klaw's Bondage Pics."

Nudist Yearbook no. 4, 1956.

Ogle, March 1956; July 1957.

Oui, May 1977.

Outré (Filmfax Presents) vol. 1, no. 3, 1995, "Bettie Page: The Art of the Pin-Up," by David J. Hogan; and vol. 2, no. 7, 1996.

Painful Memories, 1980s one-shot.

Paper, September 1988.

Peek-A-Boo 3-D, late 1980s or early 1990s.

Peep Show, Fall 1954; Fall 1955; February 1956; April 1957; May 1958.

Penthouse, December 1983.

Penthouse Forum, February 1989.

Penthouse Hottalk, February 1989.

People, January 2, 1954.

People Today, October 21, 1953; June 2, 1954; June 29, 1955; August 1956.

Pepper, vol. 1, nos. 1 and 3, 1962.

Peril, October 1956.

Perilous Bondage Assignment no. 1, 1959.

Peter Basch's Glamour Photography no. 313, 1956.

Pin-Up Photography, 1956.

Photo, November 1954; January, May 1955; March 1988.

Photo Album no. 5, date unknown.

Photo and Body nos. 5 and 10, 1957.

Photo and Form no. 7, 1960.

Photo Arts, February 1951.

Photo Arts Annual, 1952.

Photo and Fun, September 1963.

Photographer's Masterpieces no. 1, 1957.

Photographer's Odd Ball vol. 1, no. 1, 1957.

Photographer's Showcase, November 1957.

Photographing the Female Figure no. 348, 1957.

Photographing the Feminine Figure, 1958.

Pic, September 1955; May 1956.

Picture Digest, October 1957.

Picture Scope, November 1954; May 1955; March 1959.

Pin-up Photography by Charles Kell vol. 1, no. 1, Spring 1956.

Pix Annual, Spring 1955; Winter 1958.

Playboy, January 1955 centerfold; May 1955; January 1956; March 1964; January 1978; June 1978; January 1979; January 1989; December 1992, "The Betty Boom," by Buck Henry; December 1995, "The Real Bettie Page," by Karen Essex and James L. Swanson.

Playboy Presents the Year in Sex, 1988, 1989.

Playboy: The First 15 Years, early 1980s.

Pose!, September 1957; April 1959.

Presenting Bettie Page nos. 1–5, 1962.

Presenting Bettie Page at Home no. 5, 1961.

Presenting Bettie Page Outdoors, 1962.

Prude vol. 2, no. 2, 1985.

Queen of Bondage, 1962.

Quick, August, 1954; January, August, October 1955; August 1956; December 1956.

Qvinna no. 9, 1960s, Swedish publication.

Rake, January 1962.

Reflex, no. 10, 1989.

Relax, May 1957.

Revels vol. 1, no. 6, date unknown.

Rhapsody vol. 1, no. 1, 1961.

Risk, April 1957.

Rock 'n' Roll Musik Magazin, German, 1990s, "Queen of the Fifties," by Dieter Moll.

Rogue, August, October 1956; Ocrober 1957.

Rolling Stone, October 16, 1989, "The Case of the Vanished Pin Up," by Ira S. Levine.

Romp, June, August, October 1960; September 1967; April 1971.

Rugged vol. 1, no. 2, April 1957.

Ruta, Spanish no. 66, September 1995.

Satan vol. 1, no. 2, April 1957.

Satana vol. 1, no. 2, 1962.

Sate no. 1, 1957.

Satin Legs and High Heels no. 10, 1960.

Satin 'n' Lace, November 1991.

Scan, December 1960.

Scarlet, 1963.

Screw, August 22, 1988.

Secret Magazine, Belgian no. 11, November 1996, "The Return of Bettie Page," by Lou Nigro.

See, January 1952.

Sensation, February 1955.

Sha-Boom, April and May 1990.

She, September 1954; October 1957; April 1958.

Sheer Filth, U.K., no. 7, August 1989, "Bettie Page Queen of Glamour."

She Fights, 1979.

Show, September, December 1954; January 1955; May 1956.

Silky no. 3, 1960.

Sir, September 1963.

Sir Annual, Fall 1955.

Skin Diver, June 1958, "The Latest Rage With Bettie Page," by Ellsworth Boyd.

Skin Two no. 10, 1989.

Slick vol. 6, nos. 2 and 4, 1957.

Snappy, November 1955; January, March, July, November 1956; March, July, September, November 1957; May 1958; March, May, July, September 1960.

Spanking Illustrated no. 6, June 1985.

Spicy Zeppelin Stories, March 1989.

Stag, February 1955.

Stare, December 1954; February, April, June, August, October 1955; June, August, October, December 1956; February, April, June, October, December 1957; February, April 1958; June 1959; June, August, December 1961; August 1962; June, October 1963; February, April 1964; February 1965; October 1967.

Sunbathing for Health, March, August 1956.

Suppressed, September 1955; February 1957.

Sushi nos. 3–5, 1990.

Swagger, July 1957.

Tab, February, October 1955; February 1956; February 1957; February 1959; February 1962.

Tease, Various appearances since 1993 including no. 6, 1996. "Bettie Page's Agent and Lawyer Fired," Pure Imagination Publications, Marietta, GA.

Tempo, September 20, 1954; December 13, 1954; April 18, 1955.

Ten Top Glamour Photographers no. 26, 1959.

Titter, December 1951; June, October 1952; June, August, December 1953; April, June, August, December 1954; February 1955.

Topper, June 1968.

True Danger, December 1962; February 1965.

TV Girls and Gags, March 1955; March 1956; September 1956.

U.S. Glamour Presents Betty Page, 1959.

Ungawa!, British, nos. 2 and 3 1990s.

Unique no. 4, 1955.

Uncensored, August 1956.

Velvet, July 1982.

Velvet 40+ Choice Cuts, January 1989.

Velvet Spotlight 40+, January 1987.

Velvet Talks, September 1981.

The Very Best of High Society Collector's Edition, 1991.

Video, "A Rage From the Past," by B. Eder, February 1991.

Vue, October 1952; April 1956; March 1959; January 1961; March 1962.

Weird Smut no. 3, 1989.

Whisper, September 1951; January, May 1952; May, July 1953; March 1954; April 1955.

Wink, October, December 1951; February, June, August, October 1952;

February, June, August 1953; February, April, June, August, October, December 1954; February, April 1955.

Wildcat, February 1964.

World Beauties, 1965.

Zip, January 1966; January 1972.

Newspapers

Boston Phoenix, October 18, 1996, "Sane and Sexy," by Charles Taylor.

Detroit News, June 13, 1991, "Page Is the Rage," by Susan R. Pollack, Accent section, page C-1.

Metro, weekly newspaper of Santa Clara Valley, November 21–27, 1991, reprint of Karen Essex's article, "In Search of Bettie Page," from *L.A. Weekly.*

(Nashville) *Tennessean,* April 26, 1992, "Whatever Happened to Betty Page?" by Thomas Goldsmith, Style section, page J-1.

New York Times, April 27, 1997, "Fans of Bettie Page, the 50's Pinup Queen, Keep Her Image Ageless," by Stephen Henderson, Styles section, page 43.

USA Today, June 5, 1991, "The Legend of Betty Page: Pin-up Star Has Leg Up on Naughtiness," and "Mysterious Pinup Page," by Elizabeth Snead; and November 12, 1992, "Finding a Page of Pinup History," by Elizabeth Snead, Life Section, page D-1.

Merchandise, Miscellaneous

Autographed Bettie Page photos for sale, c/o Marianne Phillips, P.O. Box 129, Readlyn, Iowa 50668 (319-279-3328).

Bettie Page calendars, photo sets, postcards, magnets, trading cards, books, and magazines by photographer Bunny Yeager, 9301 NE 6th Avenue, Suite C-311, Miami, Florida 33138.

Bettie Page: The Exclusive Calendar (1995 and 1996).

Bettie Page photos, videos, photo sets from an original source. Movie Star News, 134 W. 18th Street, New York City, New York 10011-5403 (212) 620-8160.

Bettie Scouts of America, official licensed fan club. Write c/o Steve Brewster, president, 2641 S. 53rd Street, Kansas City, Kansas 66106-3365.

Betty Bisque, 8-inch tall sculpture based on Dave Stevens drawings, Graphitti Designs, Box 25070, Seattle, Washington 98125.

Betty Cardboard Stand-Up, 15 inches tall, Mother Productions, Box 325, Atwood, California 92601.

Bettie Page Embroidered Patch, Mike Broadstone, 2170 Fauber Road, Xenia, Ohio 45389-9336.

Betty Page Fetish Comix T-shirt.

"Betty Page; Jungle Queen," "Betty Page; Intimate Encounter," T-shirts and prints, by Steve Woron, The Illustration Studio.

The Betty Page Portfolio, Port Kar Industries, Oregon City, Oregon. Signed, limited edition illustrations by various artists.

Betty Page Ring, sterling silver sculpture, based on Irving Klaw photo, Netherworld, 701 N. MacQuesten Parkway, Number 122 BP, Mt. Vernon, New York 10552. May no longer be available.

Betty Page and Rocketeer T-Shirts, based on Dave Stevens drawings, Graphitti Designs.

"The Betty Page Story," play, Prop Theater, Chicago, October 1992.

Betty Print, signed, limited edition by Earl McPherson.

Betty Page Social Club, T-shirts and buttons from Toronto fetish club.

"Bunny Yeager's Bettie Page" and "Bunny Yeager's Bettie Page in Black Lace," two sets of fifty trading cards, 21st Century Archives.

Bunny Yeager 30 Postcards, 1995, small, softcover bound collection, Taschen Books, 1995.

Clayburn Moore limited edition bronze statue (fifty made).

Dave Stevens prints, "Betty's Bath," "Rocketeer and Betty."

Dress shirt with Irving Klaw Movie Star News pictures.

The Maitresse Club (U.K.) flier for "Strictly Fetish Party" in London.

My Life With the Thrill-Kill Kult—*Sexplosion!* promotional Zippo lighter.

Olivia calendars, prints, trading cards featuring art of Olivia De Berardinis.

Page Pix, Betty Page trading card set, thirty-six cards, Shel-Tone Publications, Box 45, Irvington, New Jersey 07111.

Phone cards, ARGO CITY, 136 Confair Parkway, Montoursville, Pennsylvania 17754. Designs by Dave Stevens and Bunny Yeager. Some autographed, two versions, "Bettie's Bath" or "Stockings and Black Lace." 1-800-345-9155. May no longer be available.

Talking Postcards, in box, made in Japan, mid 1950s.

Tiny colored plastic TV set viewers with pictures of Bettie (circa 1950s).

Vinyl model of Bettie as Jungle Girl.

Zero, flier for a nightclub in Barcelona, Spain.

Sources

Bettie Page, the Life of a Pin-Up Legend, by Karen Essex and James L. Swanson, General Publishing Group, Santa Monica, California, 1996.

"Bettie Page Visits the Celebrity Lounge," March 27, 1996 interview on Mr. Showbiz Celebrity Lounge website.

The Betty Pages, issues 1–9 (magazines); and *The Betty Pages Annual* nos. 1 and 2, 1988–1993; Pure Imagination Publishing, New York.

The E! True Hollywood Story: Bettie Page, From Pin-Up to Sex Queen, documentary, E! Entertainment Television, April 27, 1997.

Lifestyles of the Rich and Famous, audiotaped interview, aired November 1992.

Movie Star News, Volume One: Betty Page, The Queen of Curves (magazine), Black Cat Books, Pure Imagination Publishing, New York, 1990.

Index

··